BITTER FRIENDS, BOSOM ENEMIES

BITTER
FRIENDS,

Iran, the U.S., and the Twisted Path to Confrontation

BOSOM
ENEMIES

Barbara Slavin

ST. MARTIN'S PRESS ⚏ NEW YORK

www.stmartins.com

Book design by Philip Mazzone

Library of Congress Cataloging-in-Publication Data

Slavin, Barbara.
    Bitter friends, bosom enemies: Iran, the U.S., and the twisted path to confrontation / Barbara Slavin. — 1st ed.
        p.   cm
    Includes bibliographical references.
    ISBN-13: 978-0-312-36825-8
    ISBN-10: 0-312-36825-9
    1. United States—Foreign relations—Iran.   2. Iran—Foreign relations—United States.
3. United States—Foreign relations—2001–   4. Iran—Politics and government—1979–1997.
5. Iran—Politics and government—1997–   I. Title.

E183. 8. I55S58   2007
327.73055—dc22   2007021962

First Edition: October 2007

10 9 8 7 6 5 4 3 2 1

For Michael, Andrew, and Didi

CONTENTS

ACKNOWLEDGMENTS

THIS BOOK WOULD NOT have been written if not for Haleh Esfandiari, an Iranian-American scholar whose wisdom and warmth have inspired me for more than a decade. It was Haleh, who runs the Middle East program at the Woodrow Wilson International Center for Scholars, who first suggested that I write a book after I returned to Washington from my sixth visit to Iran in February 2006. She read the manuscript in various stages, gave sage advice, and made crucial corrections. I thank her and her husband, Shaul Bakhash, for their friendship and counsel. (Haleh was arrested May 8, 2007, and taken to Evin prison in Tehran after four months of de facto house arrest at the home of her elderly mother. It is my fervent hope that she will have been freed long before this book is published.)

Mike Van Dusen and the entire staff at the Wilson Center, from President Lee Hamilton to the library and administrative personnel and the security guards at the front desk, made me feel at home and gave me the intellectual and physical space necessary to find my voice after years of daily journalism. The Wilson Center also provided an enthusiastic research assistant, Megan Gattuso, who provided significant help.

There are many others who contributed to this book, in Iran and in the United States. Among them are Yahyia Fiuzi, an Iranian-American architect, and his beautiful and talented daughter, Pani Farkhan, who have promoted the best in both societies. Goli Emami and her late husband, Karim, made me feel at home far away from home and touched me with their intelligence and passionate concern for their country and their culture. Hadi Semati, a professor of political science at Tehran University, has enlightened countless Americans about Iran's complicated politics and patiently interrupted his own work at the Wilson Center to answer my unending questions. Iran's outgoing ambassador to the United Nations, Mohammad Javad Zarif, and former ambassador to France, Sadegh Kharrazi, provided thoughtful analysis, as did several European envoys in Tehran who, for diplomatic reasons, asked to remain nameless.

I also want to thank all my various fixers/translators, some of whom also requested that I not identify them—even though the Iranian government undoubtedly knows who they are. I particularly thank Reza, the staff of the Baztab Web site, and Leily Lankarani. Leily was with me during my interviews with President Ahmadinejad and former President Rafsanjani, and was as much colleague and friend as translator. Ebrahim Mahmoody has been my driver and companion on all my trips to Iran. He is the first person I see when I get out of the airport terminal—standing patiently with a bouquet of red roses—and the last person to say good-bye before I fly home. I can't imagine Iran without him.

On the U.S. side, Kenneth Katzman at the Congressional Research Service is perhaps the best analyst of Iran who has never gotten to travel there (a situation that I hope will be rectified). I particularly appreciate his help on the subject of the Revolutionary Guards. Vali Nasr is an outstanding scholar of Iran and Shiism and was a great source of information and encouragement. Trita Parsi, William Miller, Karim Sadjadpour, and Patrick Clawson also provided helpful details and analysis. Colin Powell, Brent Scowcroft, Richard Haass, Richard Armitage, Martin Indyk, Bruce Riedel, Flynt Leverett, and Hillary Mann are among the former U.S. officials who shared their experiences—and frustrations—in formulating U.S. policy toward Iran. I appreciate as well the access granted to me by Secretary of State Condoleezza Rice, her undersecretary for political affairs, Nick Burns, and former Iraq ambassador Zalmay Khalilzad, and the assistance of other serving U.S. diplomats who disclosed crucial details about Bush administration policy but asked that I withhold their names to avoid prejudicing their careers.

My agent, Gail Ross, taught me how to write a book proposal and extracted a first chapter sufficient to attract St. Martin's Press and its executive editor, Michael Flamini. Thanks to Michael and his staff, the publishing process has been far more pleasure than pain. Geraldine Brooks, the Pultizer Prize–winning author of *March,* is a colleague from the days when we were both foreign correspondents based in Cairo. She was kind enough to read the manuscript and to recommend it to you, the reader.

My husband, Michael Ross, our son, Andrew, and my closest woman friend, Deirdre Carson (alias Didi), provided encouragement throughout the writing process. Michael read several versions of the book and made many good suggestions; Andrew, who is turning out to be a better writer than either of his parents, also read much of the first draft and subsequent drafts, as did Didi. For their dedication to me, this book is dedicated to them.

BITTER
FRIENDS,
BOSOM
ENEMIES

INTRODUCTION

My first glimpse of Iran came courtesy of Saddam Hussein. It was New Year's 1987, near the climax of the Iran-Iraq war, and Iraqi officials had taken a group of foreign correspondents to an island in the Shatt al-Arab, the narrow waterway dividing the two countries. Through slits in cement and sandbag bunkers, we peered at the devastated Iranian port of Khorramshahr, destroyed by Iraqis at the beginning of the war and retaken by the Iranians in hard fighting. The Iraqis had just beaten back a massive Iranian offensive and wanted to show off their victory. They had left the bloated bodies of three Iranian soldiers near us, in easy range for photographers; decapitated palm trees added to the mood of desolation. As if on cue, an Iranian artillery shell fell in the reeds a few hundred yards behind us, hurting no one but providing a jolt of adrenaline and additional color for our stories.

I was based in Cairo at the time and had decided, for reasons of health and convenience, to cover the conflict from the Iraqi side. The Iranians brought reporters to the front *while* the battles were still raging; the Iraqis waited until the fighting ebbed before putting foreign journalists in harm's way. A German reporter had died of a heart attack on the Iranian front, but no journalist I knew had perished on the Iraqi side. Plus, neither the United States nor Egypt had diplomatic relations with Iran, so it was easier to get visas for Iraq than Iran. I thought about trying to go to Iran three years later, after the death of Ayatollah Ruhollah Khomeini, the leader of the Islamic revolution. By then I was five months' pregnant with my son, Andrew, and didn't want to risk being jostled or worse at Khomeini's funeral. My husband and I were packing up to move back to the United States after almost a decade abroad. Iran, I decided, would have to wait.

Seven years went by before I went overseas again as a reporter. When I joined *USA Today* in 1996, a fundamentalist Sunni Muslim faction, the Taliban, had just consolidated power in Afghanistan and was horrifying the rest of the world through, among other things, its atrocious treatment of women. My editor suggested that I do a piece looking at the situation of women in several Muslim countries. I asked if I could return to Cairo, where I had lived for four years, and, for contrast, go to Iran. I had written about the country from afar since the 1979 revolution and the seizure of the U.S. embassy. I was frankly frightened by Iran's reputation, by the harsh calls for "Death to America" at political rallies, the grim reputation of Iranian security forces for murdering dissidents, and the social restrictions that forced women to leave their homes draped in black. But I had heard from other reporters that the stories didn't do justice to most Iranians, that the politics were fascinating, and that reporting from Iran would be easier and more gratifying than from many other Muslim nations.

Iran did not disappoint. In a dog-eared notebook are my first impressions after landing at Tehran's Mehrabab airport in the wee hours of November 16, 1996. "Can taste the pollution in the back of your throat as soon as you get off the plane. No gates to the airport. Must struggle down the stairs with your luggage and board buses. A minimum of fuss at 2 A.M. and even a welcome from the Customs man. Nobody told me to pull my scarf down." My translator, Hamid Araghi, a pleasant young man who was also a stringer for a Japanese newspaper, met me with an empathetic smile. He had brought along a driver, Ebrahim Mahmoody, who was to become my faithful companion and protector on future journeys. In a fog of pollution and jetlag, I was driven along elevated expressways through a sprawling city of mid-rise concrete buildings to my hotel, a Sheraton before the revolution, renamed "Homa," the acronym for Iran's national airline. Hamid seemed offended when I told him that Tehran reminded me of Cairo. "Tehran is much cleaner," he said. Iranians, I soon learned, did not like comparisons with Arabs, even those who also came from an ancient civilization.

My first trip was brief, only a week, but it was packed with vivid moments. There was a government-organized demonstration at which protesters chanted death to another country for a change—Germany, which had just indicted several top Iranian officials for ordering the assassination of Iranian dissidents in Berlin. There was a patient Iranian reporter who drew Venn diagrams to try to explain the complexities of Iranian politics. The Militant Clerics Association is not to be confused with the Militant Clerics Society, he said. A woman intellectual I met said that for the first time since the revolution, she and her husband were thinking of leaving Iran because two writers they knew who had signed a petition protesting government censorship had disappeared, and one had been found dead in his Tehran apartment. There were DOWN WITH USA signs in my hotel and freshly repainted graffiti on the wall of the old U.S. embassy: "America is the most dangerous enemy to Islam, the Iranian nation, and human rights." But the fixtures in the hotel bathroom were still American Standard, the chef made a mean spaghetti bolognese, and there were U.S.-style snack bars playing the pop saxophone music of Kenny G and serving ersatz pizza. I met women who, despite the dreary outer garments they were obliged to wear, held significant jobs as magazine editors, lawyers, and members of parliament. One told me proudly that Iranian women were like lionesses. I resented having to wear their same uniform of a baggy raincoat and a scarf, but the costume also had its advantages. With my then dark hair and olive complexion, I thought I could blend in, so long as I didn't speak. Not that it mattered; Iranians from all walks of life were invariably friendly once they found out I was an American. Even the mayor of Tehran, Gholamhossein Karbaschi, after listing a long catalog of U.S. abuses, confided that he had visited New York twice and said, "I like your Broadway Street."

Having lived in the Soviet Union in the 1970s and China a decade later, I knew a decaying revolution when I saw one. There was the same desire in Iran for contact with outsiders and shame that a once great country had become so shabby. There was fear of government repression mixed with defiance; bitter jokes about elderly, out-of-touch leaders and queries about how to get a visa to the United States. Subsequent visits were more and more intriguing. My next trip, in 1998, followed an Iranian election in which the regime favorite had suffered an ignominious defeat and a reformist new president, Mohammad

Khatami, was trying to liberalize his country and repair relations with the West. I covered a group of U.S. wrestlers who arrived in Tehran to compete in a tournament—the first Americans officially representing their country in Iran since the seizure of U.S. hostages. When I returned to Iran a year later, the twentieth anniversary of the revolution, there were scores of new newspapers to read with actual news in them and the first Tehran Internet café to visit. Iran, it seemed, was going through a Soviet-style *perestroika* and would soon become the "normal" country the vast majority of its people wanted it to be.

It did not happen that quickly, of course. Historians will argue about the reasons. Khatami was too weak; the Clinton administration didn't try hard enough to help him; the Iranian regime was afraid that restoring ties with the United States would destroy what remained of its ideological underpinnings. Between trips to Iran I covered U.S. policy toward Iran, watching the Clinton team's failed efforts to begin high-level talks and the Bush administration's seeming initial indifference.

Then came September 11, 2001. While much of the Muslim world appeared to sympathize with the hijackers, Iran strongly condemned the attacks, and even regime radicals toned down their usual anti-U.S. rhetoric. In hindsight, the period between 9/11 and May 2003 was the most propitious time since the revolution for the two countries to reestablish ties. The two shared an enemy: militant Sunni Muslim fundamentalism, not the more nuanced Shiite variety practiced in Iran. (The two main branches of Islam split in the seventh century A.D. in a dispute over succession to the prophet Mohammed.) A dozen meetings took place between senior U.S. and Iranian diplomats, and there was acknowledged cooperation in forming a new government for Afghanistan, as well as tacit collaboration on the military side. Iran had not yet made much progress toward nuclear weapons, the United States was not bogged down in Iraq, and the moderate Khatami had just been reelected to another four-year term. Bush administration "realists" such as Richard Haass, then director for policy planning in the State Department, argued after 9/11 for a gesture to Tehran—such as an end to blocking Iran's application to join the World Trade Organization. The administration rejected such ideas. Still, in May 2003, Iran put forward a broad agenda for talks that included all the issues of concern to the

United States, from terrorism to nuclear weapons to the Arab-Israeli dispute.

Dozens of prominent Americans, including President Bush's own father, tried to convince the president to put more energy into a diplomatic path. But in Washington there was little patience for pragmatism among the ideologues who had commandeered U.S. policy and who favored a more Ramboesque approach. In 2002, Iran had found itself on an "axis of evil" with North Korea and Saddam's Iraq. The Bush administration only began offering significant concessions to Iran four years later, when the United States was in a relatively weak position because of its calamitous intervention in Iraq. By then, oil prices had risen above seventy dollars a barrel, and Iran had a belligerent new president.

In writing this book, I have benefited from extraordinary access to senior figures in both countries, including three Iranian presidents and dozens of current and former U.S. officials. In the process I have learned of repeated, largely unsuccessful attempts to narrow the differences between the two countries, and of miscalculations for which both Iranians and Americans are paying a heavy price. In going to war in Iraq, for example, the Bush administration ignored the assessment of its own intelligence community that the invasion would push Iran to redouble its efforts to acquire nuclear weapons. As of this writing Tehran may be only a year or two away from building its first nuclear bomb.

Yet Iran, in the words of a diplomat friend of mine, is not just a nuclear program, it's a country. And that country remains caught between pride in its history and independence and a desire to be accepted in the modern world. Over and over during my trips to Iran I met people who railed against U.S. policies toward Iran, then, in practically the same breath, praised some aspect of American culture or told me proudly of their relatives in the United States. In Aradan, a dusty provincial village three hours' drive southeast of Tehran and the birthplace of Iran's virulently anti-American president, Mahmoud Ahmadinejad, one of his cousins, Haj Ali Shahhosseini, an elderly shopkeeper, kept joking with me as I tried to interview him about the president, saying he was ready to "close the doors" of his store if I would take him with me to the United States.

The title of the book is a malapropism said to my husband by an Egyptian at a cocktail party in Cairo two decades ago. Meant to apply

to Arab feelings about the United States, it also captures the tortured
history of Iran and the United States. Like a long-married couple that
has gone through a bitter divorce, the two countries may never get back
together with the same intimacy, but they may acknowledge that they
have wronged each other and learn to interact in a less destructive way.
My hope is that this book will enlighten Americans about the consequences of both governments' actions and help them understand the
complexity of Iran and the need for creativity, patience, and prudence
in dealing with it. Otherwise, we will be as unpleasantly surprised by
the results of our missteps with Iran as we have been by our involvement in Iraq.

ONE

"DEATH TO AMERICA" AND
"CAN I HAVE YOUR AUTOGRAPH?"

IT WAS A GORGEOUS day for a demonstration.

The mild February air, unusually clear of smog, made the mood more like that of a picnic than a protest. Hundreds of people walked in long columns toward Tehran's Freedom Square, where a towering, arched, white concrete monument erected by Iran's deposed leader, the shah, commemorated twenty-five hundred years of Iran's existence as a unified nation. Peddlers hawked candy and red balloons, while organizers from the government passed out anti-American posters and green headbands proclaiming Iran's "obvious right" to nuclear energy. On the periphery of the square, buses disgorged workers from factories and students from local schools who had been given the day off but were obliged to spend half of it at the demonstration.

An annual ritual for more than two decades, Revolution Day (February 11) is the Islamic Republic of Iran's Fourth of July, marking the fall of the shah's last government. But instead of the fireworks most Americans look forward to on that holiday, Iranians are accustomed to verbal pyrotechnics: slogans burned into their brains since Ayatollah Ruhollah Khomeini, the beetle-browed leader of the revolution, returned to Iran from exile on February 1, 1979. "Death to America" and "Death to Israel" are perennial favorites, with calls to bring down some other government occasionally added for variety. On this particular holiday there was a new attraction: a new president, a blacksmith's son named Mahmoud Ahmadinejad. Clad in his customary antielitist attire (a cheap black sports coat over a black shirt, beige sweater vest, and gray pants), Ahmadinejad delivered an hourlong harangue about Iran's mistreatment by the United States.

A small man on a large stage, he sought to benefit from a confluence of events: the twenty-seventh anniversary of the downfall of the shah; an escalating confrontation with the West over Iran's nuclear program; protests throughout the Muslim world at the publication of Danish cartoons lampooning the prophet Mohammed; and just concluded celebrations of Ashura, the most important holiday for Shiite Muslims, commemorating the death in the Iraqi desert in A.D. 680 of the prophet's grandson, Hossein, at the hands of the army of a brutal ruler. Ahmadinejad tried to stir all these elements into a superpatriotic stew to exhort the crowd into renewed passion for Iran's Islamic government and to support for its controversial development of nuclear power. The Islamic revolution, the president declared, mirrored the valiant struggle of Hossein and his followers against those who would oppress true Islamic faith. In the same way, the president vowed, Iran would stand up to Western "bullies" who challenged Iran's "inalienable and undisputed right to produce and use nuclear energy."

"Western governments and the Great Satan [the United States] can accept insults to the prophets but it's not legal to talk about the Holocaust," Ahmadinejad continued, hammering what for him was becoming a favorite theme: the denial of the Nazi murder of six million Jews. "They use this [the Holocaust] to justify what they do to the Palestinians," he said. "They are the hostages of Zionism."

The crowd, which overflowed the square, dutifully sang patriotic songs and chanted "Death to America" and "Death to Israel" on cue. Many carried crude signs insulting Israeli and American leaders. HEY BOSH, SHUT UP declared a poster that showed a caricature of President Bush standing on a globe wearing underpants made from a U.S. flag. NUCLEAR TECHNOLOGY IS OUR LEGITIMATE RIGHT read another. THE HOLOCAUST IS A BIG LIE said a third. And, as is de rigueur on such occasions, demonstrators burned U.S. and Israeli flags and crude effigies of Uncle Sam.

Some of the signs looked handmade, but most were props handed out by government officials. Much of the fervor seemed feigned, and the crowd's attention wandered. Near a wooden scaffold where I stood with several other reporters and cameramen filming the rally, hundreds of schoolgirls bused in for the event milled about as though on a field trip to an amusement park. Over their requisite black scarves, they wore green headbands proclaiming allegiance to Hossein and support for Iran's right to nuclear energy. On their backs, over enveloping black cloaks called *chadors,* they wore signboards also declaring that Nu-CLEAR ENERGY IS OUR LEGITIMATE RIGHT. But they fidgeted and gossiped with each other other during Ahmadinejad's maiden Revolution Day speech, barely paying attention to him. And when they spied me on the platform with the other journalists, and found out I was American, they started calling out in English, "What's your name?" and "We love you!" Then dozens of the girls began passing me small scraps of paper asking for my autograph. Azam Zamani, thirteen, apologized as the "Death to America" chants rose around her. "I'm sorry," she said. "We love Americans."

Outside and inside the Iranian regime there is tremendous ambivalence about America. No other country is so fixated on the United States. No other foreign government so aspires to and fears a U.S. embrace. No other nation has provoked such a complicated response in return. Iran has been dubbed "the Bermuda triangle" of American diplomacy for swallowing up good-faith U.S. efforts to end the hostility. Iranian officials have struggled to understand domestic U.S. political pressures, while U.S. officials have tried to decipher the motives of Iranian leaders who have decried the Great Satan and funded anti-U.S. terrorists while reaching out to Washington for dialogue and respect. A few American officials have understood that Iran's harsh rhetoric, support for Middle Eastern militants, and quest for nuclear technology are predicated as much on a sense of insecurity as on a desire to dominate the Middle East. But few have been willing to try bold approaches to deal with that insecurity, for fear of bolstering a repressive government and risking political opposition in the United States.

Iranians are at least equally to blame for the long estrangement between the two countries. Hatred for the United States was a central tenet of the revolution against the U.S.-backed shah and became a habit that was difficult to break. There has been a constant fear among Iranian politicians that they would reach out to America only to be humiliated, or that rivals in Iran's complex political system would use such overtures against them. "Suppose we sit in dialogue with the United States, and they reject oil pipelines from the Caspian Sea through Iran," Abbas Maleki, a former deputy foreign minister, said in a 2001 interview, referring to U.S. pressures on Central Asian nations to send their oil west out to Turkey rather than using the shortest route, south through Iran to the Persian Gulf. "We would lose the image of Iran in the Islamic world," he said. Conservative political forces repeatedly sabotaged attempts by Iran to improve relations with the United States when the reformist Mohammad Khatami was in power. That would make him too popular, they feared, and doom their own chances for a comeback. Once in power, some of these same conservatives seemed to fear reconciliation with the United States as much or more than a U.S. military strike, which could consolidate support for the regime.

Iranian efforts to drum up hatred of the United States have waxed and waned over the years, and the lobby of the Homa Hotel was a good barometer of prevailing official sentiment. On my first visit, in November 1996, there were large gold letters over the elevator bank: DOWN WITH USA (although the spacing between the letters was off so it actually read: DOWN WITHU SA). By my next visit, in 1998, after Khatami's election, the slogan was gone at his command. In 2001, it was replaced by a discreet placard downstairs from the lobby on a bulletin board near the men's room. Attributed to the "Islamic association of Homa hotel," it said in small letters: DOWN WITH ISRAEL. DOWN WITH USA. It was put up in honor of Jerusalem Day, a pro-Palestinian event celebrated yearly by the Iranian regime on the last day of Ramadan, the ninth month of the Muslim calendar, in which the Koran was revealed to the prophet Mohammed. Two days after the holiday, the sign had vanished.

The bellmen, desk clerks, and waiters in the hotel, many of whom had worked there when it was a Sheraton, welcomed me back each time I returned to Iran like a long-lost relative. On my first visit a doorman said, "America very good" and put his two pinkies together, signaling his desire for better ties. Ten years later a bellman pulled out his old identity card from the 1970s with his name in English and his photo with long hair and sideburns. "Those were the good days," he sighed.

A poll taken in 2002 showed that more than 70 percent of Iranians wanted relations restored with the United States. The pollster— ironically a ringleader of the 1979–81 seizure of the U.S. Embassy—

was jailed, and no such survey has been taken since. Opportunities for reconciliation have come and gone repeatedly over the past twenty-eight years, especially since the 9/11 attacks by al-Qaeda terrorists. From Iran's perspective, those attacks were both a blessing and a curse. A blessing because the Bush administration declared war on Iran's two greatest regional foes: the Sunni fundamentalist Taliban regime in Afghanistan that harbored al-Qaeda and also had murdered Farsi-speaking Afghan Shiites and Iranian diplomats; and the secular Baathist dictatorship of Iraq's Saddam Hussein, which had invaded Iran in 1980 and was responsible for the deaths of three hundred thousand Iranians. A curse because those two wars brought U.S. troops to Iran's borders and briefly raised the hopes of some Iranians that a similar act of "liberation" would rid them of a repressive clerical government.

The public response in Iran to the September 11 attacks showed how different Iran, a non-Arab country, is from much of the rest of the Muslim world. While many Arabs celebrated what they saw as a long-deserved blow against the prime supporter of Israel, many Iranians held spontaneous candlelit demonstrations in sympathy with the U.S. victims. With links to a diaspora of nearly a million people in the United States, little regard for Arabs, and a cultural appreciation for innocent victims of violence, Iranians instinctively felt a connection with those who died at the World Trade Center, the Pentagon, and on the plane that crashed in Pennsylvania.

When I visited Iran a few months after the attacks, warm emotions toward the United States were running strong. Young people were sporting Gap jeans and washing down their shish kebab with "the real thing": Coca-Cola, produced for the first time since the Islamic revolution under license in the eastern Iranian shrine city of Mashhad. The drink had come to symbolize America, and consuming it in public was a political statement in favor of U.S.-Iran reconciliation. Iranian parliamentarians, previously fearful of praising Americans on the record to foreign journalists, openly advocated restoring relations with the United States. "The equation has changed since September 11," said one of them, Gholamheidar Ebrahimby-Salami, then a representative from a town near the Afghan border. Iran should "definitely" have formal diplomatic ties with the United States, he said. Mahmoud Kashani, an independent presidential candidate in the 2001 elections, said that had he been elected, "that day would have been the beginning of direct negotiations" with the United States. Even Ali Khamenei, who became Iran's supreme religious leader after the death in 1989 of Ayatollah Khomeini, suspended the ritual chant of "Death to America" at Friday prayers at Tehran University out of deference to American feelings. When they resumed, some Iranians jokingly changed the slogan to "*Margh bar Amrika-ye aziz*": Death to the *dear* America.

The Bush administration focused not on what Iran had done to help the United States but on Iranian interference in Afghanistan that American officials said ran counter to U.S. interests. Most damaging of all, on January 3, 2002, Israeli commandos seized a ship, the *Karine A,* alleged to be carrying Iranian weapons for Yasser Arafat's Palestininian Authority via the Red Sea. A speechwriter, David Frum, had suggested the word "axis" to refer to America's enemies in a draft for Bush's State of the Union address later that month. Another speechwriter, Michael Gerson, turned the word into the phrase "axis of evil," and Bush filled in the blanks with Saddam Hussein's Iraq, North Korea, and Iran.

The Bush administration appeared to have no idea what impact its words would have. Condoleezza Rice, at the time of the speech Bush's national security advisor, told me four years later that "what is funny about it is that [the phrase] didn't really catch my eye." For many Iranians, however, the remark was devastating. Those who had worked for an end to enmity with the United States and for reform in their own country said they felt like jilted lovers. Khamenei and Iranian hard-liners "used Bush's words against us," said Mohsen Kadivar, a reformist cleric. It became unpatriotic, he told me, to advocate relations with the United States. Conservatives used the speech to justify new efforts to exclude reformers from office. A clerical council that vetted candidates barred most of the reformist parliament from running for re-election in 2004 and disqualified many others who sought the presidency in 2005. Despite this draconian culling, all but one of the eight candidates permitted to run for president put forward platforms suggesting that they would reach out to the United States, understanding that would have broad popular appeal. "The mere fact that I am sitting here with you means we have no differences with the American people," Ali Akbar Hashemi Rafsanjani, the wily cleric who had previously served two presidential terms, told me in an interview in 2005 that kicked off his new campaign.

The exception was Ahmadinejad, who defeated Rafsanjani in a

runoff in June, profiting from a protest vote against one of Iran's richest men. "Our nation has no significant need for the United States," Ahmadinejad said in his first press conference as president.[1] Seven months later he expanded on his anti-American views in an interview with me, his first with a U.S. newspaper. "We have in this world six billion people," he said. "It's not an American club." The United States thinks "that no one can live without them and this is a wrong notion. We have proved we can live without them."

For all its incendiary rhetoric, Iran is the Rodney Dangerfield of Middle Eastern nations, a country that believes it deserves but has invariably been denied sufficient respect. Iranians have long felt that they were owed special attention because of Iran's location on the Persian Gulf, large oil resources, and ancient history. Even as they have confronted the United States and called for the downfall of American governments, they have watched with poorly concealed envy the growing U.S. alliance with neighboring nations India and Pakistan and the U.S. and Western investment poured into tiny Arab sheikdoms across the Persian Gulf.

Unlike Iraq, which was cobbled together by the British after World War I from the ruins of the Turkish Ottoman Empire, Iran has been a unified nation for more than two thousand years. More than five hundred years before the birth of Jesus Christ, a Persian king, Cyrus the Great, built an empire that stretched from present-day Turkey to Afghanistan. The empire crumbled, but Iranian civilization triumphed. It absorbed waves of invaders from Greeks to Mongols to Turks and Arabs, changing the invaders more than it was itself transformed.

Even Islam took on a unique form when it came in contact with Iran. In pre-Islamic times, Iran—or Persia, as it was known until the twentieth century—gave rise to a religion, Zoroastrianism, that had a single supreme God and a well-developed concept of right and wrong. Iranians still celebrate the Zoroastrian new year by jumping over fires and other pre-Islamic behavior.

Most Iranians today are Shiites, a minority among the world's 1.3 billion Muslims, who initially broke away in a dispute over who should succeed the prophet Mohammed. Shiites believe it should have been Mohammed's cousin and son-in-law, Ali, followed by other blood relatives, including Ali's son, Hossein. Shah Ismail, who ruled from 1501 to 1526, made Shiite Islam Iran's state religion, but the form the faith took—with many European and pre-Islamic characteristics—has more in common with Catholicism and evangelical Christianity than it does with the austere Sunni Islam that predominates in the Arab nations across the Persian Gulf. For example, the most important Shiite holiday, Ashura, in Iran and other Shiite centers feels like Good Friday, with passion plays about Hossein's death and parades of men and boys carrying heavy cross-shaped metal platforms, called *alamat,* adorned with symbols of the twelve most important Shiite religious figures, or *imams.* Most Shiites, known as Twelver Shiites for their reverence for these religious figures, believe that the twelfth *imam,* a young boy who went into hiding for his own protection in the ninth century, will return as a *mahdi,* or messiah, to bring justice to the world. The concept is similar to the fundamentalist Christian belief in the return of Christ and the Day of Judgment. Indeed, Christ is supposed to accompany the *mahdi* on his return to Earth.

The Shiite theme of resistance to oppression figures deeply in the Iranian psyche. In modern-day Iran, Yazid, the evil caliph whose forces massacred Hossein and his followers in the desert in the seventh century, has been compared to both President Bush and Saddam Hussein. Iranian propaganda has portrayed U.S. economic sanctions against Iran and efforts to deny it nuclear technology as part of a conspiracy against Muslims and citizens of developing nations in general. In his speeches Ahmadinejad casts the Israelis and Palestinians in a similar passion play. Injustice is to be resisted now, the Iranian leader says, just as it was by Hossein fourteen centuries ago.

Iran's history of empire and invasion has made its people welcoming and at the same time distrustful and prone to conspiracy theories about perceived foreign plots. Iranians still nurse grudges against Britain and Russia, which took advantage of Iranian weakness in the nineteenth and early twentieth centuries to wrest concessions from a failing Turkic dynasty, the Qajars. The Qajars financed a lavish and decadent court by selling off land, economic monopolies, and exclusive rights to Iran's natural resources. The sale of a tobacco monopoly to a British company headed by an army major in 1891 led to Iran's first mass protests and foreshadowed a 1906 revolt that led to the creation of a short-lived parliament.

In the twentieth century, a more disciplined monarch arose—a Russian-trained army officer named Reza Khan. He seized power in 1925 and sought to drag Iran from feudalism to modernity in the space of only a few decades. He decreed that Iranians must wear Western dress and that women must not wear the veil outside their homes, a hugely controversial edict that boomeranged a half century later when the *chador* became a rallying symbol in the Islamic revolution. Reza Shah, as he became known after seizing power, limited the traditional powers of the clergy by requiring that judges hold university law degrees and depriving clerics of the authority to notarize documents, a major source of income. He also established a network of secular schools and universities that undermined the clergy's previous monopoly over education and tried to modernize the curriculum taught to seminary students.[2] All this engendered hostility that became a foundation for clerical opposition to the shah's son.

In foreign policy Reza Shah reached out to the United States, seeking a counterweight to Russian and British influence, but also sought an alliance with Nazi Germany. Allied powers forced him to abdicate in 1941 and placed his son, Mohammad Reza, upon the throne. A weaker and more conflicted figure, the new shah continued Iran's march toward economic development and modernization, and he strengthened Iran's ties to the world's rising superpower, the United States.

He faced his first great challenge when Mohammed Mossadegh, a wildly popular and eccentric prime minister who had supported the 1906 revolution, persuaded the Iranian parliament to pass legislation in 1951 that nationalized Iran's British-run oil company. In an appeal that was a precursor to that used by Ahmadinejad to justify Iran's nuclear program, Mossadegh sought to put Iran's action in the context of postwar struggles by developing countries for a more equitable international system. He said his "movement served as inspiration to national risings of other peoples" in the Third World.[3] The Eisenhower administration, encouraged by Britain, ordered the CIA to organize a coup in 1953 that overthrew Mossadegh and put the shah back on the throne. The coup is still a source of grievance in Iran every bit as bitter as the 1979–81 seizure of U.S. Embassy hostages remains for most Americans.

The shah repaid his U.S. benefactors for rescuing his reign by acting as an American surrogate in the Persian Gulf, managing to be a close ally to both Israel and Saudi Arabia. He went on a shopping spree, buying an expensive arsenal of U.S. weapons, wasting Iranian resources in a way that aroused considerable domestic opposition. Prodded by President Kennedy, the Iranian leader also sought to show he could be a modern monarch by introducing new social reforms, including voting and other rights for women. However, the shah went too far for religious conservatives, and in 1964, he exiled their most prominent leader, Ayatollah Khomeini, after Khomeini protested a law granting immunity from prosecution to U.S. diplomats, military advisers, and their families in Iran.[4]

AMERICA HELD HOSTAGE

Opposition to the shah's policies grew, and his dreaded secret police, Savak, responded with arrests and torture, fueling protests from an increasingly broad spectrum of Iranian society, including students, leftist supporters of Mossadegh, and pro-Soviet communists, as well as Islamic socialists and fundamentalists. When the monarch's soldiers began mowing down unarmed demonstrators in 1978, the regime of the shah, who was by then dying of cancer, had begun its final descent. This time, no CIA came to his rescue. He left the country, and his last government collapsed eleven days after Khomeini landed in Tehran from Paris on a flight filled with supporters and foreign journalists.

That is the day Iran's Islamic rulers now celebrate in Freedom Square, the culmination of what they call the "ten days of dawn." Old footage of Khomeini's triumphant return and slow motorcade through Tehran amid adoring crowds plays on television over and over during the commemoration of this anniversary. The young men, with their long hair and bushy sideburns, recall the era when Iran held U.S. hostages. Americans who were politically conscious at the time of the revolution will never forget the seizure of the U.S. Embassy on November 4, 1979, and the images of blindfolded U.S. diplomats displayed like trophies by their Iranian captors. Iranian students broke into the compound through a basement window and initially held 61 Americans captive there. They eventually freed the women and minorities but kept 52 U.S. citizens hostage for 444 days.

For many Americans, the hostage crisis remains the defining event of U.S.-Iran relations, and they see no justification for this outrage. Yet the Iranian participants saw it differently. On October 22, 1979, the Carter administration allowed the shah and his family to enter the United States so that he could receive medical treatment for his cancer. Popular sentiment in Iran boiled over a week later, when Carter's national security adviser, Zbigniew Brzezinski, met in Algeria with then Iranian prime minister Mehdi Barzargan. Remembering the events of 1953, Iranian revolutionaries feared a new U.S. plot to intervene and thwart their aspirations for independence. Ebrahim Asgharzadeh, one of the leaders of the takeover, told me twenty years later that the tactic was inspired in part by U.S. student protests during the Vietnam War, and that the Iranian demonstrators intended to stay for only forty-eight hours. Khomeini and his top advisers prolonged the crisis to destroy any possibility of rapprochement with the United States and to undercut moderate supporters of the revolution. The provisional prime minister, Barzagan, resigned two days after the hostages were seized. The following spring, a new Islamic constitution enshrining Khomeini as the supreme leader of the country was overwhelmingly approved in a referendum.

The captive embassy became a sort of revolutionary tourist attraction, its value increased by nonstop U.S. media coverage and President Carter's obsession with freeing the hapless diplomats. Carter's—and America's—humiliation deepened when the United States mounted a rescue mission in April 1980 that not only failed to free the hostages but cost the lives of eight American servicemen and left behind the wreckage of half a dozen U.S. military aircraft. Khomeini agreed to the hostages' release only after the shah had died and Carter had lost the 1980 election, thereby paying for his "crime" of supporting the shah. In a final act of vengeance the Iranians did not free the hostages until a few hours after President Reagan's inauguration. Yet Iranian leaders seek to minimize the act and spin themselves as the victims. In 2005, former president Rafsanjani told me that the hostages "left Iran in a relaxed mood" and that the fault lay with the United States, which had admitted the shah for medical treatment.

Like old women comparing surgical scars, Iranian officials compete to prove whose suffering was greater. "This is where I was tortured by agents of the United States in the shah's time," said Habibolah Asgaroladi, a conservative politician, pointing to his head, where he said he was beaten by the shah's secret police in the 1970s. Americans, of course, place the blame for the breakdown in relations primarily on Iran. The United States broke diplomatic relations with Iran in 1980, and other Western nations scaled back their ties because of the embassy seizure, leaving Iran isolated when Iraqi leader Saddam Hussein, thinking Iran would collapse easily, decided to invade the country in September 1980.

Officially, the United States declared a policy of neutrality—former secretary of state Henry Kissinger famously said at the time that it was a pity that the countries couldn't both lose. However, Washington soon tilted in the direction of Baghdad, providing intelligence and weapons, including the components for the biological and chemical arms U.S. forces sought in vain after attacking Iraq in 2003. Some Iranians believe the United States instigated Iraq's invasion to avenge the seizure of the U.S. Embassy. In an interview, Iranian national security adviser Ali Larijani pointed to a visit he said President Reagan's envoy, Donald Rumsfeld, paid to Baghdad before the war. "Americans started a war in the region, provoking Saddam Hussein, and we lost two hundred thousand lives," Larijani told me. "Mr. Rumsfeld one week before the Iraqi invasion met Saddam Hussein and provoked this." In fact, Reagan did not take office until 1981, five months after the war started, and Rumsfeld didn't visit Baghdad until 1983.

In many respects, the United States and Iran have been in a state of undeclared war for most of the last three decades. While they have rarely fought face-to-face, they have exchanged bitter insults and threats and attacked each other indirectly. Iraq, it can be argued, served as a U.S. and Arab proxy in containing the spread of Iran's Islamic revolution in the 1980s. While the United States aided Saddam's Iraq, Iran created surrogates of its own to carry out asymmetrical warfare against its superpower foe. Hezbollah is the prime example. Iran organized this Lebanese Shiite militant group, whose name means "the party of God," after Israel invaded Lebanon in 1982. Besides Israelis, Hezbollah murdered 241 Americans in a truck bombing at a U.S. Marines barracks in 1983, carried out skyjackings, and seized U.S. journalists and academics as hostages in Beirut in the 1980s.

Iran also backed militants in Shiite communities in Arab nations along the Persian Gulf, including Saudi Shiites who, according to a U.S. indictment, exploded a truck bomb in front of a U.S. Air Force barracks in Saudi Arabia in 1996, killing nineteen U.S. airmen. Iran built relationships with Shiite groups opposed to the Sunni Muslim regimes of its neighbors, Afghanistan and Iraq, and had close ties with the Northern Alliance, an Afghan militia that the Bush administration relied on heavily to defeat the Taliban in 2001. And Iran organized the Badr Brigades, an Iraqi Shiite force, during Saddam's long reign, when thousands of Iraq Shiites fled to Iran to escape persecution and service in Saddam's military. One of the great ironies of Bush administration Iraq policy is that when the United States invaded Iraq in 2003, it was obliged to work closely with Shiite politicians who owed their very survival to Iran. As events in Iraq spiraled quickly out of U.S. control, thinly spread U.S. forces could do little but watch while Iranian-trained and -equipped Shiite militias filled power vacuums in southern Iraq and Shiite areas of Baghdad.

The conflict between the Bush administration's prodemocracy rhetoric and its need for tactical alliances with Iran to fight the Taliban in Afghanistan and Sunni insurgents in Iraq made it hard for American officials to put together a coherent policy to deal with Iran's growing regional power and mounting evidence that it was close to developing the ability to make nuclear weapons. It took the Bush administration until 2006 to unveil a national security strategy (its first since 2002) in which it declared that the United States "may face no greater challenge from a single country than from Iran." Yet Washington was hard-pressed to do much about this challenge, despite its bellicose rhetoric. In Bush's second term American officials worked closely with Europeans to try to increase diplomatic and economic pressure on Tehran to suspend its nuclear program, but the deepening U.S. predicament in Iraq diminished Iranian fears of possible punishment.

Iranian officials responded to American pressure with a mixture of counterthreats and overtures. "The United States has the power to cause harm and pain," Ali Asghar Soltanieh, Iran's delegate to the International Atomic Energy Agency, the UN nuclear watchdog, said. "But the United States is also susceptible to harm and pain. So if that is the path that the U.S. wishes to choose, let the ball roll."[5]

At the same time that they were issuing threats, Iranian officials put out new feelers to Washington in hopes of using their leverage in Iraq to strike a broader deal. Iranian officials agreed to one-on-one talks with American officials about Iraq, asserting that they were doing so at the behest of their Iraqi Shiite allies, but first the Iranians, then the Americans, got cold feet. The two sides finally met in May 2007 in Baghdad in an atmosphere of acrimony that held out little prospect for progress. Mostly, the Iranians sought what the Bush administration had always refused to give: recognition that after nearly three decades, Iran's system of government, however unappealing, was not about to disappear.

"We see ourselves as equal nations," said Fuad Sadeghi, a young journalist and founder of a conservative Iranian Web site called *Baztab* (Reflections). "You shouldn't expect in Iran what you saw in Libya or Iraq. If the United States enters talks as an equal partner with Iran, then it would get a good response. Iran and the States should solve their problems together."

A senior adviser to Iran's national security council, Mohammad Javad Jaffari, put it this way in an interview in the winter of 2006: "The United States in the past twenty-seven years has never needed Iran's help until now. Today, a very small group of Sunni Arabs is in conflict with the United States. Today, the government of Iraq is an ally of Iran and in Lebanon, Syria, Afghanistan, and Palestine, the United States needs Iran. Iran needs the United States, too. We can come to an understanding, but do you think there are eyes to see or ears to listen in Washington?"

Out in the provinces ordinary Iranians showed mixed emotions as tensions escalated over Iran's nuclear program. In the town of Garmsar, near Ahmadinejad's home village of Aradan, a three-hour drive east of Tehran along the old silk road to China, Zolfali Jurabloo was treating me, his first American guest, to a traditional Persian lunch. Sitting cross-legged on a carpet, dishes spread out before him on a plastic tablecloth, the sixty-three-year-old farmer served up equal portions of lamb stew and Iranian pride. "Tell Mister Bush he should not attack our homes," my host told me, referring to U.S. threats over Iran's nuclear program. More economic sanctions or a military strike did not worry him. "Even a small glass of my water is worth more than anything in the United States," he said.

After continuing in this combative vein for several minutes, the farmer, his face creased by wrinkles from years of exposure to the Persian sun, cast a hopeful and somewhat appraising eye at me as he plied me with pickled cherries. "Perhaps you can find me an American wife?" he asked.

TWO

IRAN AND THE BOMB

Buried under soft brown hills of dirt that blend perfectly into a craggy desert landscape, Iran's largest known nuclear facility is recognizable from the road only because it is surrounded by watchtowers and antiaircraft batteries. Unknown to international arms inspectors until 2002, the Natanz site, about 160 miles south of Tehran, houses a large, partially buried building designed to hold fifty thousand centrifuges—sophisticated machines that spin at high speeds to concentrate a form of uranium needed for nuclear fuel. According to nuclear experts, the plant, if operating at full capacity, could produce enough uranium for twenty-five Hiroshima-sized (10-kiloton) bombs a year.[1]

Iranian officials have insisted that they intend to use the facility for peaceful purposes only and that they would never produce uranium that could be used for bombs. But Iran's subterfuge—it concealed much of its program for nearly two decades—and a parallel effort to build missiles that could carry nuclear warheads have led much of the world to doubt Tehran's word. At the same time, Bush administration policies—declaring a right to attack countries to preempt terrorist or nuclear threats and invading Iran's neighbor, Iraq—provided potent additional incentives for Iran to seek nuclear status. In going to war in Iraq, the U.S. government ignored warnings from its own intelligence community that the invasion would spur Iran to try harder to become a nuclear weapons state.

As this book is being written it is probably already too late to prevent Iran from acquiring the ability to make nuclear weapons. By the spring of 2006 Iran had mastered centrifuge technology to the point where it was able to enrich a small amount of uranium to the level needed for fuel for civilian power plants. The same technology can make fuel for bombs. A year later, Iran had installed more than 1,300 centrifuges at Natanz and produced more than 175 tons of uranium hexafluoride, the gaseous form of uranium that is fed into centrifuges for enrichment. That's enough for more than 20 weapons.[2] Iran's progress has obliged U.S. intelligence analysts to revise their estimate of how long it could take Iran to develop a bomb, halving their worst-case scenario of 2016 to as early as 2010. According to former U.S. intelligence director John Negroponte, the Iranians "seem to be determined . . . to develop nuclear weapons."[3]

Intelligence estimates, of course, are just that; the U.S. failure to find weapons of mass destruction in Iraq demonstrated the difficulty of finding and assessing nuclear progress in secretive, authoritarian countries. As with Iraq, there is a history of both underestimating and hyping Iran's nuclear prowess. Throughout the 1990s Israeli officials repeatedly said that Iran was only a year or two away from producing weapons, and some in Israel now say that Iran could have the bomb by 2008.[4] John Bolton, a hawkish U.S. official who was undersecretary of state for arms control and international security in Bush's first term and later ambassador to the United Nations, told a 2004 audience at the Hudson Institute, a conservative Washington think tank, that Iranian officials had bragged to Europeans that they could make enough enriched uranium for a nuclear weapon in a year. Given the degree of knowledge possessed by Iranian scientists, however, they seemed likely to be able to reach the nuclear threshold even if they suspended the program during negotiations with Western countries—or the United States or Israel destroyed the known Iranian nuclear infrastructure in a military attack. "Iran may have advanced to the point where it can covertly develop nuclear weapons" even if it halts its overt program, according to Middle East military expert Anthony Cordesman.[5] Western diplomacy has focused on slowing the program down and trying to convince Iran that it will gain more by stopping short of confirmed membership in the world's coveted club of nuclear weapons states. It has not been an easy task.

THE WRONG ROGUE

The Bush administration, in the aftermath of the 9/11 attacks, identified the combination of weapons of mass destruction and terrorism as
the most potent threat to U.S. national security. But after invading Afghanistan, it focused next on Iraq, which had been caught after the first
Gulf War in 1991 with a nuclear program more advanced than it had
disclosed to international inspectors. In August 2002, as U.S. officials
were starting to beat the war drums loudly for Iraq, Natanz and another nuclear facility—a so-called heavy water plant under construction at Arak that could yield plutonium, another potential bomb
fuel—were exposed by an Iranian antiregime group based outside
Paris called the National Council of Resistance, the political wing of a
terrorist organization, the Mujahedin e-Khalq (MEK). How the group
got this information remains a topic of dispute; some U.S. nuclear experts believe that Israel was the real source. Wherever the original tip
came from, the International Atomic Energy Agency, the UN nuclear
watchdog with which Iran had nominally been cooperating since 1970,
confirmed the exile group's revelations, and Iran reluctantly began
dribbling out information about a program it had concealed for eighteen years.

The Bush administration, however, was fixated on Iraq and ignored
a U.S. intelligence community assessment about the impact of an Iraq
invasion on other would-be proliferators. Robert Hutchings, who from
2003 to 2005 headed the National Intelligence Council, an advisory
board of experts that prepares intelligence estimates on key issues for
the White House, said the council warned the administration in early
2003 that as a result of the U.S. pursuit of regime change in Iraq, "the
Iranian regime, like the North Korean regime, would probably judge
that their best option would be to acquire nuclear weapons as fast as
possible because the possession of nuclear weapons offers protection"
from U.S. attack. "I'm not sure exactly what their assumptions were
about Iranian behavior, and if the Iraq gambit had worked out the way
they hoped it would," Hutchings told me after he had left government.
"I guess they thought that this would so cow neighboring states that
they would desist from bad action."

U.S. attention began shifting to Iran only when the war in Iraq proved more challenging than the White House and civilian leadership of the Pentagon had anticipated, and Saddam's purported WMD failed to materialize. Still, the Bush administration was wary of dealing openly with Iran, a charter member of its "axis of evil." For three years the United States essentially had outsourced the Iranian nuclear issue to three European countries—Britain, France, and Germany. The so-called EU-3, hoping to prevent the United States from following the same military path with Iran that it had with Iraq, engaged in sporadic negotiations with Iran and presented an offer in August 2005 that promised a stockpile of five years of fuel for a nearly completed civilian reactor at the Iranian port of Bushehr, other trade concessions, and "a higher state of relations" between Iran and European Union members. In return, Iran was asked not to pursue its nuclear fuel program for ten years. The Europeans had delayed making an offer in hopes that Rafsanjani, the pragmatic ex-president, would win a new four-year term in Iran's June 2005 elections. But Rafsanjani lost to Ahmadinejad, a hard-liner with no experience in foreign affairs, and Iran rejected the European offer as insufficient and vague.

Even before the proposal was made the Iranians ended a ten-month voluntary suspension of their program and resumed operations at a plant in Isfahan that converted raw uranium into uranium hexafluoride gas. The Iranian game plan, in the metaphor of Robert Einhorn, assistant secretary of state for arms control under the Clinton administration, was "salami slicing. They're testing the international community. If they get a strong reaction, they can stop; if not, they can continue salami slicing." Emboldened by a relatively weak initial international response—a verbal wrist slap by the governing board of the IAEA, which urged Iran to go back to suspension but imposed no penalties if it didn't—Iran sliced off a larger chunk of salami in January 2006 and told the IAEA to take the seals off a small uranium enrichment facility at Natanz. This time the United States and Europeans were able to convince the IAEA board to vote to refer the Iranian nuclear program to the UN Security Council. But Russia and China threatened to block a UN resolution that could lay the groundwork for sanctions against Iran. Finally, in May 2006, the Bush administration offered to talk to Tehran about the nuclear program, as one of a six-nation group including the Europeans, Russia, and China. The United States also said it would consider allowing the Europeans to sell Iran civilian power plants containing U.S. technology and new airliners to replace Iran's decrepit stock. However, Iran refused to suspend uranium enrichment as a precondition for talks, even after the UN Security Council voted in July 2006 to make suspension mandatory. The Security Council appeared in no hurry to punish Iran for not complying. It took four months to pass minimal sanctions—watered down to prevent a Russian veto—forbidding exports to Iran that could help its nuclear program. A tougher resolution passed in March 2007 also failed to convince Iran to suspend enrichment.

The Bush administration sees Iran's nuclear program as a major strategic threat to U.S. allies, particularly Israel. "In Bush's view of the world, the ultimate witches' brew is WMD and terrorism," said Clifford Kupchan, an Iran expert at the Eurasia Group, a consulting firm in New York. Iran easily qualified as the most fearsome witch. According to State Department reports going back more than a decade, Iran is the leading state sponsor of terrorism, backing militant, anti-Western groups from Iraq to Lebanon and the Palestinian territories. The ultimate horror-movie scenario would be the transfer of nuclear material to a suicidal anti-U.S. terrorist with apocalyptic aims. Few experts believe Iran would do such a thing; WMD is too precious and dangerous a commodity for governments to share it with outsiders. Even without such a transfer, however, an Iran with nukes—or thought to have nukes—would be a frightening prospect. There is always the possibility that Iran would use such weapons first if it believed that it was about to be attacked. A nuclear-armed Iran would also have the confidence to spread its influence with much less fear of retaliation. Israelis would feel even more threatened than they already do because of their unresolved conflict with Arabs; some Israeli Jews might emigrate and fewer diaspora Jews would choose to make their homes in the Jewish state.[6] Shiite plurality populations in Arab countries such as Bahrain, Lebanon, and especially Iraq, might feel even more emboldened to seize power and deny rights to Sunni Muslim minorities. Shiite-Sunni divisions might also worsen to Iran's east in the Indian subcontinent. Jordan's king Abdullah has warned of a powerful "Shiite crescent" stretching from the Persian Gulf to the Mediterranean.

If Iran had nuclear weapons majority Sunni nations, such as Saudi Arabia and Egypt, might seek them, too, destroying what remains of the Nuclear Nonproliferation Treaty that has limited the nuclear club for more than three decades. The United States would have to plan for the possibility of a nuclear exchange with Iran, and chances for lethal miscalculations would rise many times over in a region that holds 60 percent of the world's proven oil reserves. "The mere possession of such instruments will alter the entire balance of power in the Middle East," said retired colonel W. Patrick Lang, the former top Middle East analyst of the Pentagon's Defense Intelligence Agency. "Iran is suddenly going to have a great deal more geopolitical oomph."[7] The United States would be left with essentially two choices, both awful: live with a nuclear Iran or start another Middle East war.

HISTORIC AMBITIONS

The United States is partly responsible for Iran's nuclear ambitions, with both Republican and Democratic administrations initially having encouraged Iran to develop nuclear power. The United States and Iran signed a civil nuclear cooperation agreement in 1957, four years after the CIA reinstalled the shah and President Eisenhower launched an "atoms for peace" program to promote nuclear energy in the developing world. Under the Johnson administration, Iran started up its first reactor, a U.S.-supplied 5-megawatt research facility, in Tehran. When Richard Nixon was in office the shah established Iran's own atomic energy agency and announced that Iran would build enough reactors to generate 23,000 megawatts of electricity by the end of the century. Under the Ford administration—when Dick Cheney was White House chief of staff and Donald Rumsfeld was in his first stint as defense secretary—Iran signed an agreement with the United States that called for the purchase of eight reactors.[8] Iran also had extensive nuclear dealings with Europe. It contracted with a German company, a Siemens subsidiary called Kraftwerk Union, to build two 1,200-megawatt nuclear reactors at the Persian Gulf port of Bushehr. During the 1970s, Iran also bought a 10 percent share in a European joint venture uranium enrichment company, Eurodif, and hundreds of Iranians were trained as nuclear scientists and technicians in the finest universities of Europe and the United States.[9]

Western nations ended all nuclear cooperation with Iran after the 1979 revolution, and Ayatollah Khomeini initially forbade continuation of the nuclear program. But the regime's view changed during the Iran-Iraq war, and Iran soon found new suppliers. In 1984, with Chinese assistance, Iran opened a nuclear research center in Isfahan, a former capital known for its matchless Islamic architecture.[10] Iran resumed working on centrifuges the following year, during the height of the 1980–88 war, after Iraq began using chemical weapons against Iranian troops. Iran did not retaliate in kind; Khomeini is said to have vetoed the use of unconventional weapons as against the tenets of Islam, which forbids the killing of innocents. Still, Iranian leaders appear to have wanted a deterrent in case Iraq developed nuclear weapons. According to Iran's belated reports to the IAEA, Tehran got its first solid offer of technical assistance in building centrifuges in 1987 from Pakistan, whose top nuclear scientist, Abdul Qadeer Khan, masterminded a black market network that later provided Iran and other customers, including Libya, with centrifuge materials and plant designs. Also in 1987, Iran lured back a top scientist who had headed a clandestine weapons program for the shah.[11] In the 1990s, Iran bought other essential components from China and Russia, and Russia agreed to complete the German reactors at Bushehr, which had been bombed and largely destroyed by the Iraqis during the Iran-Iraq war. The Russians went so far as to sign an agreement to provide Iran with an entire uranium enrichment plant, but opposition from the Clinton administration nixed the deal. Iran also tried unsuccessfully to buy heavy-water reactors from Russia, China, India, and Argentina. Einhorn told me that the Russians probably provided the design for the heavy-water plant the Iranians say they completed at Arak in August 2006. Russia also tried to sell Iran laser isotope separation technology, which is another means of enriching uranium.

Beyond trying to block these deals, the Clinton administration tried to slow down the Russian work at Bushehr out of concern that the project would provide cover for transferring nuclear materials and expertise, and that Iran would use the plant as a rationale for demanding the ability to make nuclear fuel—as Iran, in fact, later did. Carlos Pascual, a former senior official in the Clinton and Bush administrations, said the Russians used Bushehr as "a screen for the provision of illegal technology and illegal technology transfers."[12] Einhorn believes the Russian record has improved but still calls Russia the second biggest source of Iranian nuclear know-how after the A. Q. Khan network.[13]

In 2005, Russia offered to produce enriched uranium for a series of Iranian power plants and to take back spent fuel, but Iran insisted on its "right" to make fuel on its own.

One of the reasons that it has been hard to convince other nations to punish Iran for its nuclear program is because Iran's efforts to enrich uranium technically do not violate international law. According to the Nuclear Nonproliferation Treaty (NPT), which Iran signed in 1968 and ratified in 1970, all treaty members are assured the peaceful use of nuclear energy provided they do not seek to make weapons or to share weapons technologies with others. During the 1990s, when IAEA inspectors and Iraq were playing cat and mouse, the IAEA reported no substantial problems with Iran, and even got permission for short-notice inspections. Hans Blix, then head of the IAEA, said a top IAEA official was allowed to see a site in Iran's Alborz mountains after a British newspaper claimed there was a secret uranium enrichment plant there. "There were suspicions and allegations but we found no substance to them," Blix said. So it was quite a shock when anti-Tehran exiles revealed that Iran was constructing uranium enrichment facilities at Natanz and the heavy-water plant at Arak. Once the facilities were revealed, the IAEA charged Iran with not fully cooperating with the agency, and while no proof of a weapons program emerged, the U.N. body piled up numerous questions and complaints.

Iranian officials opened Natanz and Arak to UN inspection in 2003 and started to surrender information about other programs. Each visit by arms inspectors answered a few questions but invariably raised more. Access to sites and documents was often denied or delayed; inspectors complained of having to apply for new visas each time they wanted to travel to Iran from IAEA headquarters in Vienna, giving Iranian officials ample time to hide or destroy evidence. It took the IAEA several years to confirm Iran's claim that traces of highly enriched uranium found on components at Natanz and an electrical plant near Tehran were not produced in Iran and had been imported from Pakistan via the Khan black market. The nuclear agency eventually got to visit a site in northeast Tehran that was suspected of being involved in nuclear work, but only after the Iranian government had razed the place, destroying all the buildings and even hauling off possibly radioactive dirt. Iran claimed, unconvincingly, that the land had to be returned to the Tehran municipal government. The IAEA also had trouble accepting Iran's assertions that while it acquired designs for advanced centrifuges in 1995, it did not start to work on them until 2002. Iranian officials refused to provide backup documents about the original offer from Pakistan in 1987 for a less advanced type of centrifuge, and also refused to turn over a document that described how to cast enriched uranium into "halves" of metal balls that can be assembled into bombs. In the spring of 2006, an exasperated IAEA declared that it was "unable to make progress in its efforts to provide assurance about the absence of undeclared nuclear material and activities in Iran. . . . After more than three years of Agency efforts to seek clarity about all aspects of Iran's nuclear program, the existing gaps in knowledge continue to be a matter of concern. Any progress in that regard requires full transparency and active cooperation by Iran."[14] A year later, as Iran scaled back cooperation, the agency was even more in the dark.

Few experts believe that Iran went to all the trouble of concocting such an elaborate deception just to make fuel for power plants. When it resumed its research on centrifuges in 1985, work at Bushehr had been suspended and Iran had no functioning civilian power plant or any near-term prospect of having one. The same technology that can be used to make fuel for power plants can also be used for weapons; the nuclear fuel just has to be run through the centrifuges many more times. The difference between power plant fuel and bomb material lies in the concentration of a uranium isotope, U-235, whose atoms can be split apart to release vast amounts of energy in a nuclear explosion. Naturally occurring uranium, U-238, has a very small percentage of U-235; centrifuges spin uranium gas so that the lighter U-235 separates. For civilian use uranium must be about 5 percent U-235; for weapons, more than 80 percent.

Even during the shah's reign there were doubts about whether Iran was interested in nuclear technology merely as an alternative source of electricity. In the 1970s Iran was caught attempting to buy technologies with potential weapons applications, such as lasers to separate isotopes, and "collected literature on nuclear weapons design and production."[15] When caught, the Iranians—in an echo of their claims three decades later—always said their "actions were peaceful" and meant for research or civilian power plants.[16]

It is not hard to understand why Iran would want nuclear technology. It seeks to diversify domestic energy sources, allow more oil to be exported, extend its influence over the region, and to be seen as an advanced industrial and military power. Iran also wants to deter potential attackers, especially the United States and Israel, and nuclear-armed neighbors, including Pakistan.

Throughout its history Iran has often had a troubled relationship with nearby countries. Since 1979, Iran has been allied only with Syria, an Arab country ruled by a minority Shiite-derived Muslim sect, the Alawites. As a European diplomat with long experience in the region once told me, Iran "has many neighbors and not a single friend. The best relations Iran has are with Christian Armenia, a strategically insignificant country." Blix said Iran was most worried about the United States, particularly after Bush put the regime on the "axis of evil" and overturned neighboring governments in Afghanistan and Iraq. "Do they really fear an attack except from the United States? No," he said. "From Iraq, no; from Pakistan, no; from Turkey, no." Only a U.S. willingness to take regime change off the table and seek normal relations with Iran would convince Iran not to seek nuclear weapons, Blix said, and even then one could not have absolute assurance that Iran had stopped its program. "There will be a small risk left, and that's a political decision whether to accept that or not."

Beyond its strategic value, the nuclear program has taken on a growing domestic political significance, as a symbol of national pride and a substitute for the lost fervor of the Islamic revolution. Iranian leaders have pointed to the nuclear program as proof of their country's ability to progress despite the damage wrought by the Iran-Iraq war and decades of U.S. economic sanctions. "This is a historic investment," supreme leader Khamenei said in a 2006 speech marking the seventeenth anniversary of the death of his predecessor, Khomeini. "It represents our political independence and national self-confidence. It is due to the bravery of our people . . . and we should not sell out this precious resource because of the enemies' threats, and we should not be fooled by enemy bribes."[17]

The attachment to the nuclear program is as strong among so-called moderates as among so-called hard-liners in the Iranian government. Then president Khatami declared in 2004 that Iran was entitled to the nuclear fuel cycle. "It's our legitimate right and no country can prevent us from achieving it," he said.[18] His successor went so far as to stage an elaborate televised ceremony in 2006 to announce that Iran had successfully enriched a small amount of uranium at Natanz. As dancers in traditional costumes swirled around a stage clutching vials of what was said to be uranium gas, Ahmadinejad told an audience in the northeastern city of Mashhad, "I formally declare that Iran has joined the club of nuclear countries."[19] In fact, Iran ran the centrifuges for only twelve days and produced only a few grams of lightly enriched uranium; a number of the centrifuges crashed and were destroyed. Einhorn said the Iranian actions and declaration had been driven "by political, rather than technical considerations."[20]

Such subtleties were lost on the average Iranian. He might be working two or three jobs to feed his family, but at least his country would not be seen as a lesser power than Pakistan. Even before Ahmadinejad took office, most Iranians agreed that their country was entitled to nuclear technology. "Iran should have nuclear knowledge but not the bomb," said Hossein Ibrahim, a clerk in a Tehran hardware store. Others said Iran could make nuclear weapons but insisted this would be no threat to other countries. "Iranians as far as I remember are not the type to attack or invade or start conflicts," said a university student who gave only her first name, Sepideh. "Even if they want to make a bomb, it's for defense, not for attack. It comes from fear."

In plotting their nuclear strategy, Iranian officials followed closely the experience of other proliferators, especially North Korea. Confronted in late 2002 by the Bush administration about a clandestine effort to acquire parts for a uranium enrichment program, North Korea withdrew from the NPT and kicked out IAEA monitors in early 2003. It then resumed operation of a nuclear complex that churned out plutonium and amassed enough fuel for perhaps a dozen bombs. The Bush administration at first refused to talk to North Korea, then joined multinational talks and agreed in February 2007 to provide economic and diplomatic benefits in return for North Korea's promise to give up the nuclear program again. The message to Iran was clear: Become a nuclear power and no one will dare attack you; accelerate your efforts to become a weapons state and other countries will offer you many inducements to give up or limit your program.

Even after the North Koreans tested a nuclear weapon in October 2006, the penalties imposed against the regime were relatively mild: a UN resolution barring exports to North Korea that could aid its nuclear program or satisfy its leader's taste for cognac and caviar. Iraq, on the other hand, was invaded by U.S. and British troops in part because it was not yet judged to be close to possessing nuclear weapons. The North Korea model is relatively successful in that the North Koreans did everything they wanted to do without paying much of a price, said Henry Sokolski, who heads the Nonproliferation Policy Education Center, a think tank in Washington. "Moreover, they were courted" by other nations, including the United States, for breaking the rules, he told me.

A U.S. offer of civilian nuclear cooperation with India in 2006 also encouraged Iran to believe it could have nuclear prowess and foreign trade and investment, too. India had exploded its first nuclear device in 1974 and carried out further testing in 1998 but was offered absolution by Washington after it developed a lucrative economic relationship with the United States. The U.S. deal with India, which included offers of civilian nuclear cooperation, required congressional approval because it violated the nonproliferation treaty—which forbids the five acknowl-edged nuclear weapons powers (Russia, China, France, Britain, and the United States) from undertaking activities that could assist other coun-tries' nuclear weapons programs. It convinced Iran that "it's not a ques-tion of rights," Sokolski said, but of "being picked on" because it was not friendly to the United States and was perceived as weak.

Iranian officials accused Western countries of trying to impose a double standard by ignoring Israel's officially unacknowledged but widely believed possession of several hundred nuclear weapons as well as the nuclear programs of India and Pakistan, which, like Israel, never joined the NPT. As the U.S.-Iran crisis was heating up, Larijani, the Iranian national security adviser, complained, "If Americans are really overconcerned about the NPT, why are they working with India that has already manufactured the weapons?" He accused the United States of using international treaties and organizations to punish countries that chose not to follow U.S. views. "All these international rules and regulations go back to alliance with the United States," he told me in 2006. "If a country wants to be a superpower, it must respect others and not expect others to be its servants." Three years earlier Iran's then for-eign minister, Kamal Kharrazi, made a similar remark. Referring to U.S. acceptance of Israel's nuclear weapons, he said, "it is really unbelievable why Americans make themselves the yardstick for being right and wrong. Who has given them this right?"

CARROTS AND STICKS

For some in the Iranian regime, possession of nuclear technology is a potential bargaining chip, a ticket to end Iran's pariah status and estrangement from the United States. North Korea used its program this way twice—with both the Clinton and Bush administrations. Libya followed a similar route. In 2004, the Bush administration lifted restrictions on U.S. oil companies operating in Libya after Libya compensated relatives of the victims of Pan Am Flight 103, brought down by a Libyan bomb in 1988 over Lockerbie, Scotland, killing 270 people. Dealing with this hideous act of terrorism was a necessary but not sufficient reason for Washington to change policy; the turning point came in 2003 after Libya surrendered nuclear equipment it may have acquired in part to have something valuable to trade. Two years later the United States re-established full diplomatic relations with Libya, still ruled by the eccentric and thoroughly undemocratic Moammar Gadhafi.

Iran, a country of seventy million situated at the choke point of the Persian Gulf, rejected any comparison with Libya, a nation of only five million people with limited strategic value. But Iranians hoping for reconciliation with the United States saw diplomatic promise in their nuclear progress. "The completion of the nuclear fuel cycle is a very big achievement," wrote a reformist newspaper, *Shargh,* the day after Ahmadinejad announced that Iran had joined the nuclear club. "This achievement is very good capital for Iran in its possible talks with America."[21] The prospect of U.S. and European economic incentives might change popular opinion about the wisdom of going forward with the nuclear program. A U.S.-organized telephone poll of Iranians in May-June 2006 showed that more Iranians cared about reforming their inefficient economy than developing a nuclear deterrent by a factor of 3 to 2.[22]

Hossein Mousavian, one of Iran's top foreign policy experts and a former nuclear negotiator, saw talks that took place between Iran and European diplomats in 2004 and 2005 as a kind of practice run for negotiations on other issues, from terrorism to human rights, and the beginning of an end to Iran's pariah status. "The nuclear process is the first issue where after twenty-five years, Iran is sitting at table with Westerners discussing practical arrangements on the basis of international rules and regulations," he told me in 2005. "If we are successful, we can use the model for other differences." Iranians insisted, however, that they had to have their own enrichment program because they could not trust other countries to keep their promises to supply nuclear fuel. "We have a very bad experience," Mousavian explained. "In 1975 we signed an 8 billion Deutschmark contract with the Germans for Bushehr; they completed 90 percent of the project and withdrew after the revolution. We tried to get them to return for twenty years. No one can guarantee that this would not happen again. We are looking for partial production of fuel in this country. We don't want to be 100 percent dependent on the outside. What if one day you decide to stop electricity in this country? We are talking about the rights of a nation."

Larijani recalled similar experiences when I interviewed him a year later. "Before the revolution Iran had a contract with the USA for the supply of fuel for a reactor," he said. "They gave the reactor but they refused to give the fuel, even though they had received the money, and [they] never returned the money." Not only did Siemens cancel its contract to build the reactors at Bushehr; Larijani complained that Eurodif of France "didn't give us one gram of fuel," even though Iran still owns 10 percent of the company. Larijani also recalled seven years of fruitless discussions with the IAEA in the 1980s about a guaranteed supply of fuel for the non-nuclear-weapons members of the NPT. "So therefore there is no real guarantee for the supply of fuel," he said. "I think if a country has just a little brain it would not depend on the fuel from another country." Left unsaid by both Larijani and Mousavian: Iran does not have enough uranium to provide fuel for even one power plant for more than a few years, and so would have to depend on foreigners for raw materials.

THE MILITARY OPTION

Mounting economic pressure against Iran in late 2006 and early 2007 gave rise to some optimism in the United States and Europe that Iran might suspend its uranium program. At U.S. instigation, Western banks cut back dealings with Iran, and Japan and several European governments reduced credits financing their exports to Iran. Foreign investment in Iran, particularly its oil industry, declined. UN sanctions targeted Iranian arms sales and the influential Revolutionary Guards. Still, Iran continued its work at both Natanz and Arak.

At the same time the Pentagon updated planning for military strikes. According to retired Air Force lieutenant general Tom McInerney, a force of B2 bombers, F22 and F117 fighter planes, 400 nonstealth aircraft, and 500 cruise missiles could take out Iran's top nuclear and conventional military targets in 36 to 48 hours. McInerney saw air strikes as a prelude to regime change. Once the bombs and missiles had struck, "pre-planned covert forces assist the Iranian people in taking their country back with precision air support as required."[23] Lang agreed that the United States could substantially destroy the Iranian nuclear program with 1,000 sorties by bombers plus cruise missiles. He admitted that the costs would be high but said they were more bearable than a nuclear-armed Iran. "Personally, I find it so unacceptable that Iran becomes a nuclear power that if everything else fails, I would go for the air campaign," Lang said.[24]

Others stressed the difficulty of hitting numerous and dispersed targets, doubted that Iran is ripe for regime change, and warned that the consequences of a U.S. attack could be worse than living with a nuclear Iran. Oil would rise above one hundred dollars a barrel, savaging world economies. Iran might try to shut off the flow of oil from the Strait of Hormuz, panicking world markets. U.S. forces still in Iraq would be vulnerable to attack, if not directly by Iran, then by Iran-backed Iraqi Shiite militias. Anti-Israel terrorism would likely rise as would attacks against U.S. targets in the region and elsewhere by Lebanon's Hezbollah. U.S. air strikes could also bolster support for an otherwise unpopular Iranian government and could lead it to redouble efforts to build a bomb.

By 2007, the utility of an attack was questionable, since no number of sorties could destroy the knowledge in the heads of Iranian nuclear scientists and engineers. Gary Samore, a nonproliferation expert under the Clinton administration, said the longer the United States waited, the less useful air strikes would be, and the likelier that Iran had hidden facilities to enrich uranium and build weapons.

Some have suggested that Israel—which in 1981 destroyed an Iraqi nuclear reactor—would strike the Iranian program if the United States did not act. But eliminating Iran's now much more advanced nuclear program would be a vastly more difficult challenge than taking out a single Iraqi reactor. Iran is several hours flying time farther from Israel, and the distance Israeli warplanes would have to traverse, together with the number of hidden targets they would have to hit, pose a far greater logistical challenge than the 1981 raid. Israel does not have enough tanker planes for in-flight refueling, military experts note, and some of the targets might take multiple sorties to destroy.[25] Israel also lacks the ballistic and cruise missiles necessary to do the job and could not send its planes over Muslim countries en route to Iran without being detected.[26] However, there were increasing indications that Israel might act anyway and drag the United States into the confrontation, if diplomacy failed to halt Iran's nuclear progress. Bruce Riedel, an Iran expert who served on the White House National Security Council for President Clinton and both Bushes, father and son, said that Israel's military was "preparing intensively for such an operation despite its shortcomings in tankers." In the summer of 2006 the Bush administration agreed to provide Israel with new longer-range bombers. The White House, Riedel said, had sent an "amber light" to Israel to continue preparations for air strikes.

STRATEGIC AMBIGUITY

Many Iran specialists believe Iran is not necessarily interested in building or testing a bomb but aspires to a kind of strategic ambiguity—the ability to keep its enemies guessing and, if necessary, to build a weapon quickly from prefabricated components.[27] If other countries believe Iran has reached this stage of technological prowess that might be enough to enhance Iran's regional leadership and influence in the Middle East. "As long as Iran does not actually test a full nuclear explosion, it can develop and can test potential weapons and warhead designs in a wide variety of ways," Cordesman observed. "It can also prepare for underground testing and test simulated weapons . . . without exploding a bomb until it is ready for the international community to know it has actually tested a weapon."[28] Only a dramatic change in Iran's domestic politics or strategic environment might persuade the ruling clerics to set aside their nuclear ambitions.

Mousavian said the best guarantee that Iran was not developing atomic bombs would be an Iran fully reintegrated into the world economy. "If we had 100 billion euros of European investment in Iran, and if we had Iranian investment in Europe, Iran would never even think to divert nuclear enrichment because the damage would be huge for Iran," he said. Given a choice, however, Iran appeared willing to sacrifice such investment for the prestige and deterrence of becoming a nuclear state.

THREE

THE BLACKSMITH'S SON

THE SUMMONS CAME ON my last day in Iran, only hours before I was due to fly home. I had just treated my translator and driver to lunch, thanking them for their hard work and moral support throughout a frenetic trip. I had hoped to become the first U.S. newspaper reporter to interview Iran's controversial new president but was content with having snagged the national security adviser and two other top Iranian politicians who had also run for president in 2005. I was telling my translator that she could take the rest of the day off when her cell phone rang. "Be at the presidential palace at five o'clock," said a man's voice.

The downtown palace complex, one of a half dozen left behind by the deposed shah, was nearly deserted that afternoon, a national holiday marking the twenty-seventh anniversary of the triumph of the Islamic revolution. Two guards at the gate seemed surprised when I turned up with my translator. They eventually found my name on a list of approved visitors, but not my translator's, and it took about fifteen minutes to resolve the confusion. Then the guards had to find someone to operate the X-ray machine to scan our notebooks and tape recorders. Another fifteen minutes went by and I was worried that we would be late. Finally, we were directed to an ornate building across a grassy courtyard and ushered up marble stairs into a reception room furnished with plush ivory-colored damask couches and chairs. In the middle of the room was a marble fountain whose spigot had been turned off. A few bottles of mineral water and boxes of cookies had been left on a table but, unheard-of in Iran, no one offered tea; the tea servers had the day off.

Mahmoud Ahmadinejad arrived nearly two hours later, also unusual in a generally punctual country. He had kept us waiting while he performed sunset prayers and an Iranian camera crew was summoned to record his first interview with a U.S. newspaper. He looked absolutely exhausted. His small eyes were even more deeply sunken into his head than usual and ringed by dark circles. That morning he had delivered an hourlong anti-Western harangue to the Revolution Day rally in Tehran's Freedom Square, his first major public speech in Tehran since his inauguration in August 2005. I had covered the speech, assuming it would be my only chance to see him in the flesh, and chased after him after the rally ended, hoping for an exclusive quote. In the process, my shoes came off on a muddy path. They were suede and ruined forever. I was annoyed, but it struck me when I met Ahmadinejad a few hours later that he was not the sort to care about ruined shoes. For our interview he had changed from the nondescript suit jacket he had worn at the rally to an even more nondescript off-white flimsy cotton jacket, the kind you might find on a suburban American dad mowing his lawn. He had paired it with the same black shirt, beige sweater vest, and gray pants he had been wearing in the morning. Plain, almost shabby, clothing is one of Ahmadinejad's trademarks, signifying that he is a man of the people. His scraggly, poorly trimmed beard is another.

I introduced myself and said, "Pleased to meet you" in Farsi. He seemed startled and broke into a smile. After that, for the next hour, he was stoically expressionless and avoided eye contact—perhaps because I was an unrelated female or an American, or both. Most Iranians I've met are hospitable people who flatter their guests, seeking to charm them, but Ahmadinejad made no such effort. He had no small talk, answered questions with ideological stock phrases or questions of his own; it was like pulling teeth to get him to say anything positive, or even neutral, about the United States. When the allotted time was up he scurried from the room, evidently relieved that the ordeal was over.

Ahmadinejad is the new face of Iran and, to many, not a very pretty one. Under the Iranian system his formal powers are limited, and he is supposed to be mostly an administrator, absorbed in domestic affairs. Unlike the president of the United States, Ahmadinejad is not the commander-in-chief and does not direct Iran's nuclear program. Key decisions about foreign policy are made by the supreme religious leader, Ayatollah Khamenei, who is advised by a council of about a dozen senior officials that includes Ahmadinejad but is not dominated by him. Yet Ahmadinejad has made himself impossible to ignore. He has seeded his supporters throughout the bureaucracy and used the bully pulpit of the presidency to make controversial statements, threatening Israel and denying the Holocaust. He has inserted himself into Iran's complex diplomacy with the United States in interviews and press conferences and by sending an eccentric letter to President Bush in 2006—the first public overture to an American president by an Iranian one since the 1979 revolution. He has exploited his humble background to appeal to the Iranian masses and turned the nuclear issue into a symbol of Iranian pride and nationalism. He is the little man who triumphs over adversity, who stands up to the United States and shows that the ancient civilization of Iran has reached the apex of technological progress, membership in the nuclear club.

MORE CHÁVEZ THAN KHOMEINI

Much has been made of Ahmadinejad's fundamentalist religious beliefs, including frequent references to the twelfth *imam*—the Shiite Muslim religious figure who disappeared in the ninth century and whose return is supposed to herald the Day of Judgment. But a European diplomat in Tehran observed that Ahmadinejad is more "Chávez than Khomeini." By that the diplomat meant that Ahmadinejad appealed more to Iranians' patriotism than their piety, as personified by Ayatollah Khomeini, the leader of the 1979 revolution. Rather than modeling himself after Khomeini, the Iranian president has emulated Hugo Chávez, the populist leader of another oil-rich country, Venezuela. Like Chávez, Ahmadinejad has sought to build an international reputation by advocating for developing nations and challenging the global primacy of the United States. Although a minority of Iran—perhaps 20 percent—is quite religious, the imposed religiosity of the Islamic republic has turned off scores of former believers. Nationalism is the surviving ideology of the revolution, now barely remembered by Iran's youthful population. Thus Ahmadinejad casts the United States not so much as the enemy of Islam, as al-Qaeda and Sunni fundamentalists have done, but as the enemy of Third World aspirations for independence, prosperity, and modernization. "The wave of disgust toward U.S. policies is increasing," Ahmadinejad confidently declared, Chávez-like, in my interview with him. Iran, the president allowed, would be willing to negotiate with the United States, but for talks to be successful, the Bush administration would have to give up its "arrogant" behavior and accept Iran's rightful place as a major power in the Persian Gulf. "The way they have treated our people here has left no ground for talks," he said of U.S. officials. "As long as they take that overbearing position of strength and threats, nothing will happen."

A MAN OF THE PEOPLE

Who is Ahmadinejad and where did he come from? Iran's sixth president is truly a man of the people, a member of a generation forged by the revolution and burnished in the firefights of the 1980–88 Iran-Iraq war. He was born on October 28, 1956, in Aradan, a dusty provincial town about three hours' drive southeast of Tehran astride the ancient silk road connecting the medieval Western and Eastern worlds. The remains of the president's first home, a century-old mud-brick structure on the outskirts of Aradan, were still there when I visited in the winter of 2006. A traditional building, it had a single story of rooms built around a central courtyard. The mud brick was crumbling, piles of trash littered the garden, and red paint peeled from the compound's red metal gate. Ahmadinejad's father had a small grocery store in Aradan when Ahmadinejad was born, the fourth of seven children. His father couldn't make ends meet, said Haj Ali Shahhosseini, a cousin who still lives in Aradan, and the family moved to Tehran when Ahmadinejad was not quite two. The elder Ahmadinejad and his brother-in-law opened a blacksmith shop in Narmak, a working-class district in the eastern part of the capital that still has a small-town feel.

I visited Narmak on a rainy Ashura. A half-dozen childhood friends of the president had agreed to meet me there and show me where they had lived, studied, played, and prayed. Narmak is a neighborhood of low-rise apartment buildings and townhouses, small shops and narrow streets. As a child Ahmadinejad lived in a three-story attached building with a fake marble facade that in an Iranian context looked solidly middle class. He moved as an adult to a similar brick townhouse at the end of an alley only a few blocks away. His friends remember Ahmadinejad as very religious and a diligent student. One of them, Majid Karimi, told me that Ahmadinejad was a bookish overachiever who was so conscientious that he used to do homework in between pickup soccer games. When Ahmadinejad stayed over at Karimi's house, he got up a half hour earlier than his friend to review classroom notes before going to school. Even though this was in the 1970s, when the shah ruled and Western customs prevailed in much of the capital, Ahmadinejad did not drink alcohol or smoke, and he didn't chase girls. "My mother told me, 'Mahmoudy is a good boy, and it's better to be friends with him because he won't lead you astray," Karimi recalled.

Ahmadinejad was quite devout even by the pious standards of Narmak. He started going to the neighborhood mosque to pray when he was six, according to Saeed Jazi, another boyhood companion. On the night before Ashura—the high point of the Shiite Muslim religious calendar, commemorating the martyrdom of the prophet Mohammed's grandson, Hossein—Ahmadinejad would go to the mosque and wash pots and clean vegetables for stews to be cooked and doled out to neighborhood residents the next day, Jazi said. Nasser Hadian, a political scientist at Tehran University who also knew Ahmadinejad well as a child, said the future president was unusual because "he never got angry" or fought with other boys. He was not a complete puritan, however. Mohammed Burumand, another cousin in Aradan, recalled watching foreign gangster movies with Ahmadinejad and riding bikes together. Jazi said Ahmadinejad also took karate lessons and studied English at a small foreign language school in Narmak. Karimi remembered that Ahmadinejad had a unique way of hitting a soccer ball with the side of his right foot. He was a good player but neither especially popular or unpopular with the other kids, Karimi said.

Ahmadinejad's wonkishness paid off when he came in 132nd in nationwide examinations taken by 400,000 Iranian youngsters and gained entrance to university in 1976. He was so nervous, he later confided, that he had a nosebleed while taking the test. Once in university his studious habits were not strong enough to resist the political currents of the time and, like virtually all Iranian youth, he got swept up in the 1978–79 Islamic revolution against the shah. Most of his friends became leftists who sought a secular socialist republic, but Ahmadinejad "went right" toward religious radicalism, Jazi said. Despite claims by several former U.S. hostages, the future president apparently did not take part in the seizure of the U.S. embassy in 1979—although he may have visited the grounds during the 444-day saga. Abbas Abdi and Ebrahim Asgharzadeh, two ringleaders of the siege, both said that Ahmadinejad was not involved. Mohammad Ali Seyednejad, a Ministry of Education employee who knew Ahmadinejad during the 1970s, said the future president was present when plans for the takeover were discussed but argued against it.[1]

Hard as it may be for Americans to understand, had Ahmadinejad been a major player in the hostage crisis, he would have included it—indeed bragged about it—in his official résumé. For Iranian revolutionaries, seizing the U.S. embassy was a defining moment when Iran stood up to the country that had backed the hated shah and overthrown the popular prime minister, Mossadegh, in 1953. Many Iranians, including Abdi and Asgharzadeh, have since come to see the embassy seizure as a terrible mistake that isolated Iran and left it defenseless when Iraq invaded Iran in 1980. Ahmadinejad is said to have opposed the takeover not because it was morally wrong or geopolitically suicidal, but because he preferred seizing the Soviet embassy instead. At the time, his friends said, he was more anticommunist than anti-American.

The defining event for Ahmadinejad was not the revolution but the 1980–88 Iran-Iraq war. A grueling meat grinder of a conflict, it killed or injured three quarters of a million Iranians, mostly the sons of the middle and working class like Ahmadinejad. Iran was virtually alone in defending itself against Iraqi invaders. United States backing for Iraq—more than U.S. support for the shah—created Ahmadinejad's worldview and his deep-seated resentment of U.S. power. The United States and most of the rest of the world, especially Iran's Arab neighbors, backed Saddam, preferring his secular brutality to the subversive Islam of Ayatollah Khomeini, which seemed more of a threat at the time to U.S. Arab allies, all ruled by monarchs or military men. Like many religious youngsters of modest means, Ahmadinejad after the revolution had joined the *Basij,* or mobilized ones, a proregime movement of teenage and elderly volunteers from rural and poor urban areas. During the war he graduated to the Revolutionary Guards, a military organization created to protect the new government, because Iran's Islamic rulers did not trust the loyalty of the regular armed forces. The future president served as head engineer of the Guards' 6th Army Division, and later headed the Guards staff in western Iran, crossing the border at one point to the Iraqi city of Kirkuk. The war ended in a stalemate in 1988, after an American Navy cruiser shot down a civilian Iranian airliner over the Persian Gulf, killing all 290 people on board. The Reagan administration, which was escorting Kuwaiti oil tankers down the Gulf to protect them from Iranian gun-boats and mines, said the shoot-down was an accident. Many Iranians took the tragedy as a sign that the United States was now intervening directly against their civilian population, not merely supporting Sad-dam with weapons and intelligence and protecting the oil exports of Saddam's Arab allies. At that point, UN mediators finally persuaded Khomeini, by then in his last year of life, to accept a truce.

After the war ended Ahmadinejad was rewarded for his service with a series of political appointments under the administration of Iran's new president, Rafsanjani. Ahmadinejad served as vice governor and then governor of the northwestern cities of Maku and Khoy, then as an adviser to the ministry of Islamic culture and guidance (which regulates newspapers, books, films, and television), and finally, as gov-ernor of the northwestern province of Ardabil. There are also uncon-firmed reports—denied by the president—that he was the lookout for an Iranian hit team that assassinated a Kurdish dissident in Vienna in 1989. The Austrian courts began an investigation after Ahmadinejad became president but took no action against him.

Ahmadinejad's rise was interrupted in 1997 by an astonishing event in Iran's political history. For the first time since the revolution the can-didate opposed by the ruling establishment—Mohammad Khatami—was elected president in a landslide victory. Khatami loyalists proceeded to remove conservatives from senior posts in the various ministries and provincial governments. Summarily removed from the governorship of Ardabil, Ahmadinejad retreated to his old university to teach and plot a comeback with fellow conservatives.

IRAN'S NEOCONS

It didn't take them long. Khatami's efforts to liberalize Iranian society and check the power of unelected clerics and paramilitary groups were hugely popular but sparked a backlash from religious conservatives and others in the elite who feared that the Islamic revolution—and their power and privileges—would be taken from them. With the support of supreme leader Khamenei, the conservatives began rolling back Khatami's reforms. Meanwhile, a new political faction emerged among middle-aged and young conservatives. It called itself the *Abadgaran,* or "developers' coalition," and attracted religious fundamentalists, some veterans of the Revolutionary Guards and members of the *Basij.*[2] Liberal Iranians called the group "neoconservative" in an unflattering comparison to the hawkish U.S. group that backed the overthrow of Saddam and hard-line policies against Iran, and sought to expand pro-Western governments throughout the Middle East. The *Abadgaran* was also radical. It sought to bring back the ideals of the revolution, spread oil wealth more evenly in society, increase Iranian influence in the region, and achieve economic growth, in part by reaching out to China and India rather than Europe and the United States. In February 2003, the group took control of the Tehran city council after reformist candidates were disqualified from running in elections by a Khamenei-chosen body of vetters. The victors appointed Ahmadinejad mayor.

THE ENGINEER

As might be expected from a man who got his doctorate in traffic engineering, Ahmadinejad focused on the capital's obvious infrastructure problems and legendary traffic jams by building more overpasses and expressways. His ties with the Revolutionary Guards proved useful when he won their agreement to move their barracks to make way for new roads, and he also put more traffic police on the street to smooth Iranians' daily commute. Less popular were his efforts to reinstill Islamic principles at youth centers run by the municipal government. A previous mayor, Gholamhossein Karbaschi, had created the centers and encouraged young people to stage plays, art shows, and concerts; Ahmadinejad turned them into prayer halls. Billiard parlors, which had only just reappeared after two decades of banishment, had to close at 10 or 11 instead of 2 A.M. Upper-class residents of north Tehran ridiculed Ahmadinejad for his scruffy appearance; one elegant north

Tehrani called him "the chimpanzee." They laughed at him when his office banned as immoral billboards showing British soccer star David Beckham's bare legs. Rumors spread that the new mayor was such an Islamic hard-liner that he had suggested separate elevators for male and female government employees. But he won popularity in the slums of south Tehran for refusing to move to a mansion and continuing to live in his small brick townhouse at the end of an alley in Narmak, wearing inexpensive clothes and bringing his lunch to work in a bag. He extended loans to poor couples that enabled them to get married—a so-called "love fund"—cut the budget for redecorating municipal offices, and once surprised city street cleaners by getting out of his car and using his bare hands to clear a blockage in the open storm drains that run down the sides of Tehran streets. "He believes in God, and whatever he does is for God," said Mohammed Bahraini, manager of the Jamaie mosque in Narmak, where Ahmadinejad still came to pray when he was mayor and even president. "He never used to do things to please others, only God." In contrast to the corruption and nepotism endemic in Iran—both before and after the revolution—he refused to help relatives find housing. "He didn't do favors even for his family," his Aradan cousin, Mohammed Burumand, complained.

This reputation for probity—and the fact that he was a fresh political face—were the main reasons Ahmadinejad won the presidency in 2005, astonishingly his first elected office. The still popular Khatami could not run for a third consecutive term, under the Iranian constitution, and Khatami's predecessor, Rafsanjani, decided to run again. A revolutionary stalwart who used his positions over the years to make his family among the richest in Islamic Iran, Rafsanjani campaigned on a platform of reaching out to the United States, and implied strongly that he would trade Iran's nuclear program for an end to the U.S. embargo on trade and investment in Iran. Ahmadinejad didn't say much about foreign policy and focused instead on the travails of ordinary Iranians and had Iranian state television film him in his modest Narmak home. "I am proud of being the Iranian nation's little servant and street sweeper," Ahmadinejad said as he cast his ballot.[3] His main promise was to share Iran's oil wealth more fairly and put food on the *sofreh,* the cloth traditional families use to spread on the floor for meals. His slogan was *"ma metonim,"* "we can."

Iranians and foreigners alike were stunned by Ahmadinejad's

victory—most had anticipated that Rafsanjani would win. Of the half-dozen childhood friends of his I met, not a single one had voted for him. Ahmadinejad himself had apparently not doubted the result. He predicted he would win three months before the election, when few people outside or inside Iran had ever heard of him.[4] He came in second in a first round of voting and won a runoff by a strong margin of 17 million votes to Rafsanjani's 10 million. Rafsanjani supporters and Mehdi Karroubi, a reformist cleric eliminated in the first round of voting, suggested that there had been fraud in the first round, and that Karroubi should have come in second, not Ahmadinejad, and competed in the runoff with Rafsanjani.

Ahmadinejad got extra help from members of the *Basij* and Revolutionary Guards, who mobilized to get out the vote and may have padded the ballot boxes. Many Iranians stayed home, uninspired by any of the candidates, or heeding dissidents inside and outside Iran who had called for a massive boycott. That did not happen. Turnout in the first round was at least 57 percent by official tally; in the runoff, it was around 60 percent; excellent by U.S. standards though not extraordinary by Iranian ones. (The Interior Ministry initially reported 57 percent turnout in the second round, then raised it without explanation to 62 percent.)[5] Despite his decisive win over Rafsanjani, the new president was still chosen by less than 37 percent of eligible voters—not exactly an overwhelming mandate.[6]

WIPE ISRAEL OFF THE MAP

Once elected, Ahmadinejad quickly dropped any pretense of confining himself to domestic matters and began making comments indicating his contempt for the United States. In September 2005, during his international debut at the annual summit at the United Nations General Assembly, he delivered a tough speech defending Iran's right to enrich uranium, accused the United States of hypocrisy and terrorist behavior, and questioned who was really responsible for the 9/11 terrorist attacks. (The view that the U.S. government was complicit in the attacks is widely shared in the Muslim world.) Then in October, at an annual and usually little-noticed conference in Tehran called The World Without Zionism, Ahmadinejad touched the third rail for U.S.

foreign policy and questioned Israel's right to exist. "As the *imam* said, Israel must be wiped off the map," Ahmadinejad said, quoting Ayatollah Khomeini. "Anybody who recognizes Israel will burn in the fire of the Islamic nation's fury."[7] In subsequent speeches Ahmadinejad said the Holocaust was a myth fabricated to justify the creation of Israel.[8]

Many voters who had chosen Ahmadinejad over Rafsanjani quickly succumbed to buyers' remorse. The president's inflammatory remarks were undoing eight years of Khatami moderation and making Iran look again like a belligerent, irrational nation. Despite high oil revenues, Ahmadinejad's economic policies—continuing subsidies and making handouts to the poor—only increased inflation without providing jobs for the burgeoning numbers of Iran's unemployed. During frequent trips to Iran's provinces, Ahmadinejad was inundated with letters from poor and desperate Iranians seeking solutions for their personal problems.[9]

His efforts to meet popular expectations were undercut by personnel changes that removed experienced bureaucrats across the country and replaced them with loyalists, many of them unqualified for their jobs. Vali Nasr, an Iran expert at the U.S. Naval Postgraduate School in Monterey, California, called the new appointees "ideological nincompoops." Other Iranians compared the changes to a Stalin-like purge but without the blood. The personnel switches, which went deeper than usual into the bureaucracy, compounded confusion in the economy, and the parliament moved to protect the country's most important sector, the oil industry. Despite the fact that it was dominated by fellow conservatives, the parliament rejected the president's first three nominees to head the oil ministry, and Ahmadinejad had to settle for promoting the deputy minister, a veteran bureaucrat. He also failed in his efforts to replace experienced technocrats as finance minister and governor of the central bank. At his urging, the government in 2006 increased the minimum wage by 50 percent, to about $200 a month, but the salary hike led employers to eliminate 200,000 jobs; three months after the rise, wages were cut back to about $165 a month.[10]

Khamenei, worried about Ahmadinejad's inexperience, decreed that the Expediency Council, a body led by Rafsanjani that resolves disputes among government branches, would supervise both the executive and legislative branches of government. He also rebutted Ahmadinejad's comments about Israel being "wiped off the map," saying that

Iran had no such intention. "We will not commit aggression toward any nations; we will not breach any nation's rights anywhere in the world," Khamenei said in a 2005 sermon broadcast by Iranian state television on the holiday ending Ramadan, the Muslim holy month of daytime fasting.[11] The rebuttal got almost no attention outside Iran, even though Khamenei outranks the president in all matters. In June 2006, Khamenei named a new body, headed by a former foreign minister, to advise him on foreign policy—another pointed rebuke to Ahmadinejad's cabinet. Six months after the election Mohsen Rezaie, a former Revolutionary Guards commander and number two in the Expediency Council, dismissed Ahmadinejad as though the president were a boy in short pants. "He's under control inside the country," Rezaie told me. "The top decision making is done at higher levels."

Jokes about the president's appearance and his religious beliefs made the rounds of Tehran, sometimes e-mailed from cell phone to cell phone as text messages. An outbreak of cholera in the capital shortly after his election was blamed on the president washing his dirty underwear in a reservoir outside Tehran. Restrictions on the use of water in the capital were said to be caused by Ahmadinejad taking a bath. In a new version of an old joke previously used against Khamenei, two men in heaven see Ahmadinejad walking hand in hand with Jennifer Lopez. "That's his reward for a good life," says one. The other replies, "That's Jennifer Lopez's punishment." Another joke had Rafsanjani telling Ahmadinejad not to worry because officials had already named a new highway for him. In Tehran, major thoroughfares are named for martyrs—those who died in the revolution, the Iran-Iraq war, and terrorist bombings. Ahmadinejad was said to have predicted himself that he would become a martyr before the end of his term in 2009, but that comment might have been wishful thinking by his many detractors.

Ahmadinejad's reformist opponents were scathing in their criticism of the president's rhetoric about Israel and the Holocaust, his confrontational stance on the nuclear issue, and his populist economic policies. He is "destroying all the previous achievements" of Iranian leaders, said Mohammad Atrianfar, editorial director for *Shargh,* a reformist newspaper that Ahmadinejad ordered closed in September 2006 after it printed a cartoon showing the president as a donkey. Saeed Laylaz, a columnist for *Shargh* and deputy interior minister under

Khatami, said of the new chief executive, "He behaves like a rebel, not a president. Is it his job to say that Adolf Hitler was a clean guy? Is the Holocaust a real problem for the Iranian people?" He said that Ahmadinejad's economic policies were driving the country into the ground, and that "he will collapse this country in the long term." As for the nuclear issue, Laylaz said that Ahmadinejad was using it to bolster his own position in Iran and to provoke a hostile external reaction: "When you create an external enemy, you can use it as a weapon inside the country."

In a country with few reliable political polls, it is hard to gauge Ahmadinejad's popularity. The nuclear issue appeared to have worked in his favor at least initially. Most Iranians appeared to support the government's contention that their country deserved to have nuclear power and believed that the West was imposing a double standard on Iran by allowing Israel, India, and Pakistan to have nuclear weapons programs but denying Iran the right to produce uranium fuel for power plants. Ahmadinejad exploited the nationalist argument effectively, trying to model himself after Mossadegh, who nationalized the oil industry. But Ahmadinejad's confrontational rhetoric and clumsy diplomatic style made many Iranians uneasy and raised concerns that the country would become increasingly isolated. During his first few months in office, Iranians voted with their money and their feet. The Tehran stock market declined by a third, foreign and domestic investment dried up, and the brain drain of talented young people to the Arab states of the Persian Gulf and the West accelerated. European diplomats said visa applications had nearly doubled and more than $200 billion in hard currency had flowed to Dubai during Ahmadinejad's first half year in office. Newspaper editor Atrianfar said that "even if 17 million people voted for Ahmadinejad, that means that 34 million didn't vote for him. He's just preoccupied with his slogans, and the people will realize what they are told is not the reality."

In our interview, Ahmadinejad, as usual when confronted with unpleasant realities, denied them and said that his policies were not causing capital flight. "Those who have given that figure don't know the magnitude of $200 billion," he said. "We have relations with neighboring countries. There is investment back and forth. Dubai is a free-trade area. It is natural that many Iranians go there to make investments. What is important is that the result of their work comes back to Iran.

Last year, $8 billion was invested in the United Arab Emirates and $11 billion returned."

In fact, the Iranian economy was freezing up, despite the influx of record oil earnings—a mixed blessing since Iran imports 40 percent of its gasoline and subsidizes gas prices to the tune of $6 billion a year. Even in south Tehran, a poor working-class area that had been a bastion of support for Ahmadinejad during his 2005 campaign, opinion about him was mixed. Zohra Mohammedi, a twenty-three-year-old clerk in an office that arbitrated family disputes, said she was grateful to Ahmadinejad because as mayor he had made her temporary job permanent. She also spoke approvingly of the "love fund" Ahmadinejad had established in Tehran and sought to expand nationwide to give one thousand dollar loans to newlyweds. Nedar Nargisi, a high school student, told me that Ahmadinejad would "do a good job, if they let him." The "they" referred to the supreme leader and other veteran officials who had checked Khatami's power when he pushed too many changes to the system; the same people, Nargisi suggested, would also rein in Ahmadinejad. A twenty-year-old salesgirl in a cosmetics shop who gave only her first name, Mariam, was more upset by Ahmadinejad's appearance than by his policies. "Mr. Khatami, although a cleric, was always well groomed," she said. Ahmadinejad "is not up to the standards of a president."

In the labyrinthine downtown bazaar, views of Ahmadinejad seemed to depend on whether the merchants were insulated from the international economy or had to import products to assemble or sell. Asghar Mousavi, who sold household appliances made in Europe and Asia, said Ahmadinejad had done nothing for him despite a significant increase in oil prices after his election. "Every time the price of oil goes up, it's not for the benefit of the people," he said. But Habib Alizad, who sold jeans made from Iranian denim, said he approved of Ahmadinejad: "He is a clean guy and he is religious. We pray to God our leaders are successful."

As much as some Americans and Iranians wanted to see Ahmadinejad as a member of a lunatic fringe, he represented a potent constituency among the second generation of regime loyalists: those who came from humble backgrounds, did not see the United States as a political or social model to be emulated, and who regarded Iran as a country much more sinned against than sinning. It is not hard to find an

American equivalent for Ahmadinejad. In his ignorance of much of the world and his ideological/religious sanctimony, he could be mistaken for either an extreme leftist or a member of the Christian ultraright—a Jerry Falwell or a Pat Robertson. Unlike many of his childhood friends and other members of the Iranian elite, including his rival Rafsanjani, Ahmadinejad spent almost no time abroad and probably knew very few non-Muslims. His field of study—traffic engineering—did not broaden him in an intellectual sense, and he spent his entire academic career at one middling university, the Iran University of Science and Technology, in Tehran. While he was mayor he refused to meet European diplomats, although he did see China's envoy—a reflection of his interest in fostering ties with countries unlikely to criticize Iran's internal policies or question his narrow worldview.

A childhood friend said Ahmadinejad "was born a *Hezbollahi,*" the Arabic word for a member of the party of God, the name used by Iran-backed Shiite fundamentalist factions in Lebanon and elsewhere in the Middle East. In an Iranian context that meant Ahmadinejad was a zealot, someone who found fault easily in others but did not question his own behavior and beliefs. Mohsen Kadivar, a Western-educated reformist cleric who spent a year at Harvard, said Ahmadinejad was "opposed to intellectuals, who ask questions. His style is dogmatic—the opposite of analytical or critical thinking."[12] Ahmadinejad's method of dealing with criticism was to issue criticism of his own. He rebuffed questions about Iran's poor human rights record by promising to produce human rights reports about other countries' abuses. "We will be sending groups to provide reports on issues, such as their prisons, discrimination against religious minorities, assassinations, secret prisons, torture, other types of discrimination," he said.[13] On the nuclear issue, he said, Iran had done more than enough by opening its facilities to inspection by the International Atomic Energy Agency. "It is time for the Western countries to build confidence," he said, as Iran accelerated its program and began to enrich uranium.[14]

Ahmadinejad's knowledge of the United States appeared to be extremely limited. When I asked him about his first trip to the United States—a short visit to the United Nations in September 2005—he said that he hadn't been there long enough to form an impression of anything but tall buildings. It was obvious that he had no idea of what real New Yorkers were like. "Generally speaking, people are the same everywhere, and New Yorkers are no exception," he declared. "They like peace and justice and tranquility." Despite his lack of knowledge of Western political systems, the Iranian went so far as to pronounce those systems as failures. "Those with insight can already hear the sounds of the shattering and fall of the ideology and thoughts of the liberal democratic systems," he wrote in a bizarre letter he sent to Bush in May 2006. The contrast could not have been more acute with his predecessor, Khatami, who had actually studied American history and translated into Farsi the treatise on democracy by the nineteenth-century French traveler in America Alexis de Toqueville. Khatami, a midranking cleric and a descendant of the prophet Mohammed, had an enlightened view of religion and used it as a bridge to other faiths. Ahmadinejad, although not a cleric—he is the third layman to be Iran's president—used religion to diminish others.

One of the strangest political documents to come from Iran, or any country, for that matter, was the president's eighteen-page letter to Bush. Widely lampooned at the time as rambling and presumptuous, the letter was a kind of funhouse mirror image of U.S. thinking about Iran. It was also an attempt by Ahmadinejad to make himself relevant by involving himself in Iran's most sensitive diplomatic matters. Iran, he had told me, was not opposed to negotiations with the United States if the right—unspecified—conditions were met. "Iran is an Islamic country, and as Muslims the basis of our conduct is dialogue and rationality," he said. "Except for the occupiers of Jerusalem [Israel] we are prepared to talk to all countries of the world."

The letter contained passages that Bush critics could agree with, particularly the criticism of the U.S. record in Iraq and on the issue of detainees' human rights. It also contained misinformation about U.S. policies, offered no concrete solutions on the nuclear issue, and displayed a lack of self-criticism about Iran's own human rights abuses that turned what could have been an olive branch into an object of ridicule in the West. The only glimmer of self-reflection came when Ahmadinejad wrote that both he and Bush would have to answer to history and God for what they had done in office.

Did we manage to bring peace, security and prosperity for the people or insecurity and unemployment? Did we intend to establish justice or just supported special interest groups . . . ? Did we defend the rights of the underprivileged or ignore them? Did we defend the rights of all people around the world or imposed wars on them, interfered illegally in their affairs, established hellish prisons and incarcerated some of them? Did we bring world peace and security or raise the specter of intimidation and threats? ... Were we on the side of people or the occupiers and oppressors? ... And finally, they will judge us on whether we remained true to our oath of office—to serve the people, which is our main task, and the traditions of the prophets—or not?

Stanley Renshon, a political psychologist at the City College of New York, called the letter "a window into the mindset of a man whose piety easily slides into sanctimony. A man who, in spite of the high-minded appeal to religious aspirations, treats the real world in decidely black or white terms in which his word is the final judgment."[15] Bush critics might say the same about the U.S. president, and there are certainly similarities between the two leaders' thinking. Both find justification for their actions in their religious beliefs. Both demonize their opponents and appear to see a bright line between good and evil; Ahmadinejad simply defines those terms differently. Iran is good; the United States, at least under Bush, evil. Bush, Ahmadinejad suggested in his letter, is not only a bad leader but a bad Christian. "Can one be a follower of Jesus Christ (peace be upon him), the great Messenger of God, feel obliged to respect human rights, present liberalism as a civilization model, (and) make 'War on Terror' his slogan?"

A month after sending the letter, Ahmadinejad expanded on his views in a way that also was reminiscent of Bush, albeit without the latter's skillful ghostwriters. "History is the struggle between good and evil," Ahmadinejad said. "History has witnessed that the oppressors were defeated and humiliated by the oppressed people."[16] Ahmadinejad went on to compare Bush, without naming him, to the Egyptian pharaoh who refused to free Jewish slaves and so destroyed his own people. "I am telling you, if you do not abandon the path of falsehood and return to the path of justice, your doomed destiny will be annihilation, misfortune and abjectness."[17]

Bush is said to have consulted God before he ordered the invasion of Iraq; Ahmadinejad refers frequently to the twelfth *imam*. The Iranian president's 2005 UN speech ended with what appeared to be a call to

God to send this Shiite messiah soon: "O mighty Lord, I pray to you to hasten the emergence of your last repository, the promised one, that perfect and pure human being, the one that will fill this world with justice and peace."[18] A video that circulated widely in Iran later showed Ahmadinejad discussing his experience at the United Nations with an Iranian cleric. "I felt that all of a sudden, the atmosphere changed there and for twenty-seven, twenty-eight minutes all the leaders did not blink . . . as if a hand held them there and made them sit. It had opened their eyes and ears for the message of the Islamic republic," he said. He also said he felt an "aura" of holiness surrounding him.[19]

Questions arose inside and outside Iran after the UN speech as to whether Ahmadinejad was courting a disastrous confrontation with the United States to hasten the Day of Judgment or simply trying to prove his piety. Ahmadinejad's spiritual mentor, a hard-line cleric named Ayatollah Taghi Mesbah Yazdi, claimed after the 2005 election that the new president would form an "Islamic administration" and that the victory was "a clear indication of the Iranian public's support of Islamic governance."[20] But Ahmadinejad showed himself willing to bend Islamic principles to try to enhance his popularity. In May 2006, he proclaimed that women would be allowed to attend soccer matches—long a demand of Iran's female sports fans. The idea was abruptly dropped when the clerical establishment, including Mesbah Yazdi, said it would violate decency laws by letting women see scantily clothed men, but it left an impression that Ahmadinejad was not opposed to women's rights. The new president also took his wife, a high school teacher, along with him on foreign trips—something no previous Iranian leader had done. And despite efforts in the conservative-run parliament to impose a new Islamic dress code, Ahmadinejad initially did nothing to stop Tehran's young women from continuing to wear clothing resembling that of their decadent Western sisters in every detail save the token scarves upon their heads.

For Iran's conservative political establishment, Ahmadinejad was a useful tool, a lightning rod and focus for Western anger. Compared to Khatami, an urbane and charming if ultimately disappointing leader, Khamenei and the other members of the clerical establishment appeared to be right-wing authoritarians. Compared to Ahmadinejad, Khamenei looked like a moderate—a sage older man who intervenes when necessary to rein in a young radical. Ahmadinejad's comments on the Holocaust and Israel underlined this impression. The president at first seemed surprised by the negative Western reaction—after all, he was stating views prevalent among regime hard-liners and common in the Muslim world. He hadn't realized that as Iran's president, he would be taken so seriously. When he saw the reaction he kept repeating the remarks, apparently enjoying the controversy and the attention it brought him.

Ahmadinejad appeared regularly in public with a Palestinian-style checkered scarf around his neck to underline his support for the Palestinian cause. He inserted disparaging remarks about "Zionists" controlling U.S. institutions in an open letter to Americans distributed by the Iranian mission to the United Nations in late 2006. In December 2006, in his most outrageous act to date, he hosted a conference in Tehran of Holocaust deniers, including David Duke, a former leader of the Ku Klux Klan, and Hassidic Jews who reject the creation of Israel in the absence of the Messiah. "The Zionist regime will disappear soon, the same way the Soviet Union disappeared," Ahmadinejad declared.[21]

The president's anti-Israel views appear to be genuine and are broadly shared by the revolution's true believers. "They see Israel as the hidden hand that guides America against them," said Bruce Riedel, the former CIA analyst and Iran expert on the White House National Security Council. One of the reasons Khomeini opposed the shah was because of the monarch's alliance with Israel, which Khomeini viewed as a betrayal of the Muslim faith. If not for Israeli influence, many Iranians believe, successive U.S. governments would not have imposed economic sanctions on Iran. Of course, if Iran did not support Palestinian militants and threaten Israel's existence, the Jewish state might not lobby Americans so strenuously and successfully against Iran.

Many ordinary Iranians also sympathize with the Palestinians but not to the extent that they would jeopardize Iranian interests to help them. In fact, more Iranians are anti-Arab than anti-Jew, a legacy of resentment over the Arab Muslim conquest of Iran in the seventh century and of Jewish contributions to Iranian society going back to biblical times. Although thousands of Iranian Jews have migrated to Israel and the United States since 1979, small Jewish communities still live in Isfahan, Hamadan, and Shiraz and there is an appointed Jewish member in parliament. For most Iranians, Arabs are nouveau riche descendants of uncivilized desert dwellers, not to be compared with Persian sophisticates, and Iranians would prefer that their oil revenues be spent at home, not on foreign causes.

Ahmadinejad concedes that not all Iranians are enthusiastic supporters of the Palestinians. Yet in his interview with me, he insisted that "the most important problem facing the region is Palestine" and that this issue had to be resolved above all others. I lost patience as he droned on about the Holocaust and challenged him at one point: "Why don't you go to Auschwitz and see the gas chambers for yourself?" "My going there will not solve the problem," he replied. He showed the same close mindedness—even chutzpah—in an interview with the German magazine *Der Spiegel,* going so far as to tell his interviewers, "[W]e want to know whether this crime [the Holocaust] actually took place or not."[22] The stunned reporters could only insist that as Germans they might actually know the history of their country better than an Iranian traffic engineer.

Sometimes it seemed as though Ahmadinejad was more interested in courting the Arab street than the Iranian one, and that he calculated he could increase his domestic clout by gaining admiration in the wider Muslim world. His tirades against Israel and the United States were particularly popular in Arab countries such as Egypt, whose leaders have long been seen as kowtowing to Americans. But Iranians paid more attention to his failure to fulfill his promises to improve Iran's economy. Mainstream conservatives and reformers defeated candidates affiliated with the president in muncipal elections in December 2006, and Ahmadinejad's spiritual mentor, Mesbah Yazdi, failed to increase his representation in a clerical body that chooses Iran's supreme leader.

His followers' poor showing—and riots that broke out in June 2007 over gas rationing—led some Iranians to predict that he will not be elected to a second term in 2009. "He obviously is the face of the regime," said Nasr, of the U.S. Naval Postgraduate School. "But he can be sacrificed at the right time. When it comes to the nuclear issue, oil, and what Iran will do with the United States—these are above his pay station." Indeed, after the United States offered to talk to Iran, the Iranian regime, in a rare instance of message discipline, obliged Ahmadinejad to read a nuanced response from a piece of paper that had been prepared for him by his superiors. It was the first time many Iranians had seen their president wearing glasses.

As his first year in office drew to a close, Ahmadinejad tried to appear more presidential. In an interview he gave in August 2006 to Mike Wallace, the veteran CBS *Sixty Minutes* correspondent, the Iranian president smiled frequently and stuck to prepared talking points. Ahmadinejad appeared to have had some media coaching, and he did not repeat his inflammatory comments about Israel despite Wallace's goading. The United States was the problem, he told Wallace, not Iran. "They have to change their behavior and everything will be resolved."[23]

By the time he returned to the United Nations in September 2006, Ahmadinejad had gone from shy political neophyte to shameless publicity hound. He gave a half-dozen interviews, appeared at a press conference, faced down the elite Council on Foreign Relations, and delivered another tough speech to the General Assembly in which he accused the United States and Britain of delegitimizing the UN system through their domination of the Security Council. He appeared more confident—and marginally better dressed—than when I had met him, and seemed to enjoy all the attention from the media, which elevated him to Bush's level by forecasting a face-off between the two in the corridors of the United Nations. In fact, they never saw each other, appearing hours apart and addressing very different audiences. Bush was speaking mostly to a domestic audience, trying to justify his policies in the Middle East before the U.S. midterm elections. Ahmadinejad was addressing the developing world, trying to be another Castro. In the end, however, the Iranian was outdone by another Castro wannabe, Venezuela's Chávez. Bush, Chávez said, was the "devil," whose sulfurous stench still lingered at the podium of the General Assembly twenty-four hours after the American had gone. Even Ahmadinejad couldn't top that one.

FOUR

IRANIAN SQUARE DANCE

To UNDERSTAND IRAN'S UNIQUE system of government, think less of an organizational chart and more of an American square dance. The supreme religious leader—a Shiite Muslim cleric—stands in the middle, with other powerful organizations and individuals around him in a large circle. Depending on the issue, the leader draws one group or person into the center of the circle, then switches to another in a kind of political do-si-do. No figure or group is banished for good so long as it remains loyal to the leader and the system; all in the circle have the chance to influence government decisions. The dance can be slow and awkward and the steps can change in unpredictable ways.

The circle excludes many Iranians, particularly those favoring a secular government, who might command a majority in Iran if a truly free election were held. Dissidents who publicly challenge the tenets of the revolution can expect rough treatment. Within the system's confines, however, the range of ideas put forward is surprisingly wide and provides a basis for hope that Iran can evolve without having to endure another bloody revolution. The circle includes people with strongly conflicting views on domestic and foreign affairs: supporters of capitalism and a state-run economy; of price controls and the free market; of reconciliation with the United States and closer ties with China. The supreme leader, even in the days of Ayatollah Khomeini, was more arbiter than dictator, and the position has weakened considerably since Khomeini's death in 1989. Mehdi Hashemi, the son of former president Rafsanjani, told me before the 2005 vote that the position would become ceremonial, "like the king of England," if his father were re-elected. Hashemi later denied the comment and his father lost the election, but this view of how the system might change to more closely resemble Western democracies is common in Iran.

Despite more than two thousand years of autocratic, even despotic, rule, Iran has long been an intensely political place with a history of democratic activism dating back more than a century. In their first modern challenge to absolute rule, Iranians staged a nationwide boy-cott of tobacco products from 1891 to 1892—an Iranian version of the Boston Tea Party—organized by the country's clerics, who were infuri-ated that the bankrupt monarchy had given a monopoly over tobacco sales to a foreign company. The protest spawned a movement of reli-gious figures and secular intellectuals that led to the first quasi-demo-cratic constitution in the Muslim world in 1906 and made the monarchy, for a time, subservient to an elected parliament. The move-ment collapsed amid foreign intervention and internal fighting, but the democratic sentiments—and the alliance of democrats and clerics—have re-emerged repeatedly in Iranian history. This is a source of na-tional pride in Iran and one way in which Iranians distinguish themselves from the more compliant subjects of Sunni Muslim mon-archs and ex-military autocrats in the Arab world. For example, Irani-an clerics and democratic forces backed Prime Minister Mossadegh when he nationalized the oil industry in 1951; the same alliance came together with even greater power in the 1970s. Groups ranging from extreme secular left to religious right joined in the 1978–79 revolution against the shah. Many of these groups were purged in the aftermath of the revolution, but a wide spectrum of political tendencies remained.

The revolution was a true popular upheaval that overturned a ruling class led by the family of the shah, his courtiers, and a Westernized pro-fessional class and replaced it with a new elite drawn from the middle and lower ranks of Iranian society. Within this elite there have been di-visions from the start between those who cared about personal freedom and others more willing to submit to the dictates of clerics and un-elected officials. Divisions also formed over dividing Iran's oil wealth. These splits have grown more acute as revolutionary zeal has faded.

One reason for the vibrancy of political life in Iran compared to much of the Middle East is that the shah was overthrown so quickly—

in a little over a year—that no single dominant ideology or party, such as the communists of the Soviet Union or China, emerged.[1] The postrevolutionary scene was chaotic, violent, and unpredictable. The first prime minister after the fall of the shah, a Western-educated Islamicist named Mehdi Barzargan, urged that old laws be followed until new ones could be passed, but an assortment of revolutionary organizations sprang up that became laws unto themselves. These included a revolutionary council of top advisers to Khomeini, revolutionary courts that summarily executed the shah's old officials, a revolutionary guard to protect the clerics, and revolutionary committees that terrorized neighborhoods and enforced observance of strict Islamic law. Barzargan described Iran after the shah's fall as "a city with one hundred sheriffs" and his own government as "a knife without a blade." A draft constitution his government prepared was amended to give multiple religious bodies authority over secular institutions, enshrining a duality in Iranian government that continues to plague the system today. The clerical/revolutionary bodies were influenced by popular opinion but had—and continue to have—the upper hand. The final indignity for Barzargan came when Iranian students seized the U.S. embassy and his government failed to secure their release.[2] Khomeini supported the students and prolonged the hostage crisis to smoke out and weed out other opponents. Barzargan resigned and Khomeini's supremacy was confirmed.

THE SUPREME LEADER

To say that the Iranian system is unique scarcely captures its complexity. To a great extent, it is the creation of one man. Khomeini was the revolution's Karl Marx and Lenin rolled into one: a figure of enormous charisma and prestige who had earned popular support in more than two decades of opposition to the monarchy. Educated in Qom, the Iranian city that is a center for Shiite theological studies, Khomeini became politically active after the death of Ayatollah Mohammad Hossein Borujerdi, the leading religious figure of his day, in 1961.[3] Borujerdi had advocated a strict separation of mosque and state; Khomeini went 180 degrees in the other direction. He protested as an American and Zionist plot the shah's "white revolution"—liberal re-

forms that allowed women to vote, gave equal status to religious minorities, and diminished the land holdings of the Shiite clergy. He also
objected to the shah's grant of immunity from prosecution to U.S.
diplomats and military officers stationed in Iran, a humiliating echo of
the concessions bankrupt Iranian monarchs had made to Russians and
Britons in the late nineteenth and early twentieth centuries. In 1964, after publicly challenging the faith and patriotism of the shah, Khomeini
was jailed and exiled; he went first to Turkey and then to the rival Shiite center of Najaf in Iraq. There, in a series of lectures around 1969, he
introduced the concept of *Velayat-e Faqih,* or rule by the jurisprudent,
in which a Shiite cleric of recognized intellect and judgment is authorized to govern until the return of the twelfth *imam.*[4] The concept of
Velayat-e Faqih was and remains highly controversial among Shiite
Muslims. For example, Ayatollah Ali Sistani, the most revered Shiite
cleric in Iraq and, arguably, the broader Shiite world, believes that clerics should not take leadership positions in government. However,
Khomeini was so respected for his political courage and charisma—
and the shah so universally despised—that the glowering ayatollah
managed to institutionalize the position in Iran. In the throes of revolutionary fervor, Iranians voted in 1980 for an undefined "Islamic republic" (the only choices were "yes" or "no") and the following year for
a constitution that recognized the post of supreme leader.

On paper, his powers (and he must be a he) are formidable. The
leader, not the president, is commander-in-chief of the armed forces
and has the authority to declare war. The leader appoints clerics who
comprise half the members of the Council of Guardians, a twelve-man
body that has enormous influence over Iranian political life because it
reviews bills passed by parliament and vets candidates for major public
offices. The remaining six members of the Council of Guardians are
lawyers approved by parliament after being recommended by the head
of the judiciary, himself chosen by the supreme leader.

The leader also appoints the commanders of the branches of the
armed forces and the Revolutionary Guards, the powerful military and
security force that has become increasingly prominent. It is said to be in
charge of the Iranian nuclear program, and has been used by the Iranian leadership to try to export the Islamic revolution to Lebanon and
Shiite communities in Iraq and the Persian Gulf. The leader appoints
the head of the national radio and television, Friday prayer leaders

whose sermons reflect official views, and representatives to government ministries and provincial governments. He also has a number of special advisers, including former top officials, who retain influence over policies. The leader must give final approval to the list of candidates for president and can dismiss the president if he is impeached by the parliament or judged incompetent by Iran's supreme court. Impeachment has occurred once, in 1981, to Abolhassan Bani-Sadr, the first president of the Islamic republic, who unsuccessfully tried to assert the primacy of the regular government over cleric-dominated revolutionary organizations. The leader, however, can also be replaced, at least theoretically. He is chosen by the Assembly of Experts, a popularly elected body of clerics whose membership has varied from about seventy-five to eighty-six. The first assembly was elected in 1979 to draft Iran's Islamic constitution and included nonclerics. Candidates for membership, currently all clerics, must be approved by the Council of Guardians and serve for eight years. The victors of the December 2006 elections for the assembly will likely choose Khamenei's successor, and could also redefine his job.

As the man who fashioned the post of leader, Khomeini was uniquely powerful but did not always choose to exercise those powers. In the 1980s he stood aside while some of the most important issues of the day were debated. Opposing factions fought to impose conflicting systems on Iran—one favoring private property; the other, state control over the economy. Khomeini took no position, and the result was an awkward mixture of the two. Khomeini also refused to end the war with Iraq after Iranian forces succeeded in expelling Iraqi invaders in 1982. His unwillingness to give up hopes of overthrowing the regime of Saddam Hussein contributed to tens of thousands of needless Iranian and Iraqi deaths. When Khomeini grudgingly accepted a United Nations truce in 1988, he said the decision was more bitter than drinking poison.

Khomeini was seventy-eight, going on seventy-nine, when the revolution occurred, and he realized that he needed to provide for his succession. In the mid-1980s he chose a senior cleric named Hossein Ali Montazeri, but changed his mind in 1988 after Montazeri criticized the leader for prolonging the Iran-Iraq war and for permitting the summary executions of thousands of jailed members of the rebellious leftist faction, the Mujahedin e-Khalq. Khomeini died a year later, before naming another successor, and the task was left to the Assembly of Experts, which debated whether to pick one person or a collective leadership to rule in Khomeini's wake. In the end the assembly chose Ali Khamenei, a midranking cleric who had been president from 1981 to 1989. That post had been relatively weak compared to the leader and two parliamentary positions: prime minister and speaker. Under a deal orchestrated by Rafsanjani, a new constitution was written that eliminated the prime minister's job and gave executive powers to the president. Rafsanjani, who had been the speaker of parliament, became president, and Khamenei the leader.

Despite his title, Khamenei has never had the respect that Khomeini enjoyed. While Khomeini had millions of supporters who believed he was entitled to extraordinary powers, Khamenei was not even the proper clerical rank to assume the office. He was a *hojatolislam,* which means "proof of Islam," the name given to midranking students of a senior cleric, known as an *ayatollah* or "sign of God." *Ayatollahs* are supposed to achieve their stature by virtue of their scholarship and the number of junior clerics and ordinary believers who regard them as religious authorities; Khamenei was "promoted" to *ayatollah* when he became supreme leader, in a move that antagonized many of Iran's senior clerics and cast more doubt upon the legitimacy of the system. Lacking Khomeini's clerical standing and his popular support, Khamenei has had to function even more as an arbiter between different factions than as a dictator. He has also become extremely dependent on repressive institutions: the ministries of intelligence and judiciary; the *Basij,* or mobilized ones, the nationwide movement of young and elderly volunteers who fought bravely in the Iran-Iraq war but who now function mostly as vigilantes; and the Revolutionary Guards, created by Khomeini out of concern about the political reliability of the regular armed forces who had served the shah. Khamenei retained Khomeini's power to appoint prayer leaders in major towns and cities who explain government policies in their Friday sermons. And he appointed representatives throughout the bureaucracy who relayed information to him and his wishes to other government institutions. In the past he traveled around the country extensively, but age and infirmity have kept him increasingly in Tehran, where he meets Muslim and Third World leaders but rarely Westerners. Despite reports of disagreements with other top political figures, Khamenei has worked closely with three Iranian presidents: Rafsanjani, Khatami, and Ahmadinejad.

Khamenei's method has been to allow other figures to float trial balloons, then intervene to confirm or deny policy changes. For example, in early 2006, Khamenei voiced approval of direct talks between Iran and the United States about Iraq after his national security adviser, Ali Larijani, had sent out feelers for several months.[5] Khamenei appeared to change his mind and shifted his support to Iran's hawkish president, Ahmadinejad, as the nuclear program advanced and Iran faced no serious punishment from the rest of the world. But Khamenei also showed a willingness to rein in Ahmadinejad when the president attracted international condemnation and his domestic popularity appeared to wane. Iranian state television broadcast student protests against Ahmadinejad in December 2006, something that could not have taken place without the leader's approval.

Hadi Semati, a professor of political science at Tehran University, told me that when Khamenei "really wants something done and his heart is in it, he can get it done. If he wants to stop something, he can also get it done." Amir Mohebbian, editor of a conservative newspaper, *Resalat,* compared Khamenei's role to that of a U.S. president but with less power. "When there is an important problem like the nuclear issue, no one individual can make a decision," Mohebbian said.

THE PRESIDENT

In the Iranian system, the power of the presidency—like that of the leader—has varied depending on its occupant. Rafsanjani was arguably the most powerful because of his background as a key figure in the revolution. The fact that he helped make Khamenei the leader meant that Khamenei was aware that he was in Rafsanjani's debt. Rafsanjani focused on reconstructing an economy shattered by the 1980–88 Iran-Iraq war, diminished the importance of Islamic ideology, and tried unsuccessfully to restore relations with the United States by engineering the release of U.S. hostages in Lebanon and offering a major contract to an American oil company, Conoco. President Clinton, under pressure from a Republican Congress, canceled the oil deal and stiffened sanctions against Iran. Khatami dramatically eased social restrictions and improved channels between Iran and the West, but was eventually stymied by hard-line conservatives and hostility from the Bush administration. Ahmadinejad has sought to spread Iran's oil wealth more equally, to identify himself with the nuclear program, and to project a tough image to the outside world. Many of his policies appear to have backfired, but the jury is still out on what he may accomplish.

IRAN'S NSC

The president has significant institutional duties. He appoints a cabinet, subject to confirmation by an elected parliament, represents the country abroad, and is the chief administrator in domestic affairs. His interior minister names the governors of Iran's twenty-nine provinces. The president has the power of the bully pulpit—as Ahmadinejad has shown with his controversial comments about Israel and the Holocaust—but does not make key foreign policy decisions. Those are made by the supreme leader on the advice of the Supreme Council of National Security, which is comprised of about a dozen members, including the president; the speaker of parliament; ministers of intelligence, foreign affairs, and defense; heads of the various branches of the armed forces; and two representatives of the leader. According to Semati, Iran's NSC functions a bit like the American one. It has committees and advisers who prepare position papers and a process of deliberation that can be slow and intensely confrontational. "The decision-making process is more democratic than Americans think," Semati said. "If Bush wants to get something done, everyone will line up, but in Iran people will fight to the end. That's why you have a lot of gridlock."

Added to this contentious mix is a popularly elected 290-member parliament that has never been a mere rubber stamp. In fact, disputes within the parliament have sometimes grown so heated that clerical deputies have been known to knock off each other's turbans. Unlike the toothless body that existed under the shah, the parliament of the Islamic republic has the power to reject government ministers and bud-

gets and can conduct investigations. Its members, particularly committee chairmen, are frequently quoted in the Iranian press. The parliament has shifted in orientation since the revolution from leftist in the
1980s to conservative in the early 1990s, to reformist in the late 1990s,
and, after the 2004 elections, back to conservative, following the dis-
qualification of several dozen incumbent reformers by the Council of
Guardians. But contrary to some pundits' predictions and the expectations of conservatives, the 2005 election of a hard-line conservative
president did not bring peace and harmony to the Iranian political
scene. The parliament rejected several of Ahmadinejad's ministerial
nominees as unqualified and criticized the president's foreign policy
pronouncements. Mohammad Khosh-Chehreh, a member of parliament from Tehran, accused the government of incompetent diplomacy
on the nuclear issue and warned against making decisions "based on
emotions and slogans."[6] Deputies challenged the government budget
and predicted, correctly, that increased subsidies for food and fuel
would only add to inflation. Iranians have a strong antiauthoritarian
streak and a tendency to criticize others even within their own camp.
Perhaps a dozen or more senior figures believe they should be the country's leader. "We are a country of talkers and talk," Semati said. Com-
promise has had a negative connotation, implying weakness, and
"everyone thinks he is an expert."

Far from being totalitarian, Iran's system is a maze of checks and
balances. To overcome gridlock between the parliament and Council of
Guardians, Khomeini in 1988 created yet another body that only made
the political process more cumbersome. The Expediency Council—a
group of about three dozen senior regime figures, including the president, the speaker of parliament, and the head of the judiciary—is supposed to resolve disputes between the parliament, president, and
Council of Guardians and to supervise all branches of government.
Former president Rafsanjani heads the council. His deputy is Mohsen
Rezaie, the former commander of the Revolutionary Guards. In Iran,
regime stalwarts do not fade away, they simply move to another position on the circle. Both Rafsanjani and Rezaie ran unsuccessfully in the
2005 presidential elections but kept their jobs on the Expediency Council. Other losers received consolation prizes that kept them within the
circle of power. Mohammad-Baqer Qalibaf, a former Revolutionary

Guards Air Force commander and police chief, got Ahmadinejad's old job as Tehran's mayor, and is likely to run for president again; Larijani, a former head of state radio and television, became secretary of the national security council and Iran's chief nuclear negotiator. Former president Khatami and his top officials and advisers retreated, Washington-style, to Tehran think tanks, but were still consulted on foreign policy and had influence with Khamenei. After the Bush administration offered in May 2006 to join talks with Iran on its nuclear program, Khamenei added yet another layer of bureaucracy to the foreign policy decision-making process and formed a "strategic committee for foreign policy" headed by the foreign minister during Khatami's presidency, Kamal Kharrazi.[7] The implication was that Ahmadinejad's team was not up to the task of dealing with such momentous issues and, by naming this body, Khamenei was also trying to make sure that all of Islamic Iran's mainstream political forces would be onboard before any major policy shifts.

The Iranian revolution overturned the country's class structure as well as its political system. Half a million Iranians fled during the revolution and 10,000 were executed by the new government or killed in civil strife.[8] Over time the system generated a new ruling class of clerics, traditional merchants from the Tehran bazaar, officers of the Revolutionary Guards, heads of religious foundations that took over royal and private property, and technocrats, some of them Western educated. At the top of the new elite are several hundred people within government institutions and perhaps another hundred outside, including clerics in Qom. Altogether, Semati said, this elite may number about 500. Add to this thousands of government bureaucrats, the Revolutionary Guards corps of about 150,000, and the Islamic youth movement, the *Basij,* of about a million, and Iran has the equivalent, in some respects, of the Soviet or Chinese system of communist party members and apparatchiks: a relatively stable ruling class held together by patronage, ideology, and personal relationships.

WE HAVE EVERYTHING

Closeness to the top figures of the regime led to enormous increases in wealth for those who had been poor before the revolution. Khomeini's chauffeur, a former shop assistant in the Tehran bazaar, became one of the richest men in Iran.[9] So did Rafsanjani and his family, which, from a humble beginning as pistachio farmers, amassed a major stake in Iran's automobile industry and in an airline. Still firmly planted in Iran's inner circle, Rafsanjani has been a key figure in Iran from the time of the revolution, no matter what his formal title has been. "Personalities are more important than positions in Iran," said Karim Sadjadpour, an Iran analyst for the Carnegie Endowment for International Peace. After being defeated for president in 2005, Rafsanjani staged a dramatic comeback a year later when he received the most votes in elections for the Assembly of Experts, the body that chooses the supreme leader.

Iranians still speak sarcastically of the "thousand families"—once a term for the pre-1979 aristocracy. Among the new "thousand families" are many with clerical connections, including the Larijanis, the offspring of a famous ayatollah, Hashem Amoli. Ali Larijani is the national security adviser; his brothers include an adviser to the head of the judiciary, a prominent physicist, and a cleric who is a member of the Council of Guardians.

The most famous and infamous of the new elite families are the Rafsanjanis. The former president's elder daughter, Fatemeh, long had a cushy job involving women's affairs in the Foreign Ministry, and his younger daughter, Faezeh, was a member of parliament, a newspaper publisher, and head of a sports association for women. A fast-talking, self-confident young woman whose designer jeans and leopard-print scarves peek out from under her *chador,* Faezeh also toyed with running for president in 1997 but was overruled by the clerical establishment, which insisted that only men were eligible. Married young, Faezeh divorced in her thirties and, unusual in Iran, kept custody of her two children. There were limits to her influence, however. Her newspaper, *Zan,* or *Woman,* was closed in 1999 when it printed New Year's greetings from Farah Diba, the widow of the late shah. Defeated for parliament in 2000, Faezeh went to England to study for a doctorate in international relations at Cambridge University.

One of Rafsanjani's sons, Mohsen, heads the office constructing the Tehran metro; another, Yasser, is on the Expediency Council. The third, Mehdi, served in the oil industry and runs an organization promoting fuel efficiency. I met him at his offices in the upscale Jordan neighborhood of Tehran in 2005. In his thirties and university educated in Australia, he seemed the classic rich man's son—wearing an expensive blue and white striped English designer shirt that stretched a bit over his belly. He giggled frequently at his own jokes and talked expansively about politics without the caution a less well-protected Iranian might have shown. His comment about his father turning the job of leader into a ceremonial position like "the King of England" caused a huge uproar in the Iranian press after it was published in *USA Today.* When I asked him whether the Rafsanjani family wanted Rafsanjani to run again for president, Mehdi said, "No," because "we have everything" already—unwitting confirmation that Rafsanjani had used his years of high office to enrich his clan. The image of the rich man's son was completed when Mehdi got up from a chair to go to his desk and revealed that he had been sitting all the time we had been speaking on a thick wad of Iranian cash.

Unlike the Soviet Union or China, Iran has no single ruling party. Instead, there are a half-dozen recognized political groupings that are less formal parties in the Western sense than tendencies, usually identified with key political figures. After the revolution, pro-Khomeini forces sought to create one dominant party, the Islamic Republican Party, and they suppressed previously active communist, leftist, and secular groups that had been key supporters of the revolution. But the ruling party was riven from the start by differences, particularly over the direction of the economy, and Khomeini dissolved the group in 1987. Since then, several political organizations have formed that range from right to left, from socially repressive to prodemocratic.

Designers of Venn diagrams have had a field day trying to depict Iran's political groupings, which defy comparison to parties in the West and change as frequently as the images in a kaleidoscope. In their fractiousness and willingness to create new political factions—and the number of individuals who think they are suited to lead the country—Iranian government officials most resemble Israelis—a comparison neither might appreciate.

As of this writing, the major political forces in Iran include:

MILITANT CLERICS ASSOCIATION: Many conservative clerics are affiliated with this group, which includes the leader, Khamenei; a longtime head of the Assembly of Experts, Ayatollah Ali Meshkini (until his death in July 2007); and a former speaker of parliament, Ali Akbar Nateq Nouri, who ran unsuccessfully for president in 1997. The group is socially conservative but favors private enterprise and a cautious foreign policy that will not jeopardize the stability of the system.

DEVELOPERS' COALITION: Ahmadinejad comes from this right-wing faction, which some Iranians have nicknamed the neoconservatives for their back-to-the-revolution cultural views and hawkish foreign and defense policies. The group gained considerable power with Ahmadinejad's election but began splitting less than a year later because of policy disagreements and the disappointment of members who did not get important jobs in the new administration.

EXECUTIVES OF CONSTRUCTION: A pragmatic, probusiness group, it was set up in the mid-1990s under the leadership of then president Rafsanjani and might best be compared with the "realist" wing of the U.S. Republican Party as exemplified by the first president Bush. It strongly supports foreign trade and investment and tolerates a certain amount of social freedom.

MILITANT CLERICS SOCIETY: Not to be confused with the Militant Clerics Association, this clerical body was once far left and included leaders of the 1979 hostage crisis as well as former president Khatami. Under the Khatami administration, many of these same clerics became Iran's most ardent reformers.

ISLAMIC PARTICIPATION FRONT: Led by former president Khatami's brother, Mohammed Reza Khatami, this group backed a free press, cultural liberalization, and renewed ties to the United States. It is the largest reformist party, but went into decline after the 2004 parliamentary elections and the 2005 presidential contest.

THE NATIONAL TRUST: Mehdi Karroubi, once a member of the Militant Clerics Society, formed this party in 2005 after being defeated for the presidency. It appears to be largely a personal vehicle for Karroubi, who served as speaker of parliament during the 1990s.

CONNECTIONS

In all societies, connections with high officials can be helpful; in Iran, they are a necessity. To go through the front door of an institution is useless; the back or side door or even the window is nearly always the more effective route. Connections that worked when one faction was in power become worthless when a new group ascends to office. For a journalist to obtain an interview with a top figure, for example, he or she must know someone with associates in that office; it is not sufficient to apply formally through the Ministry of Islamic Culture and Guidance, which is nominally in charge of the foreign as well as domestic press. An elaborate vetting process is also required, as are repeated trips to Iran to prove one's interest in the country. I had traveled to Iran four times before I got my first major interview, with Rafsanjani, in 2005. Before the interview I was quizzed by a close family friend, then met twice with Rafsanjani's son Mehdi, once with the former president's brother, Mohammad, and once with Rafsanjani's favorite journalist, Mohammad Atrianfar, chief of the editorial board of the reformist newspaper *Shargh*. Before interviewing the national security adviser, Larijani, in 2006, I met at length with one of his deputies. My 2006 interview with Ahmadinejad came after repeated meetings with conservative journalists who had contacts in the president's office. "Personal connections will expedite your case but they won't make or break it," said Kian Tajbakhsh, an urban planner and adviser to the World Bank who lives in Iran (and was jailed in 2007 on spurious charges of spying).

Lacking direct experience with American officials, Iranians often assume that the U.S. system works like theirs. Many Iranian officials tend to distrust official channels and would rather send messages through private emissaries than address the Bush administration through the Swiss embassy in Tehran, which represents U.S. interests in the absence of formal diplomatic ties. Iranians also practice a kind of Kremlinology, scouring photos of U.S. presidents to try to figure out who the most important advisers are. Iranians have told me that Stephen Hadley, Bush's second-term national security advisor, must be more influential than Secretary of State Condoleezza Rice because Hadley is photographed next to Bush on foreign trips. When Larijani wanted to signal Iran's readiness to hold direct talks with the United

States, he went out of his way to praise Hadley to me but sent no greetings to Rice, even though she was Hadley's boss in the first Bush term and has had more impact on shaping U.S. policy toward Iran in the second term.

A backlash against Iranian reformers toward the end of the Khatami presidency brought into the center of the circle an influential group of younger Iranians once exiled to the periphery. Iran's neoconservatives triumphed to some extent because of the growing influence of their namesakes in the United States. Bush's "axis of evil" comment, in his 2002 State of the Union address, delighted U.S. neoconservatives but was enormously damaging to the reform movement in Iran. Iranian neoconservatives argued that the Bush administration simply pocketed Iran's assistance in overthrowing the Taliban regime in Afghanistan in 2001, and that Bush's remark proved that the United States would never accept Iran as a regional power or partner. Emboldened by the reformers' weakness and aided by a voter boycott, the neocons swept municipal elections in 2003 and staged what amounted to a coup in parliamentary elections the following year. The Council of Guardians, dominated by hard-liners, disqualified about three thousand candidates, including eighty incumbent members of parliament.[10] The ousted reformers staged a sit-in at the parliament but attracted little popular support. (This was not the first time the council has acted to change Iran's political direction. It did the same thing in 1992 to purge radical leftists who had controlled the parliament following the revolution through the Iran-Iraq war.[11])

The pendulum kept swinging to the right as Iranian neoconservatives built upon their parliamentary and municipal council victories to capture the presidency in 2005. After his victory, Ahmadinejad brought his friends and allies into the inner circle. Just as he had been fired as governor of Ardabil, a province in the northwest, after Khatami's election in 1997, Ahmadinejad dismissed thousands of veteran bureaucrats around the country and replaced them with cronies, including many veterans of the Revolutionary Guards. Iranians complained that the cuts went too deep and that the new officials were not qualified to do their jobs. Rafsanjani told a group of clerics that "a tendency in Iran is trying to banish competent officials and it is harming the country like a plague."[12]

The criticism was ironic in view of the fact that Rafsanjani and his generation were scarcely more qualified to hold positions of responsibility after the revolution. Shaul Bakhash, a professor at George Mason University and a former journalist who covered the shah's overthrow, wrote that the revolutionaries took over a government with "strong administrative traditions and capabilities." The new bosses stripped away the top layer of the bureaucracy but had to be taught by the career civil servants who remained how to "write budgets, to keep the national accounts and to negotiate foreign trade agreements." As so often happens after political upheaval, the "revolutionaries" slowly turned into bureaucrats like the ones they had replaced.[13] Saeed Laylaz, the former deputy interior minister under Khatami, predicted that Ahmadinejad's appointees would eventually learn how to fulfill their responsibilities and ideology would lose out to the practical realities of governing. "The Islamic Republic of Iran is like a factory," he told me. "For twenty-seven years, this factory has received super *Hezbollahis* [rightwing religious zealots] and delivered handsome technocrats."

Tajbakhsh, the World Bank adviser, had another metaphor for Iran: a soccer team where talent is an important, but not the most important, qualification for membership. The owners of the team are Shiite clerics who require that coaches and players follow certain religious practices in order to participate. The team turns out to be relatively successful, although not as good as it could have been with different ownership and different rules for membership.

Still, the system has staying power. It has a network of social services and means of social control that penetrate more deeply into the hinterlands than the monarchy ever did. Governance is inefficient by Western standards but compares favorably with other Middle Eastern regimes. For example, Iranian officials are usually punctual, an exception in the region, and tend not to break appointments at the last minute, like some Saudis do. Most government departments follow written rules and procedures. Corruption is endemic when large sums of money are involved such as major oil or construction contracts. In 2005, Transparency International ranked Iran eighty-eighth in the world in terms of corruption, worse than Egypt and Syria (the United States was seventeenth).[14] But petty bribes are less prevalent in Iran than in many other countries in the Middle East. Tajbakhsh, who moved to Iran several years ago after two decades in the West, said he has never had to pay a bribe to register a deed, get married, or handle other normal transactions. During six visits to Iran in ten years I was hit up only once—by an employee of the Ministry of Culture and Guidance—for a fifty dollar "fee" to visit a cultural center for Iranian youth. I avoided that person from then on. I also managed to escape several "agencies" created by ex-ministry employees that charged hefty sums to set up appointments with Iranian officials for inexperienced foreign journalists.

Iranians complain with reason that the bureaucracy can be cumbersome and slow. Sadjadpour recalled needing approval from a dozen different ministries to secure his exemption from military service. "They have to get the OK from so many institutions that they can be almost paralyzed with indecision," he said. Yet the system muddles on and Iranians appear to value stability over radical change.

ELECTORAL POLITICS

Bush administration officials have criticized Iran's government as undemocratic, even totalitarian, but the labels give short shrift to a system that has developed elements of democracy and more freedom of expression than any other Middle Eastern state with the exception of Israel, the Palestinian territories, and, although its ultimate fate is still far from certain at this writing, the "new" Iraq. Barry Rosen, a former U.S. embassy hostage, called Iran "the most democratic of authoritarian states in the region and also the most erratic." The system appears to provide just enough political choice to keep Iranians from turning off it completely. Elections are far from free but produce results that have frequently surprised political analysts, and Iranians have gotten into the habit of going to the polling booth. Khatami's 1997 election was a great boon to the system. The establishment candidate, Nateq Nouri, the lackluster speaker of the parliament, suffered a humiliating defeat. Turnout was huge by American standards, about 80 percent, of which Khatami won 69 percent. Khatami went on to disappoint his enthusiastic supporters but was still re-elected in 2001 by an even larger margin—80 percent—although turnout was lower, about 67 percent of eligible voters. Ahmadinejad's election was also unexpected; Rafsanjani or a reformist candidate had been predicted to win. Still, the Bush administration rejected the 2005 vote before it was held. "Today Iran is ruled by men who suppress liberty at home and spread terror across the world," Bush said. "Power is in the hands of an unelected few who have retained power through an electoral process that ignores the basic requirements of democracy."

U.S. officials noted that the Guardian Council rejected all but eight candidates for president. But perhaps more astonishing than the rejection was the fact that more than one thousand Iranians sought to run, five times the number who applied in 1997. Among the presidential hopefuls was a seventy-year-old woman who said she was motivated by the high price of onions and a man who wore a giant garbage bag to show that he would be a slave to the Iranian people. Despite Bush's dismissal of the process, the choice offered to Iranians was fairly broad. Rafsanjani, the ultimate pragmatist, led the field. Three candidates ran as reformers: a cleric, a former minister of higher education, and a former Khatami vice president who spoke out in favor of human rights and social liberalization. Former education minister Mostafa Moin said during the campaign that Iranian women should no longer be obliged to cover their hair, crossing what had been a red line for the regime since Khomeini forced women to wear the veil after the revolution. There were two conservative candidates besides Ahmadinejad: Larijani, then the head of state radio and television, and Qalibaf, the former police chief. (Rezaie, the former commander of the Revolutionary Guards, dropped out to avoid giving the victory to reformers.) According to the government, at least 57 percent of eligible voters took part in the first round of voting, a possibly inflated figure but still respectable by international standards. And for the first time in Iranian history, a runoff election was held because no candidate won a majority in the first round.

The campaign was the liveliest Iranians had ever experienced. Candidates plastered Tehran with colorful posters, supporters wore headbands proclaiming allegiance to their favorites, and there was widespread use of the Internet. All the candidates had official Web sites as well as other sites run by supporters. One of two clerics competing, the reformist Karroubi, had his photos cropped in such a way that people could not see his turban—recognition that many Iranians are fed up with clerics in politics. Rafsanjani's campaign featured teenage girls in slinky Western-style outfits. In one provocative commercial girls were shown roller-skating with their long hair, barely bound by

Rafsanjani headbands, rippling in the wind. Qalibaf ran a slick television advertisement that showed him in a crisp uniform piloting an Iran Air flight. Sadjadpour said the ad was modeled after a trailer for the Tom Cruise movie *Top Gun;* the idea was to show Qalibaf as a heroic figure who would save Iran.

Television was crucial to Ahmadinejad's victory. His campaign video contrasted his modest two-bedroom home in Narmak, the working-class suburb in southeast Tehran, with the palatial residence of Tehran's previous mayor, Karbaschi, in upscale north Tehran. Ahmadinejad's son was shown laughing when asked where the family kept its Jacuzzi. Ahmadinejad also swayed voters by traveling the country in a small bus and promising to distribute the country's oil revenues more equitably. It was not exactly democracy, but it was also not one-party or one-man rule. Iran has "democratic features," said Richard Haass, the former top official in the Bush State Department who is now president of the Council on Foreign Relations. "You've got electoral elements and some distribution of power, but the appointed elements are way too powerful and the playing field is pretty tilted."

The 2005 presidential election confirmed that "elections actually do matter in Iran . . . in terms of the possibility of unexpected results, important changes in policy direction, and changes of political cadres," said Farideh Farhi, an Iran analyst from the University of Hawaii.[15] Reformers were forced back on the fringes of the circle but made a modest comeback, along with moderate conservatives, in December 2006 municipal elections, as Ahmadinejad's economic policies fell flat.

Dissidents want a referendum to eliminate the office of supreme leader or make it largely ceremonial. The power of the position could diminish after Khamenei dies. Or it could become even more important if Rafsanjani succeeds Khamenei. Rafsanjani became acting head of the Assembly of Experts, which chooses the leader, after its chairman died in July 2007.

The country could also become less democratic if Iran faces a military confrontation with the United States. Much as Americans have sacrificed personal rights to allow their government to prosecute the war on terror, Iranians would likely accept an even more repressive system if the country was attacked over its nuclear program. Military figures, particularly from the Revolutionary Guards, would become even more prominent, accelerating a trend that is pushing Iran toward the politics of its neighbors, Pakistan and Turkey, where the military has been a key institution for decades. In Tehran in 2005 and 2006, I heard a number of people, particularly in the lower middle class, express nostalgia for the days of Reza Shah, the father of the ousted shah. The elder Pahlavi was a Russian-trained former officer who modeled himself after the founder of modern Turkey, Kemal Atatürk. Vali Nasr, of the Naval Postgraduate School in Monterey, California, said this nostalgia points to a central paradox in Iranian politics. "There is a desire for continuity of electoral practices and yet the need for a strong hand," he said. The result, he said, is likely to be "an uneasy coexistence between Putin-like strong men and elected parliaments."

Prone to criticize their own system, Iranians also point out that the U.S. system is not without flaws. They are quick to bring up the human rights abuses committed at Guantánamo and Abu Ghraib and the chaos in Iraq that followed the U.S. toppling of Saddam Hussein. Conspiratorial by nature, they question the true nature of American democracy and suggest that Americans are naïve to believe that they are really in control of their own political fate. "We have a Guardian Council and everyone knows them; you have one, too, but nobody knows them," Rafsanjani's son Mehdi told me after Bush's re-election. The U.S. council vetting candidates, Mehdi said, is "people with money. In the future, we will become like you."

FIVE

GUARDIANS OF THE REVOLUTION

Mᵧ ᴅʀɪᴠᴇʀ ɪɴ ɪʀᴀɴ is not easily fazed. A burly man in his late forties who had been a wrestler in his youth, he has driven journalists around Iran since the 1979 revolution and there is little about the country that surprises him anymore. But on a frosty morning in February 2006, he was experiencing something new and, he said, unnerving—entering the private precincts of Iran's Revolutionary Guards. We had driven northeast of Tehran, above the smog line of pollution that covers the capital like a dingy blanket, to a green and wooded park area called Lavisan-Shian. There, beyond barbed-wire fences and military checkpoints, was the private residence of Mohsen Rezaie, the former commander of the Guards. Rezaie stepped down in 1997 but his influence remains strong, a reflection of the power of the institution he headed for sixteen years.

Rezaie's house was a rectangular structure of concrete and stucco that looked more like an office or a barracks than a home. Our meeting was held in a large but drab reception room furnished with two parallel rows of imitation leather and chrome chairs, the sort you might find in an airport tourist lounge. The room was clearly used frequently for meetings, and plates of English cucumbers, oranges, and cookies were set out on sidetables along with the requisite cups of tea. I sat waiting with my translator for only a few moments before Rezaie entered the room, surrounded by a half-dozen aides. A middle-aged man with a hint of a paunch and a stubbly beard, Rezaie might be perfectly cast in an Iranian version of *The Sopranos*. He sat down on one of the chairs opposite me without shaking hands but, in a country where officials also avoid the eyes of unrelated women, he fixed me with an intense stare before launching into what sounded like a well-rehearsed monologue. He laid out two scenarios for the future of U.S.-Iran relations: reconciliation that recognized Iran's influence in the Middle East and right to nuclear energy or dire consequences if the Bush administration sought to put more pressure on Iran. This was a "golden time for the Americans" to resolve their differences with Iran about the nuclear issue and other matters, Rezaie said. But if the United States "decides on harsh measures, everything would be changed overnight and there would be serious problems" for the United States throughout the Middle East, he warned.

PART MILITARY, PART MAFIA

The Guards' leaders seem to occupy permanent spots in Iran's inner circle. After he left the Guards in 1997, Rezaie became secretary of the Expediency Council, the group of about three dozen senior regime figures that resolves disputes between the branches of government. In 2002, he founded a news Web site, *Baztab,* or Reflections, that has become a must-read source of information about the conservatives who dominate the Iranian government. Wilfried Buchta, a German scholar of Iran, calls Rezaie "one of the 12 most powerful men" in the country."[1] "He's legendary," said Kenneth Katzman, a Middle East expert at the Congressional Research Service and author of a book on the Guards. "The Guards was very disorganized when he took it over, and he made the organization what it is today."

Commissioned on May 5, 1979, three months after the overthrow of the last government of the shah, the Guards was intended to be a people's militia to safeguard the ideals of the Islamic revolution. It has evolved into something far more powerful and unique in the annals of military organizations. With about 150,000 active members—the top third of the nation's military—plus thousands of influential veterans, the Guards combines the vanguard military mission of the U.S. Marines, the internal and external security and intelligence activities of the old Soviet KGB, the economic muscle of a Japanese trading consortium, and the black market expertise of the Cosa Nostra. The Guards protects Iran's top leaders and is in charge of its nuclear program and missile development. Its members and veterans rival Shiite Muslim clerics as the most influential figures in Iran today. Ahmadinejad is a former Guards officer, as are about half the members of his cabinet, two thirds of Iran's governors, and a third of the members of parliament. Ex-guardsmen head Islamic foundations that control a significant portion of Iran's wealth and chair corporations in charge of major construction projects. Rezaie, for example, built a fortune for himself in construction and other businesses in his native Khuzestan, Iran's oil-producing southwest province on the border with Iraq.

While many outside Iran see the Guards as a bastion of anti-Americanism, the reality is more complicated. In its early years, the Guards was responsible indirectly for the worst terrorist act against Americans before the advent of al-Qaeda—the 1983 Marine barracks bombing that killed 241 Americans in Beirut. But the Guards has also produced some of Iran's most outspoken dissidents, including Akbar Ganji, a crusading journalist who exposed the regime's worst human rights abuses. The Guards has suspended anti-American activities when ordered to do so by Iran's civilian and clerical leaders, indirectly collaborated with the United States in overthrowing the Taliban in Afghanistan, interfered massively in Iraq both for and against U.S. allies, and produced politicians, such as Rezaie, who have suggested a "grand bargain" with the United States that would acknowledge Iran's role as a major strategic player in the Persian Gulf. If the United States and Iran ever reconcile, a substantial portion of the Guards will have to be onboard. They are the men who know where the bodies are buried because they are the ones who buried them.

Mohsen Sazegara, an anti-shah activist who studied in the 1970s at the Illinois Institute of Technology in Chicago, was present at the creation of the Guards. He was among scores of young Iranians who joined Khomeini after he was expelled from Iraq in 1978 and moved to the Paris suburb of Neauphle-le-Château. Sazegara, who was on Khomeini's historic flight back from Paris to Tehran on February 1, 1979, had no military experience but figured that the Iranian revolution would require a people's army on the order of the Viet Cong. "We didn't expect such a quick victory," Sazegara told me in 2006. "We thought there would be a long battle with the shah's army and the

United States." After overthrowing the old government, the Guards, in Sazegara's view, would blend back into the population and become a reserve force like the U.S. National Guard, to be called upon in cases of national emergency. Sazegara and several other activists wrote a charter for the Guards and incorporated a variety of armed groups that had opposed the shah. Most of these groups drew their membership from the children of traditional, religious families newly entered into the urban middle class.

The Guards functioned first as an internal security force, putting down ethnic unrest in the northern Azeri city of Tabriz and in the Kurdish areas in Iran's northwest.[2] Then it moved to suppress rivals to Khomeini in Tehran, including communists and the Mujahedin e-Khalq, the Islamic leftist group that broke with the Iranian regime and later disclosed Iran's nuclear progress. The Guards also became embroiled in the takeover of the U.S. Embassy, providing backup after militant students seized the compound on November 4, 1979. A group of Americans who managed to escape the embassy was caught and marched back into captivity by Guards members.[3] After the failed U.S. attempt to rescue the hostages in April 1980, the captives were moved to Guards bases around the country to preempt another rescue effort.[4] In a reward for Guards services, the spacious U.S. Embassy compound was later turned into a high school for Guards Air Force cadets and plastered with anti-American slogans, such as "Down to World Arrogance!" Few Iranians pay any attention to the slogans anymore, but the government dutifully repaints them every few years and the compound remains in Guards hands.

WAR AND TERRORISM

The 1980–88 Iran-Iraq war transformed the Guards from an internal security force into an army that paralleled and then grew stronger than the regular armed forces. When Iraq invaded Iran in 1980, hoping to take advantage of Iran's revolutionary chaos, the conventional Iranian army was a shambles; thousands of its officers had been executed or fled. Iranian leaders hastily recalled junior officers, and the Guards put together a new popular force called the *Basij,* or mobilized ones. Made up of conscripts as young as ten or eleven recruited around the nation from rural areas and urban mosques, the *Basij* used these youngsters as unarmed cannon fodder in a new kind of warfare in which thousands swarmed across minefields to overwhelm Iraqi forces with human wave attacks. Around the necks of these unfortunate youth were plastic keys promising immediate admission to Heaven for those who died fighting the Iraqi invaders. Tens of thousands of young Iranians perished this way. Once the Iraqi lines had been breached, regular army forces followed up with tanks and artillery. The Guards also drafted older, educated Iranians with expertise needed to flesh out a professional military organization.

By the spring of 1982, the Iraqis had been driven out of Iranian territory and the war could have and should have ended in a draw. According to Sazegara, Rezaie and Rafsanjani, who was then speaker of the parliament, convinced Khomeini to take the war inside Iraq to protect Iranian cities against another Iraqi offensive. Khomeini needed little convincing. In a paroxysm of vengeance and ideological zeal, he prolonged the conflict in hopes of overthrowing Saddam. At this point the Guards changed from a force defending against foreign aggression to an organization actively seeking to export the new Iranian form of government.[5] The Guards formalized the new role by creating a fifth branch, after an air force, ground force, navy, and *Basij:* the Qods, or Jerusalem force, responsible for subversive activities abroad. The goals were to implant an Islamic revolution in Iraq, where Shiites were the majority; to support the Palestinians against Israel, and to create militant Shiite Muslim parties in other countries with substantial Shiite populations, including Lebanon, Bahrain, and Saudi Arabia. The Qods force also killed Iranian opposition figures abroad. "They were the ones who did Iran's wet work overseas," said Steven Simon, a terrorism expert who served in the Clinton National Security Council, using spy jargon for assassinations.

This dark side of the Guards brought it into confrontation with the United States and Israel through a variety of Arab surrogates. The most potent was Hezbollah, or the Party of God, the movement of Lebanese Shiite Muslims. Iran had long-standing religious ties with Lebanese Shiites, whose clerics had intermarried with Iranians for centuries and sometimes studied in Qom. Iran's new government also had excellent relations with the Palestine Liberation Organization, which had bases in Lebanon and provided training to several hundred future

Guards before the revolution. So the Islamic regime reacted quickly to help its allies after Israeli forces invaded Lebanon in June 1982. Israel had hoped to implant a friendly government in Lebanon that would expel Palestinian guerrillas who had been firing rockets on northern Israeli communities. Instead, the Israelis fostered a new and more potent enemy. Despite the ongoing war with Iraq, Iran sent about one thousand Guards to Lebanon's Bekaa Valley and put together Hezbollah from a splinter faction of a secular Shiite group, Amal.[6] Hezbollah went on to become a major social and political as well as military organization, responsible for increasing the political clout of the largest and most downtrodden sector of the Lebanese population. The party also organized relentless attacks on Israeli soldiers and their Lebanese allies that led Israel to withdraw from southern Lebanon in 2000 and inspired a new Palestinian uprising in the West Bank and Gaza later that year. Hezbollah's summer 2006 raid into Israel—killing eight Israeli soldiers and capturing two—provoked a major confrontation that killed hundreds of Lebanese and scores of Israelis and heightened tensions between Iran, the United States, and Israel.

U.S. support for Israel in its campaign against Hezbollah in 2006 was more than an expression of the long U.S. alliance with Israel. It was an indirect war against Iran in part motivated by revenge. Although suicide attacks have come to be identified with the Sunni Muslim al-Qaeda, Hezbollah introduced the technique in the early 1980s in a series of bombings against U.S. and European forces who had intervened in support of a pro-Israeli Lebanese government. Attacks in 1983 against the U.S. Embassy, the Marine barracks, and a French military compound killed 361 people, including 258 Americans. A group that called itself Islamic Jihad took responsibility but appeared to be a front for Hezbollah.[7] The mastermind was Imad Mughniyah, a Lebanese Shiite trained by the Revolutionary Guards. Mughniyah, never formally charged in the Beirut bombings, was indicted for murder in the 1985 hijacking in the Middle East of a TWA flight during which a U.S. Navy diver was killed. Mughniyah was also implicated in the bombings of two Jewish centers in Argentina in 1992 and 1994 that caused the deaths of 124 people, and he was linked to the kidnapping of more than a dozen Americans in Lebanon in the 1980s.

The Revolutionary Guards may have also had a hand in the 1996 bombing of a U.S. Air Force barracks in Saudi Arabia that killed nineteen Americans and wounded five hundred. Iranian intelligence officials are alleged to have recruited Saudi Shiites on pilgrimages to a religious shrine in Damascus, Syria; Revolutionary Guards are said to have trained the bombers in Lebanon's Bekaa Valley and provided the explosives for the blast.[8] Two members of the Guards reportedly met with the suspected terrorists—members of a group called Saudi Hezbollah—shortly before the bombing. Louis Freeh, who headed the FBI at the time, charged that the bombers received passports at the Iranian Embassy in Damascus and were paid $250,000 by an Iranian Guards general, Ahmad Sharifi. Freeh also claimed that two leaders of the attack received sanctuary in Iran.[9] Then attorney general John Ashcroft declared in 2001 that "elements of the Iranian government, inspired, supported, and supervised" the attack, even though no Iranians were among fourteen people—thirteen Saudis and a Lebanese—indicted by a U.S. grand jury. Iran has denied any involvement with the bombing and rebuffed a request by President Clinton in 1999 for assistance in solving the crime, a move that set back chances for U.S.-Iran reconciliation.

TIES WITH AL-QAEDA

The Bush administration sought to justify its 2003 invasion of Iraq by claiming links between Saddam's regime and al-Qaeda. In fact, Iran's ties with al-Qaeda appear to have been more extensive, and the Guards was in charge of cultivating them. According to the congressionally appointed 9/11 Commission, the Qods force had contacts with al-Qaeda beginning in the early 1990s in Sudan.[10] Al-Qaeda leader Osama bin Laden had relocated to Sudan from Afghanistan after the end of the decadelong Afghan war against Russian occupation. (Bin Laden subsequently moved back to Afghanistan after the Sudanese, under U.S. and Saudi pressure, expelled him in 1996.) In the early nineties the Qods force was already training assorted Islamic radicals in Sudan, which had a militant Muslim government eager to be seen as a major player in advancing the cause of radical Islam. According to the 9/11 Commission, the Iranians and al-Qaeda reached an "informal agreement to cooperate in providing support—even if only training—for actions carried out primarily against Israel and the United States.

Not long afterward, senior al-Qaeda operatives and trainers traveled to Iran to receive training and explosives."[11] Al-Qaeda recruits also went to Lebanon's Bekaa Valley in 1993 for additional instruction and "showed particular interest in learning how to use truck bombs, such as the one that killed 241 U.S. Marines" in Beirut in 1983.[12] It is possible that some of that Iranian/Hezbollah expertise assisted al-Qaeda members who attacked two U.S. embassies in Africa in 1998, killing twelve Americans and more than two hundred others.

The links with Iran proved even more useful to bin Laden three years later. According to the 9/11 Commission, eight to ten of the Arab "muscle" men who carried out the September 11 attacks crossed Iran en route from Afghanistan to Arab countries between October 2000 and February 2001. However, the commission "found no evidence that Iran or Hezbollah was aware of the planning for what later became the 9/11 attack."[13]

The September 11 attacks appear to have stunned Iran as much as they did the rest of the world, and they provided the opportunity for the first real military cooperation between the United States and Iran since the 1979 revolution. Iran had long-standing grievances against the group that had hosted al-Qaeda, the Taliban, which strongly discriminated against Afghanistan's Shiite minority. Iranian officials had begun a propaganda campaign against the Taliban in the mid-1990s, focusing on the fact that the Afghan group's human rights record was even worse than Iran's, and women were forced to drape themselves in public from head to toe. (An Iranian friend told me at the time that "I had to laugh when they criticized the Taliban. That was Iran five years ago.") In 1998, Iran sent two hundred thousand troops to its border with Afghanistan, and the two countries nearly went to war after Taliban forces murdered eight Iranian diplomats and a journalist in the Afghan city of Mazar e-Sharif, along with scores of Afghan Shiites. Rather than confronting the Taliban directly, Iran became a major backer of the Northern Alliance, the coalition of militias from Afghan minority groups opposed to the Taliban.

In an e-mail interview in 2005, my first contact with Rezaie, he provided new details about Iran's role in helping to overthrow the Taliban in 2001. According to Rezaie, Iranian Revolutionary Guards advisers were present at the fall of the Afghan capital, Kabul, in November 2001. His account was confirmed by American sources. Gary Schroen, head of the CIA's Afghan team, told me that two Iranian Guards colonels were attached to the Northern Alliance commander, Bismullah Khan, when U.S. Special Forces arrived in Kabul in September 2001. "There was never any [U.S.] interaction [with the Iranians], but we saw them," he said. Iranian advisers were also spotted by Americans in Mazar-e Sharif, at Kunduz, scene of a major battle, and in the western city of Herat. A former senior officer in the Qods force told me that the U.S. military erred by trusting Pakistani forces during the initial stages of the Afghan war. "Pakistan was feeding the U.S. Air Force wrong information to get the United States to bomb the Northern Alliance instead of the Taliban," he said. "Iran, through its [Afghan] friends, gave accurate positions to the U.S. Air Force."

Iran expected to be rewarded by the United States for its assistance, or at least not to be punished. The Bush administration, however, while appreciating Iran's support for the Northern Alliance, worried about the growing Iranian presence in western Afghanistan, where Revolutionary Guards members appeared to have free rein. A senior U.S. official complained to me in early 2002 that members of the Qods force were helping al-Qaeda members escape Afghanistan through Iran. The U.S. administration also reacted strongly after the Israeli capture on January 3, 2002, of the *Karine A,* the ship allegedly carrying Iranian weapons to the Palestinian Authority. It is possible that the Qods force sabotaged efforts by then president Khatami to improve relations with the United States by authorizing the arms shipment to the Palestinians without his knowledge.[14] Hezbollah operations chief Mughniyah was said to have supervised loading the weapons onto the *Karine A* while the ship was in Iranian-controlled waters near an island in the Persian Gulf where the Guards had private ports.[15]

FILLING THE VACUUM IN IRAQ

The controversy over the Guards' role in Afghanistan and in support of the Palestinians was soon eclipsed by the unintended consequences of the U.S. invasion of Iraq. Despite the assurances of Vice President Dick Cheney, among others, that Americans would be greeted as liberators, U.S. forces quickly found themselves targets in a multisided unconventional war. By toppling Saddam and disbanding the Iraqi Army and Saddam's ruling Baath Party, the Bush administration created a political and military vacuum ripe for exploitation by Tehran and the Revolutionary Guards. Just as the Guards had created Hezbollah to fight the Israelis, it had organized a party and militia in the early 1980s comprised of Iraqi Shiites who had opposed Saddam's regime and fled to Iran at the beginning of the Iran-Iraq war. The group, the Supreme Council for the Islamic Revolution in Iraq (SCIRI), was led by a Shiite cleric, Mohammad Baqr al-Hakim, and had a fifteen-thousand-member Iranian-trained militia known as the Badr Brigades.

After Saddam was toppled, Hakim returned to Iraq and was assassinated by a car bomb in August 2003 in the Shiite holy city of Najaf. A rival Shiite faction led by a young cleric named Moqtada al-Sadr was initially suspected of ordering the killing, later blamed on Sunni extremists. Iran adjusted quickly to Hakim's death and began distributing money and arms to Sadr and other Shiite leaders while continuing to support SCIRI under the leadership of Hakim's brother, Abdel Aziz. U.S. officials complained that Iran and Hezbollah, at Iran's behest, were also teaching Iraqi militia members how to blow up Iraqis and U.S. and British troops with improvised explosive devices.[16]

The Iran-Iraq border was poorly patrolled, and thousands of Iranians came as "pilgrims" to Najaf and another Shiite holy city, Karbala. It was not difficult for Guards members and other intelligence agents to infiltrate the country. Lawrence Wilkerson, former chief of staff to secretary of state Colin Powell, said he was told by British authorities that the Iranians sent two thousand Guards members and paramilitaries into southern Iraq behind U.S. armored columns in March 2003. "The Iranians got security from our logistics tail and began taking Basra before we had even reached Baghdad," Wilkerson said.

According to Katzman, the Guards found a new playground in Iraq and "bought off everybody," including Sadr's militia, the Mahdi Army, the Fadhila Party that governed the southern city of Basra and its all-important oil terminals, the Badr Brigades, and groups that called themselves Iraqi Hezbollah and Islamic Amal. Sunni militants also appeared to find temporary refuge in Iran on occasion in their efforts to avoid capture by U.S. and allied Iraqi forces.[17] In 2005, Guards commander general Yahya Rahim-Safavi bragged that the U.S. effort to implant a friendly government in Iraq had failed. Following the collapse of the Soviet Union, "the U.S. tried to make the world unipolar," he said. "However, it failed because today's world is multipolar. Islamic states can form an alliance and become a global power."[18] The Iranian Guards seemed likely to have major influence in Iraq no matter which Shiite politician or group consolidated power, whether the country remained united or fell apart.

Other Bush administration policies in the Middle East inadvertently strengthened the influence of the Guards. Hezbollah grew stronger after Syrian troops, under international pressure, ended a thirty-year occupation of Lebanon in 2005 following the assassination of a former Lebanese prime minister, Rafik Hariri, allegedly by pro-Syrian terrorists. The Guards provided thousands of rockets and medium-range missiles to Hezbollah, which the group fired into northern Israel to devastating effect in the summer of 2006. The Guards also maintained a strong relationship with Palestinian Islamic Jihad and sought to cultivate the image of an alliance with a more popular Palestinian group, Hamas, which won Palestinian parliamentary elections in 2006.

BIG BUSINESS

The Guards' influence abroad was mirrored by growing power within Iran, especially after Khomeini died and was succeeded by Khamenei. Lacking Khomeini's charisma and spiritual credentials, Khamenei relied on the Guards and *Basij* to bolster his rule, and he expanded their influence in government. Rafsanjani, who had become president, also perverted the nature of the Guards by insisting that government organizations, where possible, become self-sufficient, Sazegara said. This was in part a reaction to Iran's isolation during the Iran-Iraq war. With the United States and most other countries backing Iraq and reluctant to deal with Iran, the Guards was obliged to produce its own arms and ammunition, and also got involved in smuggling to augment Iran's meager arsenal.[19] In its 2006 war with Israel, Hezbollah demonstrated the sophistication of these Iranian-made weapons, including medium-range missiles, pilotless drones, antitank weapons, and a ground-to-sea rocket that damaged an Israeli ship.

Guards members became an important element in Iran's civilian economy, too, founding construction companies similar to the U.S. Army Corps of Engineers to build roads and repair Iran's war-damaged infrastructure. In charge of Iran's border security, the Guards became expert smugglers, taking advantage of several exclusive harbors on Kish island, a free-trade zone across the Persian Gulf from the United Arab Emirates, also a legendary center for no-questions-asked commerce. By 2004, the Guards was reputed to operate seventy-two illegal docks and smuggle in more than $9.5 billion in goods a year.[20] The Guards was said to be involved in importing alcohol—banned by the Islamic government—as well as appliances and automobile and airplane parts.[21] In 2004, the Guards closed a new international airport outside Tehran an hour after the first plane landed. The official explanation was that the Turkish company hired to operate the terminal had ties to an Israeli firm, but the real reason appeared to be that the Guards wanted a bigger share of the revenues from customs and duty-free sales.[22]

A law introduced into the Iranian parliament in 2006 gave priority for government contracts to Guards- and *Basij*-run companies, and Guards firms also became involved in oil and gas exploration. In the space of just a few weeks in 2006, the government awarded Guards companies more than $5 billion in civilian contracts: more than $2 billion to develop a huge offshore gas field between Iran and the Arab Gulf state of Qatar; a $1.3 billion contract to build a pipeline between the field and southeastern Iran; and $2 billion to expand Tehran's subway system.[23] A general who headed up the Guards' economic operations said the organization had completed more than $3 billion in major construction projects and was working on another $2 billion. The Guards, he said, devoted 70 percent of its resources to military contracts and the remainder to civilian projects.[24] The Revolutionary Guards are now a business as much as they are a military organization, according to Shahram Chubin, an Iran expert at the Geneva Center for Security Policy. He compared the Guards to China's People's Liberation Army of fifteen years ago, before private capitalism had expanded significantly in that rising Asian nation.

ROLE IN POLITICS

With economic and military power comes political clout. Men with connections to the Guards have increasingly become involved in government, supplanting to some extent the clerics and bazaar merchants who dominated the ruling elite after the revolution. Guards and the *Basij* get preferential treatment when they apply to universities, and tens of thousands have used their paramilitary credentials as stepping-stones to jobs in the bureaucracy.[25] Frederick Tellier, a researcher at the Institute for International and Strategic Studies in Paris and a former attaché at the French embassy in Tehran, wrote that the Guards "now provide a kind of ideological filter for the recruitment, selection and socialization process of future conservative leaders in the Islamic Republic."[26] The change has been especially striking since conservatives began a political comeback in 2003. Iraq war veterans dominated the race for municipal elections in Tehran in that year, and the new council named Ahmadinejad as mayor, giving him a foundation for his run for president. Guards members sought to make him a successful mayor by agreeing to move military bases within Tehran to provide room for new expressways to help alleviate Tehran's hideous traffic. In 2004—after 80 incumbent reformist deputies were barred from running by the Guardian Council—conservatives with a background in the Guards or *Basij* took a third of the seats in the 290-member parliament. Of the top 30 finishers in Tehran, 10 were veterans of the Iran-Iraq war.[27]

The Guards completed their sweep of the nonclerical portions of Iran's government the following year. Four men with Guards backgrounds—Ahmadinejad, Rezaie, Larijani, and Qalibaf—all won approval from Iran's ruling clerics to run for president, although Rezaie dropped out at the last minute to avoid eliminating the chances for a conservative to win. By allowing so many Guards members to run, leader Khamenei "let the genie out of the bottle," Sazegara said. "Because he wanted to oppose the reform movement, he invited them [the military] into politics. When people enter politics backed by guns, you have no tools to push them back. They have money as well, and organization."

The growing presence of Guards veterans in the regime has led some to suggest that Iran is experiencing a creeping coup. Iran has a history of military leaders who become kings, including Reza Khan, the Russian-trained officer who founded the Pahlavi dynasty in 1925. Tellier wrote that a "military junta [is] a distinct possibility."[28] Others disagreed and said that the Guards has shown no inclination so far to overturn a structure that gives it its justification for being.

Decision making in Iran is a collective enterprise, and the Guards have a voice but not a veto on national security policies. Any move toward a Guards coup would likely be checked by the regular army—and vice versa. However, this dualism has dissipated in recent years. According to Clinton administration terrorism expert Simon, "There's an increasing integration of the Guards and the regular parts of Iran's general purpose forces. They train more together and do more joint procurement." The top leadership has also become interchangeable. For example, Ali Shamkani, a Guards veteran, served for several years as defense minister in charge of both the Guards and the regular military. Ahmadinejad's defense minister, Mostafa Mohammad-Najjar, was also a senior Guards commander in charge of Middle East operations from 1982 to 1985, when Iran began to spread its influence into Lebanon and the Arab states across the Persian Gulf. There remains a division of labor between the Guards and the regular military, with the Guards in charge of unconventional weapons, air defenses, and regime protection. But Iranians can be drafted into either force, depending on which outfit needs their particular skills. Apart from the Qods force and those involved in the most sensitive weapons programs, "there has been a kind of normalization of the Guards role within the overall defense framework," Simon said. If Iran were to be attacked, he added, "they'd have an integrated plan for defense."

In our interview in 2006, Rezaie disputed the notion that the Guards had increased its political power dramatically since 2003. He said that military veterans had long played a major role in the Iranian government, and the only difference was that "sometimes the media talks about it more." A crucial test of the Guards' power could come in the transition period following Khamenei's passing as supreme leader, when the Guards could be a kingmaker.[29]

Many outside observers assume that Guards members and veterans are all conservatives opposed to liberalizing the regime or improving ties with the West, but, as so often is the case with Iran, the situation is more nuanced. Like the American military, the Guards leadership tilts to the right while the rank-and-file are more moderate. In 1994, local Guards commanders refused to use force to put down riots in the city of Qazvin, northwest of Tehran. In 1997, 73 percent of the Guards—4 percent more than in the general electorate—voted for Khatami when he scored his upset victory for president.[30] The Guards leadership reacted fiercely when the cleric-led system appeared at stake during student riots in 1999 that followed the closure of a popular newspaper and an assault by vigilantes associated with the supreme leader on student dormitories. Twenty-four Guards commanders wrote Khatami a letter criticizing him for being too lenient with the students, warning that "our patience is exhausted" and demanding that the president "act in accordance with your Islamic and national mission."[31] After Khatami reversed course and came down on the side of suppressing the protests, Guards commanders were obliged to retract the criticism and pledge loyalty to the president.[32]

Guards members seem more overtly religious than many Iranians, but that actually reinforces diversity within the ranks, because in Shiite Islam believers can choose the cleric who will be their personal spiritual adviser. For example, Grand Ayatollah Montazeri, the moderate dismissed by Khomeini as his designated successor, retained a strong following among Guards members even after he became Iran's most prominent dissident cleric.[33] According to Paul Pillar, a CIA veteran and former Middle East chief on the National Intelligence Council, which advises the U.S. president, it would be hard to identify a Guards position on issues such as reconciliation with the United States. "You've probably got debates within the Guards just as in other Iranian organizations," he said.

Rezaie's political evolution illustrates how so-called hard-liners within the Guards can change their views. In 1997, he antagonized both Khamenei and Rafsanjani by calling for creation of an anti-American axis with Syria and Iran's old rival, Iraq.[34] Following Khatami's election, Khamenei fired Rezaie and replaced him with Rezaie's deputy. Rezaie, who had been willing to deal with Iraq, then began to show interest in reaching out to Islamic Iran's other great foe, the United States. In May 2003, he took part in a conference in Athens attended by about one hundred European, Middle Eastern, and American foreign policy experts, including Flynt Leverett, a just-retired senior official on the U.S. National Security Council. According to Leverett, Rezaie proposed a security and cooperation organization for the Middle East and South Asia in which the United States and Iran would take part, patterned on the Organization for Security and Cooperation in Europe. That body brought together democratic and Soviet-bloc countries during the Cold War and now promotes security and good governance in former Soviet-bloc nations. It is unlikely that Rezaie would have made such a suggestion without approval from the supreme leader.

In his e-mail interview with me in 2005, arranged by the *Baztab* Web site to promote his presidential candidacy, Rezaie was extremely conciliatory toward Americans. He said that Iran's economy was the most critical problem facing the country, not the threat of attack by the United States as often claimed by Iranian propaganda. He called for a greater emphasis on private enterprise, more economic cooperation with the West, and liberalization of Iranian government restrictions on dress and social behavior. Asked if the United States and Iran could open talks with a view toward restoring diplomatic relations, Rezaie wrote, "Everything is possible." If the Bush administration were to make a "rational offer to Iran, I believe a real transformation will take place in relations between Iran and America," he said.

In our face-to-face interview the following year, he repeated his overture, and said there was a need for "a rational, brave person" to solve the problems between the two countries. "This needs bravery and the U.S. government should not be afraid," he said. "I think Mr. Bush is afraid. Reagan showed more courage."

Rezaie has never visited the United States, but his son Ahmad spent several years in America in the late 1990s and was a vocal critic of the Iranian regime. Ahmad had fled Iran, disgusted by his upbringing as the child of a feared official. He told *The New York Times*'s Elaine Sciolino that he hated a job given to him by his father that gave him the right to stop and search private cars. "I told my father, 'If you treat young people this way, you're doomed,'" he said.[35] Ahmad flew to the United States in 1998, made the rounds of think tanks in Washington, and lived for a time with Kenneth Timmerman, a harsh critic of the Iranian government. Timmerman described his former houseguest as "a very gentle, sensitive young man with a great deal of integrity and personal courage." Patrick Clawson, an Iran expert at the Washington Institute for Near East Policy, recalled Rezaie as "an unhappy young man who had become highly disillusioned and angry at the system." Ahmad eventually returned to Iran through the efforts of his father, faced no judicial punishment, and stayed out of politics. Mohsen Rezaie accepted responsibility for his son's defection, giving a contrite speech in which he said that he had "avoided forming close emotional ties with family members in order to prevent doubt and weakness" during the Iran-Iraq war.[36] Coincidentally or not, Rezaie's opinion of America appeared to change after his son returned to Iran. Rezaie denied, through an aide, that his son's defection had any impact on his views. The aide said that Rezaie's strategic vision had gradually changed on its own.

Despite his overtures to the United States and his moderate social outlook, Rezaie is still considered a conservative in the Iranian political context. In our 2006 interview he criticized the Khatami administration, which he claimed had made numerous concessions to the United States and Europe on the nuclear issue without getting anything in return. However, Guards veterans include several men who became prominent reformers and members of the Khatami camp. Among them was Khatami's minister of power and electricity, Habib Bitaraf, who was also a leader of the U.S. Embassy seizure. Another former Guards member and holder of U.S. hostages, Ebrahim Asgharzadeh, became a reformist member of Tehran's first elected city council. Hamid-Reza Jalaiepour, publisher of a series of reformist newspapers during the Khatami presidency, commanded the Guards in two cities in Iran's restive Kurdish region in the 1980s.[37] Iran's most celebrated dissident also served in the Guards. Akbar Ganji was jailed for six years in 2000 after writing a series of articles about the role of Iranian leaders and the Guards and intelligence apparatus in the murder of Iranian writers and dissidents in the mid-1990s. The Guards' repressive activities within Iran and support for terrorism abroad have damaged the prestige of the organization, according to Sazegara, who left the Guards soon after it was formed, served in other top positions in Iran, and eventually turned against the regime. "During the war, the Guards were respected and everyone knew that they sacrificed their lives for the country," he told me. Despite the institution's loss of prestige, Sazegara said many of those serving in the Guards now are "very good people, who don't agree with Ahmadinejad or Khamenei."

Most Iranians long ago lost their revolutionary zeal, and the Guards were not immune to liberalizing trends in society. Saeed Laylaz, the former deputy interior minister, told me after Ahmadinejad's victory that the only thing that united the Guards was "economic benefits. Otherwise there is no ideology unifying them." That might account for the fact that Guards leaders were not publicly very supportive at first of

Ahmadinejad, whose belligerent comments about Israel and the United States initially depressed the Iranian stock market and scared off foreign and Iranian investors. For some members of the Guards, a climate of crisis with the West might seem attractive, since a closed economy favored their companies over foreign ones and bolstered the feeling that they were needed for the nation's defense. But growing trade and investment might produce big commissions for other well-connected veterans, and a general collapse of the Iranian economy under sanctions would benefit no one. "Think about the Indonesian, Pakistani, and Turkish militaries," suggested Vali Nasr, the Iran expert at the Naval Postgraduate School. "They have their hand in the till individually and collectively. They benefit from economic isolation in certain ways but would also benefit from an opening of the economy."

Apart from Rezaie, one of the most interesting people I have met in Iran is Mohammad Javad Jaffari, a Guards veteran who serves as an adviser to the country's Supreme Council of National Security. A veteran of the Iran-Iraq war in his midforties, he has a large scar on the side of his neck that looks as though it was caused by shrapnel. Apart from the scar, Jaffari is a handsome man with a neatly trimmed beard and an open, earnest gaze. During several meetings in 2006 he told me that the time had come for the United States and Iran to work together to stabilize the Middle East. The father of three children, it appeared that he had seen enough war and figured that Americans had as well. Iran would be a more reliable ally for the United States, he suggested, than the Sunni Muslim dictatorships of the Arab world. "I think Americans and Shiites can have an understanding because Shiites are logical and Americans are, too," Jaffari said. "If we sit together, we can solve the problems of the Middle East."

A GRAND BARGAIN OR ELSE

His pitch was similar to what I heard from Rezaie, albeit without the threats. Rezaie held out both an olive branch and a sword. In part because of U.S. blunders, he said, Iran had strengthened its regional power to the point where the two countries could now deal with each other as equals. But if the Bush administration chose to try to punish

Iran, Iran would retaliate in Lebanon, Afghanistan, and Palestine, he said, and the United States would pay a heavy price. I thought of what Rezaie had said when Hezbollah and Israel went to war a few months later as the United States escalated a campaign against Iran in the United Nations. His overture appeared meant to have been an offer that the United States could not refuse.

SIX

THE REFORMERS

Baharak Hajiahmadi was nearly crying with excitement as she waited at the Ahmadiyeh mosque in the working-class Tehran neighborhood of Resaalat. The year was 1999 and posters put up on nearby streets proclaimed that Mohammad Khatami was coming to the mosque that evening. The fifteen-year-old Hajiahmadi had run home to tell her mother and then sprinted back to join scores of others eager to see their president. Khatami had been elected nearly two years earlier and had already improved the political and social atmosphere within the country and the way in which Iran was viewed from abroad. But he was facing growing obstacles from repressive forces in the regime, and his supporters wanted to encourage him not to lose heart.

Hajiahmadi had written Khatami a letter and she read it to me as we waited in the female-only balcony in the mosque: "We youngsters love you more than you know and we will always pray for your life and your success. If all the world turns its face from you, I will not. It is a while that I haven't seen your smiling face. I hope to see your prophetic face smiling again."

The mosque was new but small and it was oppressively hot and stuffy inside. The walls were freshly whitewashed and mosaic tiles brightened the front of the main hall facing the holy city of Mecca. A large picture of Ayatollah Khomeini hung to the right of the lectern, with an equally large photograph of his successor, Khamenei, to the left. The main hall was filled, shoulder-to-shoulder, with men and boys sitting cross-legged on cheap machine-made carpets. The women were ushered up a flight of stairs to a balcony that looked ready to burst from the weight of so many bodies. Several hours passed as the women chatted companionably and admonished small children to behave. Occasionally, the ladies rustled their raincoats and cloaks to seek relief from the heat by coaxing what little air there was to circulate underneath their Islamically correct outer garments. Finally, after what seemed like an eternity, the crowd of men downstairs began to stir. Hands went up as people began pointing to the front of the mosque.

Khatami was there, having entered without fanfare and so quietly that few noticed him at first. He was sitting cross-legged on the floor to the side of the lectern, chatting with new clerics, putting turbans on them, and kissing them on both cheeks. Women and children clambered onto chairs and bent precariously over the balcony rail to get a better view, and a little girl waved a red carnation. "Khatami, you are our hope," the audience chanted as the president rose to speak. "Khatami, we support you."

The president smiled shyly and urged the crowd to hush. "You are not here for me, you are here for your country and your heritage," he said. "I ask you to always pray for the people giving service to your country instead of shouting for me." Then he introduced another speaker, Qorbanali Dorri-Najafabadi, who had been forced by Khatami to resign that very day from the post of intelligence minister to take the blame for a series of killings of intellectuals by regime forces opposed to the president's reforms. "My brother and my friend, Mr. Dorri, will talk because I am so busy," Khatami said, gesturing toward the man he had just fired. "God be with you," he told the audience before turning and abruptly leaving the mosque. A chastened Dorri apologized to the crowd and to the Iranian public for failing to stop the murders. "I was doing my duty to the best of my knowledge and ability," Dorri said.

Hajiahmahdi was crestfallen that Khatami had left so quickly. "I was hoping he would talk more and linger, but this was quite a privilege to hear his voice and see him," she said. Having no affection or respect for Dorri, she and the others in the mosque turned to leave as soon as the president had departed. The crowd may have been disappointed, but in hindsight, Khatami's actions that day were a high point of his presidency. He had succeeded in putting Dorri on the spot and showing that the Khatami administration—unlike previous Iranian regimes—intended to govern the country according to the rule of law. An investigation ordered by Khatami into what became known as the "serial murders" of writers and aging liberal activists proved that members of the intelligence ministry had been involved. The killings appeared meant to show Iranians that they should not get too hopeful that their new president would change the way Iran was ruled. It took Khatami a month of lobbying other regime heavyweights to get rid of Dorri.[1] Dorri's successor, Ali Yunesi, went on to preside over a cleanup of the intelligence ministry, and the murders stopped. It was a rare bureaucratic victory against regime forces threatened by Khatami's platform and popularity.

From the regime's point of view, Khatami was an accidental president, a midranking cleric and scholar of philosophy conversant in German and English who had been forced to resign as the minister in charge of culture and press in 1992 because the parliament thought him too liberal; in two terms in the job, he never closed a newspaper or banned a book. He had spent the next five years as director of the Iranian National Library and was truly more at home in the world of ideas than in Iran's cutthroat politics. When he agreed to run for president in 1997, he did not expect to be victorious, and Iranian pundits predicted that the regime favorite—Nateq Nouri, the conservative speaker of the parliament—would win. But Iranians were taken with Khatami's smiling visage and his pledges to give more freedom to young people and women, and to improve Iran's relations with the outside world. Elected in a landslide of nearly 70 percent, he seemed, at the beginning, incapable of putting a foot wrong. He was shown on television riding a bus to work on National Clear Air Day, surprising a woman passenger by plopping down beside her with no bodyguards in view. The image contrasted sharply with that of Iran's supreme religious leader. On the same day that Khatami rode the bus, Khamenei was shown traveling outside Tehran with an ostentatiously large entourage and addressing sycophantic, orchestrated crowds. Handsome and well groomed compared to Khamenei and most Iranian leaders since the revolution, Khatami got credit even for the weather when it snowed or rained in normally dry and polluted Tehran.

IRAN'S MARTIN LUTHER

Khatami did not invent Iran's reform effort, known as the Second of Khordad Movement for the day on the Persian calendar when Khatami was elected, although he came to personify it. The reform campaign had been gathering intellectual momentum since the senseless carnage of the 1980–88 Iran-Iraq war. Religious intellectuals who supported the 1979 revolution began to have doubts about the autocratic and idiosyncratic system created by and for Khomeini. But they suppressed their criticism while the regime was fighting for its very existence against Iraqi invaders and confronting a violent internal opposition led by the Mujahedin e-Khalq, the leftist guerilla group that had sided with Iraq.

The key figure in critiquing the new Islamic system was the son of a Tehran grocer named Hossein Dabbagh. Religious but not a cleric, Dabbagh—who later wrote and lectured under the pen name Abdulkarim Soroush—was an ardent supporter of the revolution who had studied Western philosophy in London in the 1970s. Returning to Iran after the revolution, he was named by Khomeini to a "cultural revolution" committee that sought to reshape Iran's university curriculum in ways acceptable to the new theocracy. Soroush, who quit the committee in 1984, said later that his main motivation was to curb radical students and allow the universities to reopen and continue to teach normal subjects, such as math and science.[2]

As his revolutionary ardor faded, Soroush began to espouse a modern interpretation of Islam not only compatible with but dependent on democracy. He challenged the right of Shiite clerics—including Iran's supreme leader—to be seen as infallible interpreters of religious law, and said there was no room for compulsion in religion or politics. His scholarly articles in a magazine for intellectuals called *Kiyan,* or "universe," and his lectures at Tehran's Research Institute for Human Sciences began to attract a wide following and greatly influenced not only Iran's reform movement but Islamic thinkers around the globe. By the mid-1990s, he had become so influential that Iranians and foreign scholars compared him to Martin Luther—the father of the Protestant reform movement against the Roman Catholic church. During a speech in 1995 commemorating the takeover of the U.S. Embassy, supreme leader Khamenei spent more time condemning Soroush's views than criticizing the United States.[3] Threatened by Soroush, the regime dispatched young vigilantes allied with Khamenei from a group called *Ansar e-Hezbollahi,* followers of the party of God, to disrupt Soroush's lectures. *Kiyan* was shut and Soroush has worked abroad since 2000. But his ideas have inspired scores of fellow reformers and dissidents in Iran, including Saeed Hajjarian, a top adviser to Khatami, and Akbar Ganji, the crusading journalist who has called for a campaign of civil disobedience to overturn the Islamic regime. In an open letter to Soroush from prison in 2005, Ganji wrote that "our generation is greatly indebted to you. Through you, we became familiar with modernity and different approaches to religion and the idea of the righteous man."[4] *Time* magazine named Soroush to its annual list of the one hundred most influential men and women in 2005, calling him "the leading intellectual force behind the Islamic republic's pro-democracy movement."[5]

In 1997, Soroush was ecstatic about Khatami's election and saw it as a reflection of pent-up desire for change in Iran that would have lasting effects. "I think the clergy should take a lesson from this election," he told CNN's Christiane Amanpour. "They have to change their orientation towards people, because so far the authorities thought that on the part of them, it is just to order, and it is on the part of people to obey the orders."[6] Soroush said Khatami had the power to push for reform because of his electoral mandate, but added, "of course the opposition is not that weak."

The early days of the Khatami era were truly a time of euphoria in Iran, a Tehran spring particularly for women, young people, and intellectuals. Relations improved with foreign countries and there was an explosion of personal and press freedoms. Suddenly, there were scores of newspapers with actual news in them, the government stopped confiscating satellite dishes, and artists felt freer than they had in years. Ali Mohammadi, a twenty-five-year-old Tehrani, told me that he stayed up to 3 A.M. just to read all the new publications, and journalism became the hot profession for educated youth. Traveling to Iran as a foreign correspondent no longer felt like dropping into a black hole for unfiltered information. CNN and the BBC became accessible in Tehran hotels and anti-American slogans dating from the revolution were removed from hotel lobbies. Khatami used Iran's chairmanship of the Organization of Islamic Countries in 1997 as an excuse to refurbish those hotels and to present a new and moderate image of Iran to the outside world. He called for a "dialogue of civilizations" with the West and tolerance of opposing ideas within Iran. Instead of blaming the "Great Satan," as Iranian officials called the United States, for all of Iran's troubles, Khatami wrote, "Let us not doubt that unless we undergo an inner transformation, we cannot expect external forces to solve our problems for us."[7]

HOSTAGE HOLDERS BECOME CONCILIATORS

The reform movement expanded to include a number of former leftists in the Iranian political context, including several who had organized and led the 1979 takeover of the U.S. Embassy. In a striking reversal, they sought to be seen as conciliators. Khatami named as one of his vice presidents a woman, Massoumeh Ebtekar, whom reporters had dubbed "Sister Mary" when she acted as a spokesperson for the hostage holders during the embassy crisis. In her new job she was responsible for the environment. Both the United States and Iran "should have regrets for all of what happened," she told me. "Why can't we work together as equals?"

As the world approached the twentieth anniversary of the Iranian revolution, there was a concerted effort by several former hostage holders to explain and atone for their youthful behavior, and to use it as a bridge for improving relations with the United States. Abbas Abdi, ringleader of the embassy seizure, was particularly courageous, going so far as to meet one of the former hostages, Barry Rosen, in Paris in the summer of 1998. The two shook hands and addressed a conference sponsored by a Cyprus-based peace group, the Center for World Dialogue. Over dinner in a Paris restaurant on their last evening together, Abdi "privately apologized for what he had done to myself and my family," Rosen, a former embassy spokesman, told me. "Abbas is a really bright and thoughtful person," he said. The reunion "turned out to be so unbelievably positive."

The rabble-rousing hostage holder had become a contemplative figure, tempered by age and disappointment in the system he had helped consolidate. When I interviewed Abdi for the first time in 1999, he was 43, with soft brown eyes and thinning hair, and was the father of five children ranging in age from 6 to 20. "If a person does not make changes as he ages, he must be a piece of wood," he said. He said he still felt it had been his duty to take part in the embassy seizure to prevent the United States from continuing its historic pattern of interference in Iran's political development. At least now, he said, Iran had no one to blame but itself for the way in which it was governed. That said, he acknowledged the naivete of those who had held 52 Americans hostage for 444 days. "In the days of the revolution, we were shouting and screaming for liberty, but we did not know what it meant," he said.

Abdi was optimistic that the reform movement would succeed, and he urged the United States to leave Iran alone, apart from easing sanctions or other economic pressure. "I always have this fear that the presence of Americans in Iran will discourage or slow down the trend of democracy here," he said. "Give Iran a little bit of time on its own to make democracy a fundamental principle and a pillar." He and other reformers were looking to the political process permitted under the Iranian constitution to consolidate the gains already made by Khatami. Iran's first democratic muncipal elections were scheduled later that year—the provision providing for them in the constitution had not been implemented previously—and a new parliament would be chosen in 2000 to replace one dominated by conservatives. "My vision is that the parliamentary elections will be carried out in a satisfactory manner, and two years after that we will be ready for relations with the United States," Abdi said. (In fact, Iran offered in 2003 to begin broad negotiations with the United States, but the Bush administration, confident of victory in Iraq, rejected the overture. Abdi, meanwhile, was sentenced in 2003 to five years in prison for organizing a poll that showed that 74 percent of Iranians wanted to restore ties with the United States. He was released in 2005 and now lives quietly in Tehran.)

Ebrahim Asgharzadeh, another hostage holder turned reformer, in 1999 was planning to run for the Tehran city council, and he said that the municipal elections across the country would begin to build democracy from the ground up. "When every little village has its own council, people can demand better roads and facilities, and they will come to democracy automatically in their minds," he told me. Like Soroush, however, both Abdi and Asgharzadeh had become the target of attacks by members of the *Ansar e-Hezbollahi*. Abdi was beaten in Qom after returning to Iran from his meeting with Rosen; Asgharzadeh was set upon by *Hezbollahi* in the ancient western city of Hamadan when he tried to give a lecture there in December 1998. They beat him with iron bars, broke his glasses, and tore his suit. "The concept of democracy is a very serious matter in my country," he said, with some understatement.

There were other danger signs early in Khatami's tenure, and they were compounded by strategic errors by his supporters and by economic factors beyond his control. Unfortunately for the new president, world oil prices hit their lowest point in a quarter century, plummeting from seventeen dollars to ten dollars a barrel after Asian economies overheated and crashed in 1998. In an interview in 2006, Khatami cited the sudden drop in oil prices as one of the lowest moments of his presidency. "We were forced to calculate the price of oil for our budget at eleven dollars a barrel, and all of our programs faced problems," he said. "With two days left before the Iranian New Year, the trade minister told me that we had only forty-eight hours of wheat reserves left in the country, when we should have had at least three months. I couldn't sleep for five or six nights."

Khatami may have lost sleep but others in his entourage appeared oblivious. A Western diplomat in Tehran warned in the winter of 1998 about the "cockiness" of the people around Khatami and their lack of expertise or interest in economics. Credit was scarce in the private sector and import licenses almost impossible to obtain, the diplomat said. Where businessmen previously could raise $1 million from merchants in the bazaar in 24 hours, it now took several weeks to put together the cash. Iran at that point did not have a unified exchange rate and maintained several rates for various purposes, including importing grain and selling oil. For those transactions, a dollar was worth 1,750 Iranian rials, but on the raging black market that most Iranians were forced to use, the sawbuck bought 6,500 rials. Relations with Europe and the United States began to thaw, but the Clinton administration had tightened economic sanctions before Khatami's election and was not willing to take a dramatic step—such as lifting an oil embargo or unfreezing Iranian assets still in the United States since the revolution—that would give the Iranian economy and Khatami's presidency a boost. Khatami's government, meanwhile, had no control over religious foundations that controlled billions of dollars of Iran's oil revenues with no accountability to him or Iran's elected parliament.

ALIENATING RAFSANJANI

There were strategic political mistakes, as well, that isolated the president and his supporters. Flush with victory, they turned against not only right-wing religious conservatives but pragmatic figures such as Rafsanjani, the adroit politician who was a key figure in the revolution and had served as president from 1989 to 1997. Rafsanjani had begun the process of economic reform after Khomeini's death, and had begun to liberalize religious restrictions on society, for example permitting radio and television to broadcast classical and other instrumental Western music for the first time since the revolution. The *chador,* the all-enveloping black tent that became a required uniform for women after the revolution, had given way to fashionable raincoats and designer scarves, and women began appearing in public wearing discreet amounts of makeup. Rafsanjani had appointed technocrats, many of them educated in the West, as cabinet ministers, valuing competence over ideological qualifications, and encouraged Iranian exiles to return to reclaim their property and invest in the country. Most crucial of all, Rafsanjani had helped engineer Khatami's victory by switching the allegiance of the Rafsanjani political grouping, the Executives of Construction, to Khatami and away from Nateq Nouri, the candidate backed by the supreme leader. Still, Khatami supporters, particularly those who had been left-wing radicals, never fully trusted Rafsanjani, whose main interest appeared to be promoting himself and his family. Society might have eased up slightly under Rafsanjani, but during his presidency Iranian intelligence agents assassinated dissidents in Europe and intellectuals in Tehran, and the aura of violence and corruption around him was difficult to dispel. Even Khatami sought to distance himself from Rafsanjani after the election. A Western diplomat in Tehran told me that Khatami had refused to attend a lavish farewell party for Rafsanjani because the new president was appalled at the expense.

By alienating Rafsanjani, reformers were left defenseless when conservative forces began their counterattack shortly after Khatami's election. The judiciary—which under Iran's political system is controlled by the supreme leader—first brought corruption charges against officials working for Gholamhossein Karbaschi, Tehran's mayor and the manager of Khatami's campaign. Karbaschi, who had been named to his post in 1989 by Rafsanjani, was an extremely capable administrator, with a liking for double-breasted blue blazers, who had created parks and cultural centers for Tehran and tried to untangle its monumental traffic. He had also made enemies among major landholders and speculators by introducing a property tax in Tehran. Prosecutors summoned him repeatedly for questioning, and in the spring of 1998, he was formally charged with corruption and embezzlement. In an interview a few weeks before his indictment, he compared his plight to that of President Clinton, then facing impeachment over lying about his relationship with a White House aide, Monica Lewinsky. "The measures they have taken against me have been less intense than the opposition against Clinton," he said. "But we also have many here like [special prosecutor Kenneth] Starr." Karbaschi was sentenced that July to five years in prison and banned from political office for twenty years. The sentence was later reduced to two years but his political career was destroyed.

Other Khatami allies faced harrassment and prosecution as conservatives sought to intimidate the new president. The parliament, still dominated by conservatives, impeached Khatami's liberal interior minister, Abdollah Nouri, in June 1998. One charge they raised against him was that Nouri had fired 1,689 officials who worked under the previous minister and had replaced them with "ideologically unreliable" people.[8] (Among those purged was Ahmadinejad, then the governor of Ardabil province in northwest Iran; after his election as president in 2005, his ministers turned the tables and threw out thousands who had worked for the Khatami administration.) Nouri resigned and Khatami named him a vice president in charge of social affairs and development, a post that did not require parliamentary approval. In November 1999, however, Nouri was tried and convicted by a special clerical court on a hodgepodge of charges, including endorsing relations with the United States and Israel.[9] The parliament also targeted Khatami's broad-minded minister of culture and Islamic guidance, Ataollah Mohajerani, blaming him for what conservatives viewed as an epidemic of critical newspapers and articles challenging the Islamic regime. An absurb dance began in 1998 in which the judiciary would close reform newspapers, which would then reopen the next day under new names with the same management, staff, and editorial slant. In 1999, the parliament deprived the culture minister of the right to license new publications, effectively neutralizing this reformist tactic.

Not satisfied with court cases and impeachment proceedings,

Khatami's opponents turned to violence in an effort to discredit the new president by showing that he could not fulfill the most basic task of government—maintaining law and order. In the fall and winter of 1998–99, a half-dozen Iranian intellectuals were brutally murdered, including an elderly couple, Dariush and Parvaneh Forouhar, stabbed to death in their Tehran home. Dariush Forouhar had been head of the Nation of Iran Party, which had supported the nationalist government of Mohammed Mossadegh in the 1950s. Forouhar had spent more than fifteen years in prison under the shah, backed the 1979 revolution, and served as minister of labor in the first government after the shah's fall. His party was semitolerated by the Islamic regime because of this background of opposition to the monarchy, but Forouhar was harassed because he opposed the theocratic system and advocated a democratic, secular government.

Others murdered in the fall of 1998 included two middle-aged writers who had been among 134 intellectuals who had signed an open letter to Rafsanjani in 1994—after the death in jail of another intellectual—urging greater freedom of expression. Iranian newspapers were full of rumors that the other signatories would also be killed. It was at this point that a translator friend of mine in Tehran said that she and her husband, both in their sixties, were for the first time considering leaving Iran for good. "We have never felt so scared," she said, not during the revolution nor the Iran-Iraq war, when Scud missiles were falling on Tehran. For once, Khatami rose to the challenge and delivered an impassioned speech to students in which he warned that Iran was in danger of succumbing to "religious fascism."[10] He named a committee to investigate the serial murders, and in January 1999, the intelligence ministry admitted that "rogue" staffers had committed the killings. A month later, the minister, Dorri, resigned and apologized to Iranians after Khatami thrust him forward at the Ahmadiyeh mosque.

A subsequent trial convicted several intelligence officers for the murders. The purported head of the conspiracy, a deputy intelligence minister named Saeed Emami, was found dead in his prison cell in the summer of 1999 after allegedly killing himself by swallowing hair-removal cream. Officials who testified at the trial, which was closed to the public, said Emami had been under orders from Iran's "foreign enemies" to kill the intellectuals and damage Iran's international reputation.[11]

Ganji, the investigative reporter, published a series of blockbuster articles in reformist newspapers alleging that the murders had high-level approval. He also blamed Rafsanjani for sanctioning prior assassinations and accused him of prolonging the Iran-Iraq war. Ganji's articles, and other stories delving into the corruption of the former president's family, so discredited Rafsanjani that he technically lost his bid for a seat in February 2000 parliamentary elections and his hopes to become speaker of the parliament, a position he had held and made influential in the 1980s. In the parliamentary voting, the former president came in thirty-first but was declared to have come in twenty-ninth in Tehran, entitling him to one of the city's thirty seats. Angry and embarrassed, he declined the post.

At the time, several Iranian political analysts warned that the Khatami camp had made a dreadful mistake by allowing its supporters to target Rafsanjani. The former president, who retained power as head of the Expediency Council, the body that mediates disputes between government branches, drew closer to Khamenei; Khatami, although subsequently elected to another four-year term, became little more than a lame duck. Hadi Semati, the professor of political science at Tehran University, said Ganji and Abdi, then editor of another paper that targeted Rafsanjani, *Salam,* were swept along by the popularity of their articles and should have thought more about the consequences of alienating so powerful a figure. "They bought into the public mood," Semati said. "They mistreated a potential strategic ally." Rafsanjani's son Mehdi told me in 2005 that "reformers made a big mistake to fight against my father." Because of the antagonism they created, Mehdi said, "we lost eight years" in which Iran could have resolved many of its problems. Ganji, however, was unrepentant, even though he was jailed in 2000 and spent six years in prison because of his investigative journalism. "I should have written much more," he said a few months after his release.

IRAN'S TIANANMEN

The event that most discredited the Khatami presidency among the Iranian people took place a little more than two years after his election and only six months after his triumph over the intelligence ministry.

On July 7, 1999, the parliament passed the bill restricting the Khatami administration's ability to license newspapers, and a special clerical court closed *Salam*. Students gathered to protest peacefully on the campus of Tehran University, and hundreds of police and *Ansar e-Hezbollahi* retaliated by storming a dormitory that night, flinging several students from their balconies, killing at least one and injuring and arresting scores. Outraged youngsters took to the streets in major cities across the nation and demonstrated by the thousands for a week in downtown Tehran in the biggest public protests since the 1979 revolution. Store windows were smashed and looted; students threw stones at police and torched pictures of the supreme leader. Khatami, who had initially condemned the assault on the students, reversed course on July 13 and accused the students of "attacking the foundations of the regime" and warned that they would be "repressed with force and determination."[12]

Vali Nasr compares the attack on the students to the Chinese suppression of young democracy advocates in Beijing's Tiananmen Square in 1989. Khatami, he says, should have stood with his followers in the street like Boris Yeltsin did atop a tank to stop a Soviet counterrevolution in 1991.[13] But while it is easy to criticize Khatami, the president acted to save lives and to prevent a possible coup. Twenty-four commanders of the Revolutionary Guards had written him a letter during the riots warning that "our patience is exhausted" and that "if you do not make any revolutionary decisions and act in accordance with your Islamic and national mission, tomorrow may already be too late."[14] Khatami considered resigning but was convinced by his supporters to stay; the commander of the Revolutionary Guards, Yahya Rahim-Safavi, then publicly declared his allegiance to the president.[15]

In our interview in 2006, during a visit he paid to the United States, Khatami described the crackdown on students as the low point of his presidency. "A great evil was done to the university and students," he told me, his expression sorrowful and contrite, as we sat on gilded furniture in the New York apartment of Iran's ambassador to the United Nations. Still, Khatami defended his reversal of position, claiming that forces "not in pursuit of freedom took advantage of the rioting for other purposes, and the security of the country meant that we had to confront this rioting." Khatami also said that he intervened to prevent those arrested as alleged ringleaders from being executed. They "were not the people who caused this," he said. The harsh treatment of the students and Khatami's failure to protect them damaged the reform movement, the former president acknowledged. "After that, the conditions became a lot more security-oriented and the environment for the reform movement became even more constrained," he said.

Reformers went on to sweep parliamentary elections the following year, but the victory was pyrrhic and the balance of power remained with the institutions not subject to popular mandate. When parliament tried to increase the president's powers, it was blocked by the Guardian Council. Over the course of Khatami's presidency, the council vetoed 111 of 297 bills he had approved.[16] Among them was a bill that would have barred the council from disqualifying candidates for parliamentary and presidential elections. This power proved to be among the most potent tools in stymieing the reform movement.

Killings of writers and old liberal activists stopped after Khatami replaced the intelligence minister, but in March 2000, less than a month after reformists swept parliamentary elections, a gunman believed to be linked to hard-line conservatives tried to assassinate Khatami's chief political theorist—and rumored source of newspaper leaks about the serial murders—Saeed Hajjarian, outside his office at the Tehran city council. The assailant, who was riding on the back of a motorcycle, fired point-blank into Hajjarian's face, then fled. The getaway motorcycle was the size allowed for use only by Iranian police, and guards outside the office did not chase the gunman or his driver, heightening suspicion that the hit was officially sanctioned.[17] Hajjarian survived and went through a painful convalescence, but the reform movement did not recover.

When Khatami came to the United Nations six months later, he was a chastened, apologetic figure. He told journalists over scrambled eggs and fresh fruit at a New York hotel that it was unfair to compare Iran, with its history of twenty-five hundred years of autocratic rule, to other nations with long-standing democracies. "Our people are in a rush to realize what they want, but reality may not be conducive to it right away," he said. He rejected any comparison of himself to Mikhail Gorbachev, the Soviet Communist Party leader whose reforms preceded the collapse of the Soviet system. Khatami made it clear that he was not questioning the foundation of the regime, in which the supreme leader has the final say on all major issues. The following year Khatami agreed under pressure from his supporters to run for re-election, but all sense of triumph and optimism had been drained from his campaign. Asadeh Moaveni, an Iranian-American journalist who was then covering Iran for *Time* magazine, wrote that Khatami broke down in tears when he announced his decision. "If I had my way, I would try to serve Iran outside government," the former head of the National Library said. "My assets are limited. I have a tiny bit of capital and that's people's regard for me."[18] Khatami won by an even higher margin than previously—78 percent of votes cast—but turnout was about 67 percent compared to a record 80 percent in 1997.

Emboldened conservatives, sensing the public mood of disillusionment with the reformers, began a comeback in 2003 by manipulating the electoral process to disqualify incumbents from running in municipal, and then parliamentary, elections. Electoral participation dropped but the conservatives didn't seem to care. Only 12 percent of eligible Tehran voters took part in the election for the Tehran city council that chose Ahmadinejad as mayor and laid the groundwork for his successful presidential run. Crusading journalism ceased with the imprisonment of Ganji, Abdi, and others and the closure of outspoken newspapers. The repression turned several reformers into outright dissidents, among them Ganji and Mohsen Sazegara, the newspaper publisher who in his youth had been among the founders of the Revolutionary Guards. Ganji suggested and Sazegara took up the idea of an Internet campaign for a referendum on abolishing the Islamic republic.

The conservatives, meanwhile, intensified their bureaucratic assault against the reform movement. In the 2004 parliamentary elections, the Guardian Council disqualified thirty-six hundred reformist candidates, including eighty incumbent members of parliament.[19] The discarded reformers tried to gain a reversal of the decision by staging a sit-in at the parliament but attracted little popular support, and the protest fizzled.

In the presidential vote that followed in 2005, the council at first tried to remove all but one reformist candidate, then relented and permitted two other reformers to run, to give the voting a greater semblance of legitimacy. (Khatami, having served two consecutive terms as president, was not eligible to run.) At least 40 percent of a demoralized electorate boycotted the elections, and those who took part split their votes among seven candidates. One of them, the moderate cleric Mehdi

Karroubi, attracted some support by promising to give the equivalent of fifty dollars a month to everyone over eighteen. He alleged later that there had been fraud, and that he should have made it into the runoff. Instead, Ahmadinejad was said to have come in second and faced the first-round leader, Rafsanjani, in the runoff, which Ahmadinejad won by 10 million votes. Ahmadinejad played on the reformers' failure to emphasize issues of economic justice, and profited from a protest vote against Rafsanjani, seen as too old (he was seventy at the time) and resented because of his wealth and past involvement in terrorism and domestic human rights abuses. Iranians may also have tired of a divided government and the constant squabbles between the president's office and the supreme leader, and decided that it was better to hand a victory to the conservatives and hold them accountable for all policy decisions.

AYATOLLAH KHRUSHCHEV

In the aftermath of the election, reformers engaged in much soul-searching about the reasons for their defeat. Some blamed a boycott campaign encouraged by dissidents outside Iran. Others said the reformers erred by emphasizing civil over economic rights, by pushing too quickly to change the system, and by alienating Rafsanjani and other pragmatists within the system. "We needed to slow down and consolidate," Semati said. "We didn't read well the public mood and spent too much time arguing with each other within the movement." Many said that the fault lay with Khatami and his Hamlet-like indecision about continuing to serve a regime that so patently contradicted his calls for freedom and respect for human rights. Khatami's "emphasis on the rule of law in the absence of constitutional reforms had the effect of tightening the grip of the country's unelected clerical rulers, who used the judiciary and the appointed Guardian Council . . . to stiff-arm reform," Nasr wrote.[20]

At several points Khatami could have carried out his threats to resign—to protest the 1999 crackdown on students and the repression of other demonstrations in 2003. But he appeared to believe that his continued presence would be a force for moderation and that the system still contained the potential to evolve toward a more genuine democracy. Although he came two decades after the revolution, he resembled the moderates who figured prominently in the regime from 1979 to 1981 and the Mensheviks swept aside by the Bolsheviks in Russia seventy years earlier. The noted historian of revolutions, Crane Brinton, could have been describing Khatami when he wrote of the Russian socialist, Alexander Kerensky: "The eloquent compromisist leader seems to us a man of words, an orator who could move crowds but could not guide them, an impractical and incompetent person in the field of action."[21]

Still, there is no doubt that Iran changed for the better under Khatami. Where once the regime summarily executed its opponents by the hundreds and murdered writers in their beds, the Iranian government at least made a pretense of following laws and procedures. Dissidents, while arrested and even tortured, generally survived and were released upon serving their sentences. Mohsen Kadivar, the reformist cleric who was jailed for eighteen months in 2000 for accusing authorities of creating an "Islamic kingdom" instead of a republic, said Khatami had made a positive difference. "Three or four years ago, we were killed in the streets, now we go to prison," he said. "Reforms here go millimeter by millimeter." Khatami stepped down at the end of his term as Rafsanjani had before him—making them among the few living ex-presidents in a region where leaders tend to rule for life. Under Khatami, the regime became more sensitive to criticism from abroad, especially from human rights groups. Although many newspapers were closed and others reverted to self-censorship, pockets of criticism remained, especially on the Internet, and Iranians became more politically mature and self-confident. "You can't take the society back," said Mohammad Atrianfar, head of the editorial board of *Shargh,* the reform-leaning newspaper that was shut in the fall of 2006 and allowed to reopen nine months later. Hajjarian, slowly recovering from his wounds, compared the reform movement to a relay race. "When I am out of breath, someone will come and take the baton from me and run the next one hundred meters," he said.[22]

Khatami, despite his regrets, believes that his presidency made a major contribution to Iran's political development. Asked his proudest moment as president, Khatami described a scene at Tehran University in 2005 when students confronted him and criticized him harshly for his failures. "I said, 'thank God that I have seen the result of my reforms,'" he told me in 2006. "In a Third World country where the slightest criticism could lead to someone losing their life, I am happy to see in Iran that someone can make the harshest criticisms against the top power of the executive and not be persecuted or arrested." Of course, the same could not be said of those who criticized the supreme leader. Khatami conceded that while he hoped that such tolerance of opposing views "could be seen in all branches of government, I only had limited powers."

Asked what Khatami's legacy was, Saeed Laylaz, the deputy interior minister in Khatami's first term, said: "Freedom in private life is the main achievement of Khatami." The Ahmadinejad administration, he predicted, would not be able to turn the country back and Iran—provided it was not attacked by the United States—would continue to evolve toward greater democracy and accountability. As for those who opposed reform, Laylaz said, "Iranian civilization is too big for their mouths." Khatami admitted that many Iranians had become apathetic about politics but said that "the underlying current for progress still exists" and Iranian leaders would ignore it at their peril.

Still, the Second of Khordad Movement did not fulfill Iranians' expectations. At least as of this writing, the elected portions of Iran's government remain subservient to the indirectly elected top leadership and, despite some modest reformist gains in the 2006 municipal elections, all sectors of the regime are dominated by conservatives who opposed Khatami's attempt to create a kinder, gentler Islamic republic. Despite overwhelming public support, Khatami lacked the vision and the courage to institutionalize change. Khatami himself admitted in 2000 that he was no "Ayatollah Gorbachev" who would overturn Iran's theocratic system. "I am Khatami, not Gorbachev," he told reporters at the United Nations. "I did not come in the name of reform. I had some suggestions." Indeed, he was more an Iranian Nikita Khrushchev, who smoothed the regime's rougher edges but left the system intact.

SEVEN

CHILDREN OF THE REVOLUTION

On my first trip to Iran a decade ago, I met a lovely young woman who was fluent in English and worked for a travel agency in Tehran as a guide. She had what seemed to be a pleasant enough existence, doing a job that allowed her to travel around the country and meet interesting people. In her off-hours she moved easily among friends and relatives in the upper-class districts of northern Tehran. Her large extended family was close and welcoming and took turns inviting relatives for gargantuan lunches on Friday, the Muslim Sabbath. She had had numerous boyfriends, both Iranian and foreign, and went to parties every week where the liquor flowed and youngsters danced to the latest Western music. She was confident and poised and had learned, it seemed, how to deal with the hassles of the Islamic republic's bureaucracy and the occasional vice squad vigilante who turned up at private homes in search of a bribe. But when I met her again a year later, on my second trip to Iran, she was much different. A party she had been to had been raided by the police, and she and the other guests had been arrested and hauled off to jail in the dead of night. Something had happened to her then, something that so offended her dignity and sense of security that she wouldn't tell me what it was—ten lashes with a leather strap, perhaps, or a gynecological exam to determine her virginity. Maybe it was just the knowledge that she could be arrested for the "crime" of having fun that finally made her snap. Whatever the reason, she had decided to emigrate to Europe.

She had had enough of living two lives—one almost Western, the other Islamically correct. She wanted to live somewhere, she said, where she could be the same person all the time.

A combination of factors has produced the greatest challenge facing the Iranian government today: the sheer number of its young citizens. Thanks in part to the regime's success in improving public health, the population has doubled since the revolution, and more than two thirds of Iran's 70 million people are below the age of 30—including many babies born during the Iran-Iraq war. The fertility rate rose then, as female participation in the workforce dropped because of new religious restrictions and women heeded exhortations by Khomeini to replace the youngsters dying in droves on the Iraqi front. Exposed to global cultural trends on satellite television and the Internet, and acutely aware of what they are missing, these Iranian boomers are impatient with their parents and angry at the regime but uncertain how to change their country. The political reform movement of the mid and late 1990s only heightened their expectations, and many young people have succumbed to drug addiction and depression, while others have become cynical, apolitical careerists. The brightest and best connected, like my tour guide friend, have left Iran, and many more would go if they could. A nationwide poll in 2005 by Iran's government-run National Youth Organization found that 44 percent of young Iranians would emigrate if given the opportunity. Yahyia Fuizi, a U.S.-educated architect who returned to Iran in the mid-1990s after a long and successful career abroad, told me that he had lost more than forty staff to jobs overseas. "I train them and they escape," he said.

Young people have been pivotal in Iranian history. They have been at the forefront of the country's political changes since the turn of the last century, when they played a major role in the 1906–11 revolt that briefly turned Iran into the region's only constitutional monarchy. The youth of Iran came out again en masse to support Mossadegh when he nationalized Iranian oil in 1951. The 1979 revolution would never have succeeded without the tens of thousands of young Iranians who demonstrated across the country and risked their lives to overthrow the shah. They plunged into politics and joined dozens of antigovernment organizations—Islamic, democratic, and socialist, and combinations of all three, producing the most lively political discourse Iran had ever experienced. Student gatherings, sometimes masquerading as poetry

readings and lectures, preceded the mass street protests that finally toppled the regime.[1] Other youngsters joined underground guerilla
groups that attacked regime officials and their supporters. Hundreds
of young people were arrested, incarcerated in Tehran's dreaded Evin
prison, and tortured by the shah's secret police. Thousands more Iranians studying abroad, primarily in the United States, organized demonstrations that were inspired by their own history of student activism as
well as foreign protests against the U.S. war in Vietnam and in support
of human rights. The spectacle of these kids being teargassed by
Washington police in front of the White House in 1977 while the shah
met President Carter helped build support in Iran and around the
world for the revolution.

Returning home after the shah's government fell, these youngsters
were full of energy and optimism about the new Iran they were determined to create. Yet within months their revolution was hijacked by
clerics who imposed new kinds of repression in their efforts to create a
new Islamic youth culture. Universities were closed for two years while
liberal professors were purged, the curriculum was Islamicized, and
secular student groups were disbanded. Textbooks were rewritten to
glorify the revolution, the Shiite religion, and martyrdom.[2] Women
and girls as young as nine were forced to drape themselves in dark,
shapeless robes; the legal age of marriage was reduced to nine, and entire professions, such as judgeships, were barred to females. At schools,
sports events, and beaches, the sexes were segregated. Music, art, chess,
even whistling in public became a crime. Khomeini, the septuagenarian
leader of the revolution, decreed that public gatherings of any kind,
apart from religious events and anti-American and anti-Israel demonstrations, were forbidden. Not that there was much to celebrate during
his reign. Iraq attacked Iran in 1980 and Khomeini, seeking the overthrow of Saddam Hussein, refused a truce until 1988.

No cultural revolution so drastic could last, and with the end of the
war and Khomeini's death in 1989, the situation for young Iranians began to improve. The 1997 election of Khatami coincided with the coming of age of the wartime baby boom and triggered a significant
relaxation of social restrictions. Before Khatami, vice squad vigilantes
on motorbikes regularly harassed women and girls whose clothing was
considered insufficiently Islamic. The crackdowns were concentrated
during summer, when women might be tempted to wear cooler and

more revealing clothes, and during the Muslim holy month that includes Ashura, the commemoration of the death in the seventh century of the prophet Mohammed's grandson, Hossein. In 1996, an Iranian friend confided that two women she knew had been sentenced to seventy-four lashes each for wearing bad *hijab,* the word in Farsi (and Arabic) for the veil. Under Khatami, the dress code began to relax and the sort of intrusion into private life that so alienated my tour guide friend became rarer. The regime appeared to have made a tacit decision to allow Iranians more personal space, provided that they did not meddle in opposition politics. "Khatami was brought to power by the youth so he owed them something big," said Mehrdad Mashayekhi, a professor of sociology at Georgetown University. "At least in the first two years of his presidency, he created circumstances in their favor."

Khatami was one crucial factor; globalization another. Starting in the midnineties, satellite television, the Internet, and pirated CDs brought the world increasingly into Iranian homes, from the latest Hollywood movies to hard rock and rap. The first time I went to Iran, Michael Jackson was all the rage, followed in swift succession by the Backstreet Boys, Pink Floyd, Eminem, Metallica, Guns N' Roses, and 50 Cent. None of this music could be performed in public. Still, the contrast between public and private lives became less stark during the Khatami presidency. In 1999, the regime staged its first pop music festival in twenty years, and traditional and quite sensual Persian music began being played at concerts and a growing number of restaurants. Male singers could perform, although mixed dancing in public is still taboo, as are women singing solo unless their audience is all female. In upscale north Tehran there was a construction boom in Western-style shopping malls and food courts where young Iranians could stroll and text message each other to arrange dates. Young people affected the dress styles of their musical idols, and even girls joined gangs that they called "heavy" (for heavy metal) and "rap."[3] They cruise the streets in cars, stage drag races, and hold parties on Ashura, though that is meant to be a time of mourning. Even the poor take advantage of Islamic holidays and sports victories and defeats to go outside and flirt discreetly. The June 21, 1998, victory of Iran over the United States in a World Cup match in Lyons, France, triggered a nightlong celebration in Tehran and other cities the likes of which the country had never seen, as young women threw off their head scarves and boogied in the streets. The sexual revolution hit Iran with a vengeance in the mid-nineties, and young women bragged to me about their conquests with stunning bravado in a nation where extramarital relations—if proven—can result in death by stoning. "We see in Iran a movement for joy among children of the revolution who have started to reject everything the state embraces," Mashayekhi said. "Whatever the state tries to promote is rejected."

THE PINK REVOLUTION

Inspired by images on the Internet, in Western fashion magazines, and on satellite television, Iranian young people have managed to subvert a once strict Islamic dress code. Khomeini would be horrified to see how young women look on the streets of Tehran and other big cities less than three decades after the revolution. Instead of wearing nunlike head coverings and the shapeless black *chador,* many choose bright colors and tight tunics over skinny jeans and capri pants, barely observing traditional Islamic requirements to cover all but their hands, face, and feet. Girl students have created a three-tiered style that Iranians call "Saturday, Sunday, Monday" in which a short jacket or sweater is layered over a tight tunic and pants. Scarves slip back to show generous amounts of hair, and in the summer, painted toenails gleam under skimpy sandals. Some young women wear far too much makeup, and the hair that shows outside their scarves is often artificially streaked blonde. Nose jobs have become popular among both young men and women, as though making themselves look less Middle Eastern would change their lives. A translator friend of mine, Goli Emami, complained, "The more you look at the people in the streets, they don't look like Iranians anymore."

I arrived in Tehran in the winter of 2005 to find young women awash in pink: scarves, jackets, sweaters, bags, and shoes. The color became especially fashionable that year in Europe, and the trend moved to Iran before it made it to the United States. Wearing pink was more than a fashion statement. It was a silent protest against a regime whose favorite shade was the color of death, an effort by the young to make life in Islamic Iran less grim. Unable to defeat the trend, the government tried to co-opt it and painted city buses pink and purple. Incredibly, in 2005, slogans on street banners praising the anniversary of Khomeini's return to Iran in 1979 were also lettered in pink.

These cosmetic improvements certainly made Iran look less dreary, but only served to make the younger generation hunger for more. A twenty-six-year-old English teacher I met during the winter of the "pink revolution" was bored by the minimal pleasures available in Tehran, desperate for real employment, and working odd jobs to make ends meet. "This life is like death," he said. He amused himself by telling vulgar jokes about Iranian leaders that reminded me of the cracks young Russians used to make about aging Soviet political figures in the 1970s and 1980s. One of his cleaner jokes went like this: "Khomeini made a will before he died and said, 'Give my beard to Rafsanjani, my hand to Khamenei, and my balls to Khatami.'" Rafsanjani, the former president, looks very Asian and has almost no facial hair; Khamenei, the supreme leader, nearly lost a hand in a terrorist bombing after the revolution; while Khatami is criticized for not standing up to hard-liners and working harder to advance political and social reforms.

TOO FEW JOBS, TOO MANY DRUGS

Young Iranians might be less resentful of the restrictions on their lives if they had more economic security. Despite record oil earnings in recent years, Iran's state-dominated economy has failed to create enough jobs that pay the several hundred dollars a month needed to support a family at a basic level. To keep pace with those entering the labor force each year, Iran needs to generate eight hundred thousand jobs but is producing only four hundred thousand.[4] In 2006, according to Mohammad Jahromi, minister of labor and social affairs, nearly half of young people between the ages of twenty-five and twenty-nine were unemployed, and fewer than one in ten of these youngsters had hopes of starting their own businesses. "The only solution to the problem of unemployment is the attraction of domestic and foreign investment," he said.[5] To lure the level of investment that would solve the problem would require the Iranian government to pursue less confrontational foreign policies and more transparent and consistent regulations at home.

The regime's success in raising the educational level of Iranians has also contributed to the frustrations of the young, by creating expections that it cannot meet. More than 9 out of every 10 Iranian children between the ages of six and fourteen can read and write, thanks to government investment in primary education, and they will not be satisfied with menial or make-work jobs when they are adults.[6] The number of university students has also increased, from about 140,000 in 1979 to more than 1 million, and women now outnumber men on Iran's campuses by about 3 to 2.[7] Iranians complain about the quality of the education and the difficulty of gaining admission to universities. There are quotas for the politically well connected and the children of police, Iraq war veterans, and members of the Revolutionary Guards and *Basij,* the youth group that enforces loyalty to the regime. Even these youngsters have trouble finding good jobs once they graduate.

The frustrations engendered by rising literacy, social restrictions, and lack of employment have serious consequences for Iranian society. A slogan I once heard in Tehran at a government-orchestrated rally said that the greatest achievement of the revolution was "to raise God-seeking youth." Yet Iranian youngsters are violating the tenets of their faith in increasingly self-destructive ways. Alcohol abuse is common among rich kids, whose families purchase liquor easily on the black market. Poorer young people turn to drugs, especially heroin and opium, which are readily available. Drug addiction is not a new problem in Iran, but it has gotten worse since the revolution, when the regime banned alcohol and control over Iranian borders broke down. In 1980, a year after the revolution, then president Bani-Sadr estimated that 10 percent of Iranians were taking narcotic drugs.[8] In 1998, when American wrestlers returned to Iran for the first time since the revolution to compete in a major championship, one of the slogans displayed prominently in Tehran's Freedom stadium read: "Fight drug addiction."

Opium and heroin have become especially easy to obtain since the revival of poppy cultivation in Afghanistan following the 2001 U.S. invasion of that country and the toppling of its fundamentalist Taliban government. Iranian officials assert that they have lost numerous soldiers and Revolutionary Guards fighting drug trafficking on the Afghan border. But there are persistent reports that members of Iranian law enforcement organizations are also profiting from the trade and that Iranian officials would rather see young people dulled by dope than challenging the regime. Indeed, by the government's own admission, there are at least 1.2 million heroin addicts in Iran—as many as there are in the United States.[9] On a per capita basis, however, this means that Iran's rate of heroin addiction is 400 percent greater than it is in the United States. By comparison, Pakistan, another Islamic nation where alcohol is not openly sold to the general public, has fewer than a million addicts, even though its population is more than twice that of Iran. Britain, with 60 million people, has about 340,000 opiate abusers.[10]

Glazed-eyed young addicts are a common sight in Tehran's public parks and on hiking trails in the Alborz mountains to the city's north and east. A large downtown park across from the former Interconti-nental (now *Laleh* or Tulip) hotel is notorious for drug dealing, and an epidemic of car thefts and other petty crimes has been blamed on ad-dicts in search of money for a fix. An Iranian acquaintance told me she was shocked in 2006 when she visited the grave of her father and found the cemetery littered with discarded syringes full of blood. Addiction has contributed to prostitution and HIV/AIDs. According to one Irani-an newspaper, there were nearly eighty-five thousand prostitutes in Tehran alone in 2002; 40 percent of female drug addicts in Iran were HIV positive; and two teenage prostitutes spread the virus to eleven hundred men in six months.[11]

Other, semiofficial estimates suggest that the problem is even worse than the official figures indicate. In 2005, the government newspaper *Iran* put the number of addicts at 2 million. It quoted then deputy health minister Mohammad Khabbaz as saying that addiction caused 55 percent of Iranian divorces, 65 percent of child and spouse abuse cases, 40 percent of the burglaries, and 70 percent of the AIDS cases in the country.[12] Officials said the number of those afflicted with AIDS was thirty-seven hundred, but the real figure was believed to be much higher.[13] One Iranian newspaper wrote that 13 percent of high school students and 20 percent of university students were hooked on narcotic drugs. "More funds should be set aside for the prevention of HIV/AIDS," the English-language *Iran Daily* wrote, "encouraging healthy activities through sports and the arts; in other words keeping the young and active sections of the population engaged in some initiative or other so that they don't go astray."[14]

Iranian officials have tried at times to give the young places to enjoy themselves legally and in public. The former mayor of Tehran, Gholamhossein Karbaschi, was particularly proud of the cultural centers he set up in the capital's poorer neighborhoods. I visited one in 1996 in a former slaughterhouse district in southern Tehran where, according to Karbaschi, Iranians had once feared to venture after dark because of a high crime rate. The Bahman Cultural Center on the grounds of the former slaughterhouse had a resortlike feel, with whitewashed buildings, bright murals, tree-lined paths, and gardens. It had four auditoriums seating two thousand people, including a five-hundred-seat movie theater named for the silent-film star Charlie Chaplin. There was a symphony orchestra with one hundred musicians, several art galleries showing modern abstract works, classes in aerobics and English, a swimming pool (with segregated swim times for men and women), a library, and places to play chess. There was also a small theater for dramatic arts. When I visited, youngsters were doing a dress rehearsal for a nonmusical version of *Les Misérables*—suitable for Iranian audiences because the women were fully covered in period dresses and bonnets. During its heyday, the Bahman center attracted thousands of kids a day, according to its then director, Morteza Kazemi. It has since lost popularity. Karbaschi was arrested, tried, and convicted on what appear to have been exaggerated charges of corruption. Ahmadinejad, appointed mayor in 2003 before his election as president two years later, tried to give the cultural centers a more religious cast and Iran's young people drifted away.

MOUNTAIN RETREAT

Geography has given Tehran's youth an escape hatch in the arc of mountains ringing the capital from northeast to west. In the winter the slopes are snow-covered and majestic, and the air is unpolluted and crisp. Religious vigilantes tend to stay away or relax their standards, and Iranian young people get to act their age, throwing snowballs at each other and sitting together in cafés drinking tea and inhaling fruit-flavored tobacco through gurgling water pipes. There are several ski resorts that I was told were rather good, although as a nonskier, I passed on boarding the creaky cable cars that took people to the slopes. I preferred trudging up the steps cut into the rocky paths in one section called Darband, stopping at open-air restaurants, and eating shish ke-bab while admiring the mountain views. On the road to another popu-lar resort called Tochal, an enterprising Iranian had set up a paintball range and a bungee-jumping ride for kids that proudly displayed the label of its manufacturer, Aspen Creations. Said Rahimi, a young engi-neer I met at Tochal, told me he couldn't afford the twenty-three dol-lars fee to go skiing but that the walking renewed his spirits. "You have several things to do on the weekend in America but in Iran, it's lim-ited," he said apologetically.

The mountains are usually a safe place to do interviews without at-tracting undue attention from the authorities; Iranians seem to imbibe a bit of bravery along with the clean air. In December 2001, Iranian youngsters were particularly audacious. Khatami had just been re-elected president and there was a wave of sympathy for Americans fol-lowing the 9/11 terrorist attacks. Young men and women had poured into the streets of Tehran in a spontaneous show of support for the United States, and then demonstrated again, more violently, following the loss by Iran's soccer team to Bahrain in a World Cup qualifying match. Three teenagers I met a few weeks later in the mountains had taken part in the soccer riots, and one had spent two weeks in jail. "I would do it again," this youngster told me in Farsi, adding for empha-sis in English: "I don't give a shit." He and his companions were decked out like punk rockers, all in denim, and their hair was stiff with gel. One of them wore a long fake gold chain that swung from his jeans pocket below his knees. "There is no place to go, not even a nightclub," said the boy, a nineteen-year-old named Payman. "Our fathers tell us about what it used to be like in this country. Now we have to rely on our fathers for money, and a car is a young man's dream." One of his companions, Farshid, also nineteen, said, "This is the most free place we have, and even here we're a bit scared. We are miserable people compared to other countries."

THE KHATAMI EFFECT

There was a fleeting period, after Khatami was first elected, when Ira-nian young people seemed to have more hope. The voting age in Iran is only fifteen, so younger voters were instrumental in his victory.

Khatami had a gentle and unaffected way of speaking, and he touched young people as few Iranian leaders had. Iranian youth related to him almost as they might a rock star, with teenage girls squealing and crying in his presence. "He understands the words of the young, and his words go back to our hearts," Molood Mehrabian, a twenty-one-year-old, told me in the winter of 1999 as we waited in the female-only balcony of the Ahmadiyeh mosque for Khatami to speak. "The way he talks is different, and he has lots of new ideas," she said. A middle-aged woman in the throng, Azam Heydari, said she had three children, two daughters and a son, and she had voted for Khatami for their sakes. "Our children have no future in this country," she told me. "I want him to provide a better future."

Older Khatami supporters believed that Iran's rising generation would force the country's leaders to become more democratic and responsive to the concerns of the youth. "This new generation is seeking development and change, and will eventually impose its ideas on the society," Ebrahim Asgharzadeh, the former firebrand who helped organize the 1979 seizure of the U.S. embassy, told me in 1999.

By then, however, a conservative backlash against Khatami had already begun, and religious hard-liners who controlled the judiciary began shutting down reformist newspapers. The turning point came on July 7, 1999, and, as so often in Iranian history, the primary actors—and victims—were Iran's youth. The judiciary had closed the reformist newspaper *Salam,* which had become extremely popular for publicizing the dirty deeds of Iran's intelligence establishment: the murders of intellectuals in Tehran and of dissidents in Europe. Scores of students gathered to protest the newspaper's closure and staged a peaceful rally at Tehran University. That evening, several hundred plainclothes thugs descended on the university dormitories, beating students and flinging a few from third-floor balconies. At least one student was killed, three hundred were wounded, and more than a thousand were arrested that night and during nearly a week of demonstrations and riots that followed.[15] The cover of the *Economist* magazine displayed what became the iconic picture of the events: a long-haired, handsome student brandishing the bloodstained shirt of a dead companion. Ezzat Ebrahimnezhad was the student who had died, and his handsome friend, Ahmad Batebi, was among four students sentenced to death, later commuted to fifteen years in prison. Shirin Ebadi, the Nobel Peace

Prize–winning lawyer and human rights advocate, described meeting Batebi several years later when he was on a brief furlough from jail. "The young man with the coffee-bean eyes and red bandanna, whose Che Guevara looks made the photo even more memorable . . . had put on weight and his hair was shorter. . . . His very body language radiated defeat."[16]

Political protests stopped for a time, but there were other catalysts for defiance. In Iran as in most of the world (apart from the United States), soccer is a national obsession, and the qualifying matches for the World Cup have become pretexts to party in the streets. In the fall of 2001, the demonstrations began innocently, then turned violent after the 1–3 loss to Bahrain. Boys and girls shouted, "Long live freedom," blasted rock music from their cars, and chanted slogans in support of the United States and Reza Pahlavi, the son of the late shah, who lives in exile outside Washington. Police cracked down and arrested scores of revelers after some of them began throwing stones and Molotov cocktails in the streets of downtown Tehran.[17] As in the soccer demonstrations of 1998, politics seem to have had less to do with the outbursts than the youngsters' need to let off steam. At the United Nations a few weeks after the riots, Khatami told me and a few other reporters at a press breakfast that the protests were "not pro-American or anti-Iranian. It's natural, not political. Our people want joy."

Students turned out again by the thousands at campuses across the country in 2002, after a court sentenced a history professor, Hashem Aghajari, to death for giving a speech in which he advised Iranians not to blindly follow hard-line interpretations of Islam as though they were monkeys, not humans. The protests and adverse international reaction to the sentence so embarrassed Iran's ruling clerics that the country's supreme court decided on clemency. Aghajari was retried and freed in 2004.[18] When Khatami addressed students later that year, he was heckled by youngsters who chanted, "Khatami, what happened to your promised freedoms?"[19]

As the regime cracked down on newspapers and demonstrations, technology provided a new outlet for political and personal expression. The Internet was introduced in Iran in 1992 as an academic tool, and its use began to expand rapidly with government encouragement after Khatami's election five years later. In the winter of 1999 I visited what the proprietors claimed was Tehran's first Internet café. It was just before Valentine's Day—a Western holiday that Iranian youngsters had decided to make their own to protest restrictions on contact with the opposite sex—and the Internet CoffeeNet was packed with young people sending greeting cards to their boy- and girlfriends via e-mail. By the end of the year there were more than one thousand Internet cafés in Tehran alone. Initially it was difficult and expensive to get an Internet connection at home; then computers became more affordable and Internet service expanded to meet demand. By 2004, there were 5.5 million Internet users in Iran and 10 computers for every 100 Iranians.[20]

Blogs debuted in 2002, thanks to an Iranian-Canadian named Hossein Derakhshan, a computer whiz kid who had written technical columns for Iranian newspapers. After most of the reformist papers were closed by order of the authorities, Derakhshan came up with a way to use Farsi with free weblog software and provided instructions on his bilingual site, www.hoder.com. The technology caught on so quickly that Farsi became the third most common language in the blogosphere, according to researchers at Stanford University. By 2006, there were believed to be 100,000 active blogs in Iran, and Internet users may have reached 15 million.[21] It took the regime a little while to figure out how to deal with the phenomenon. In 2003, it began arresting bloggers who posted criticisms of the government; the following year, the parliament passed laws banning "cyber crimes," and authorities began blocking thousands of political sites. Derakhshan was detained briefly in 2005, when he returned to Iran to cover the presidential election campaign. He was forced to sign a letter apologizing for his blog commentary before being allowed to leave the country.[22]

Still, the Internet remained a safety valve for young people yearning for connections with each other and the outside world. Hiking in the mountains outside Tehran in 2005, I met a twenty-one-year-old woman studying computer software who boasted that she had her own blog and e-mailed people in dozens of countries. "I know Brad in Carolina, he's very handsome," she said. "I met three guys here on the Internet and arranged meetings with them." I gave her my card, and by the time I had gotten back to my hotel and checked my e-mail, she had already sent me a note, and we arranged to have coffee later that week. She could have been a college student from any other country. Except for the silk scarf that, by some miracle of physics, kept slipping off her hair without completely falling off.

Those who would like Iran's government to collapse before the country acquires nuclear weapons put a great deal of faith in Iran's restive youth. But the regime has become much more effective at preventing and containing protests, and not all Iranian young people are disaffected. During the last presidential campaign Ahmadinejad attracted votes from working-class young Iranians impressed by his calls for social justice, and the president tried to keep their affection through his policy of handouts to the poor and his "love fund" that offered low-cost loans to newlyweds. Among the regime's continuing supporters are nearly a million members of the *Basij,* or mobilized ones, the volunteer force of mostly young people that defends government policies and informs on protest groups. Thousands of other young men belong to *Ansar e-Hezbollahi,* the vigilantelike offshoot of the *Basij* sent to rough up students and others critical of the government. Though many young Iranians seem mesmerized by the West, there has also been a resurgence of folk religion and devotion to the so-called twelfth *imam.* The Jamkaran mosque outside Qom, Iran's theological center, attracts tens of thousands of young people who drop prayers into a well where, legend has it, God provides divine answers to worldly problems. More than a third of Iranian youth polled in 2006 by an American pollster said that they would like their country to become more religious and conservative, compared to just over a quarter who said they would prefer a more secular, liberal society.[23] While most of those who turn out for Friday prayers at Tehran University appear middle-aged or older, I met plenty of youngsters there who prayed with emotion and chanted "Death to America" with apparent fervor.

Support for the United States appeared to drop in Iran after 2003 as a result of the carnage in Iraq, and President Bush became only marginally more popular in Iran than in the rest of the Muslim world. "I can't look at Bush because he makes war and commits crimes against humanity," said Zohra Mohammedi, twenty-three, as she attended Friday prayers in the winter of 2006. The U.S.-organized telephone poll of Iranians in May–June 2006 found that older Iranians were more likely to admire the United States than those under the age of thirty, and more youngsters said they would rather see the Muslim holy city of Mecca than New York. Nearly a third of those polled aged eighteen to twenty-nine said the government it admired the least in the world was the Bush administration. They preferred England and Russia to the U.S. government by a margin of 2 to 1; Russian leader Vladimir Putin was the most popular foreign leader, followed by then French president Jacques Chirac.[24]

Student activism associated with Iran's reform movement declined after Ahmadinejad's election, but there remain outlets for what I would call the loyal opposition. In the winter of 2006, I visited the offices of *Baztab,* a conservative Web site that means "Reflections." Mohsen Rezaie, the former commander of the Revolutionary Guards and unsuccessful candidate for president in 2005, provides money for the site, which employs about fifteen young Iranians. The offices are in a modest fifth-floor walk-up apartment in a middle-class neighborhood of Tehran, and the computer technical staff, interestingly, are all female. The men are bearded, the women modestly clad, and they work together without apparent embarrassment or tension. When I interviewed him, Fuad Sadeghi, thirty and one of the founders of the site, was bristling with political opinions and questions about the United States, including why it chose to support Israel. Wouldn't it be fairer, he asked, for all Jews and Palestinians to vote on what sort of country Israel/Palestine should become? Although his site generally supported Iranian government policies, it was shut down for a month in 2005 for leveling charges of corruption against a senior official, and it has printed numerous items critical of Ahmadinejad. Sadeghi, bearded and chubby, was proud of the Web site's independence and said that he was optimistic about Iran's future because "the responsibility is going to the younger generation." Many others in his age group, however, appear to have lost faith that the system will change quickly enough to satisfy their personal aspirations. The main regime-tolerated student movement, the so-called Office for Consolidation of Unity, urged young Iranians to boycott the 2005 presidential elections, arguing that voting would legitimize an authoritarian system.[25]

LOSING INTEREST IN POLITICS

Most of the young Iranians I've met are turned off on politics, regard-
ing it as a closed game for regime supporters. One of my young friends
has become a barometer for me of his generation's expectations. Seven
at the time of the revolution, he comes from a family that he described
as religious but tolerant. He first learned English by watching American cartoons and sitcoms on television before the revolution, then
gained fluency by listening to the English-language broadcasts of the
Voice of America and the British Broadcasting Corporation. When I
first met him, in 1998, he was bearded, conservative in his social views,
and hopeful for the future of the Islamic system. When I saw him on
subsequent visits he was more Western in his appearance and behavior,
more cynical, and less interested in political life. "Why should I care
about Palestinian politics when I don't even care about my own?" he
told me when I asked his opinion of Ahmadinejad's comments about
wiping Israel off the map. "We should solve our own problems," he
said. "Our regime is far worse than Israel's." He had voted, along with
most Iranian young people, for Khatami in 1997 as a protest against the
establishment, but did not vote in 2001 or 2005. He said he was not disappointed by Khatami's failure to change the system because "I never
expected him to do anything for Iran. The government found a way to
deceive the people again."

My friend got married at thirty but divorced within a year. His wife,
it seemed, wanted more material possessions than he could provide. He
gave up his first career as a journalist because the pay was poor, and he
said he no longer felt he could have any influence on his country's policies by writing articles. He went into business and prospered, at least
judging from his appearance. When I first met him he was rather
scruffy, with a stubbly beard and inexpensive clothes. The last time I
saw him he was clean shaven, had a stylish haircut, and was wearing a
well-tailored gaberdine suit. He shook my hand in the lobby of the hotel, still a rather bold gesture in Iran, and ushered me into a new Peu-
geot for a drive around the city. He told me he had just taken his first
visit abroad, to the United Arab Emirates, gone to a bar, and had his
first glass of Scotch. While there he also went to the U.S. Embassy to
inquire about a visa but was put off, he said, by the rudeness of the local staff. You could see in his face the conflict between his pride as an

Iranian and his dissatisfaction with what his country had become. He would concentrate now, he said, on getting rich and enjoying life to the extent possible while ignoring the machinations of Iran's rulers. And he was still thinking about leaving Iran.

As the mother of a teenager, I sympathize with the plight of these young Iranians and also with their parents. From the slums of south Tehran to the fashionable districts of the north, from the old capital of Isfahan to the theological center of Qom, mothers and fathers spoke to me about their worries for their children, wondering how they would manage to lead fulfilling lives in the Islamic republic. One of the saddest legacies of the revolution has been the way in which it has divided families between parents in Iran and children who go abroad in search of more freedom and economic opportunity. The Iranian diaspora numbers perhaps 5 million, nearly 1 million in the United States alone, and most of its members have left parents, aunts, uncles, and grandparents behind. Iranians in general are close-knit people, willing to sacrifice to give their children a better life but deeply troubled by the lack of regular contact. I have many friends in Iran who see their children and grandchildren once a year, if that. Some Iranians did not return home for two decades after the revolution, and many still fear harassment or worse by the regime's security forces.

The conflict between the desire to keep one's children close and to see them prosper strikes all manner of Iranians, from a foreign ministry official who asked me to help get his son into an American-affiliated university in the Middle East to Nobel laureate Shirin Ebadi. Ebadi, one of Iran's few female judges, had refused to leave the country when she was dismissed from her job after the revolution, and she cut ties with many friends who had fled rather than stay and struggle to reform the Islamic regime. She stayed in Iran even after she had been imprisoned for her human rights work and still faced the threat of another jail term or worse. Then her elder daughter, Negar, informed her parents that she wanted to go to Canada to complete her education as an electrical engineer. The Ebadi family spent weeks debating whether Negar should go, concerned that she might choose not to return. Ebadi didn't want to lose her daughter, and she didn't want Iran to lose the contribution her daughter might make. But she also didn't want to deprive her daughter of the chance to fulfill her potential. "I knew it wouldn't be Montreal's sidewalk cafés and summer jazz festivals that might keep her there," she wrote. "It would be the chance to work in an atmosphere where her contribution was respected, where she was constantly learning from her colleagues. How seductive it would be, I thought, for her to wake up in the morning, put on a crisp suit, and walk down a bustling street without a veil, feeling herself part of a global culture that was dynamic and full of life."[26]

Ebadi let her daughter go.

EIGHT

THE MULLAHS

T HE IRANIAN CITY OF Qom is famous for two products: a sweet
brown pistachio brittle called *sohan* and Shiite clerics known as
"mullahs." A two-hour drive south of Tehran, Qom (pronounced like
"comb") is a sun-baked city of single-story houses, small shops, gold-
domed shrines, and whitewashed seminaries. The narrow streets are
filled with mullahs in long beige tunics under gauzy black cloaks, and
women, who, unlike their more risqué sisters in Tehran, generally wear
chadors, billowing black veils. Besides their cloaks and tunics, the mullahs are also distinguishable by their white or black turbans, the latter
color signifying that the bearer is descended from the prophet Mohammed and deserving of particular deference in Shiite Islam. There
is a saying in Iran that Tehran is Iran's brain, Isfahan its heart, and
Qom, its soul.

I first went to Qom in 1999, stopping briefly on a journey from
Tehran to Isfahan. A modern four-lane highway leads from the Iranian capital through a stark and beautiful landscape reminiscent of the
American Southwest, with unusual rock formations of red sandstone
and black basalt. Qom appears suddenly in the desert, like a medieval
mirage, with its turbaned mullahs and women in black, minarets, and
cupolas, but it is not completely divorced from modernity. In 1999,
peddlers in the bazaar were hawking shopping bags bearing the name
Titanic, after the movie, a huge hit in Iran as well as in the United

States. Many of the mullahs were riding motorbikes, their tunics tucked between their legs in a less than dignified fashion.

Reporting in Qom was tricky, particularly for a woman and a foreigner to boot; clerics were reluctant to be seen talking to women unrelated to them. My driver, who calls Qom "the mullah factory," had the bright idea of rolling down the window as we drove through the bazaar and asking one of the young products of this factory to get in the front seat of the car. We picked up a serious-looking, white-turbaned clerical student of twenty-four, who spoke to me and my female translator (in the backseat) as we drove around the town. He turned out to be an Iraqi from Basra who gave his name as Abu Ahmad Saedi. He had been in Qom for six years pursuing an education that would have been difficult in his native country under the regime of Saddam Hussein. The young mullah said he was studying with a noted ayatollah, Kazem al-Haeri, also the mentor of a young Iraqi Shiite leader, Moqtada al-Sadr, who would later rise to prominence after the U.S. invasion of Iraq. Saedi found Qom to be much more comfortable than his homeland, then under international sanctions. His fellow students came from dozens of countries, including China, Afghanistan, France, and even the United States, he said. Saedi's views about America had been shaped by U.S. air strikes and sanctions against Iraq and by the lectures he had heard from Ayatollah al-Haeri, a hard-line conservative with no love for the United States. "There are no Americans in America," the young mullah said. "They are all from somewhere else and they are sucking the blood of other people. They are the Great Satan and they are killing our children in Iraq."

Modern Middle Eastern politics have elevated the stature of Qom, which would otherwise pale in significance to the Iraqi city of Najaf, site of the tomb of Ali, the prophet's cousin and son-in-law. Shiites—the word means "the partisans"—believe that Ali and his progeny should have succeeded Mohammed and revere his close relatives and descendants as saints with a special ability to interpret God's law. Even though the most important Shiite shrines honoring these saints are in Iraq, more than half of the world's 130 million Shiites live in Iran. In the sixteenth century, the ruling Safavid dynasty, seeking to distinguish its subjects from their Sunni Muslim neighbors, imposed Shiism as the state religion. The Safavids built a magnificent capital at Isfahan and also boosted the fortunes of Qom, already notable for a large mosque that holds the remains of Fatemeh Masoumeh, the sister of the Imam Ali al-Reza, the eighth leader of the Shiites. Qom is also the site of a major seminary, the Faiziyeh, which was refurbished in the 1920s, when Najaf was in turmoil after the collapse of the Sunni Ottoman Turkish empire and Britain ruled the new country of Iraq.

Vali Nasr, author of a book on Shiism, compares the rivalry between Najaf and Qom to that between Harvard and Yale. Senior clerics go back and forth depending on the political circumstances in each country; currently the most revered figures are in Najaf but Qom has more seminaries, Nasr said. It's been a pattern in history that when Najaf's fortunes fall, Qom's fortunes rise. Many clerics in Najaf fled to Qom after the British suppressed a Shiite uprising in Iraq in the 1920s; Ayatollah Khomeini, the leader of Iran's 1979 revolution, went to Najaf in the 1960s after he was forced into exile by the shah. Saddam Hussein, Iraq's Sunni dictator, expelled Khomeini at the shah's request in 1978, earning Khomeini's undying enmity. Several prominent Iraqi ayatollahs fled to Iran during the 1980–88 Iran-Iraq war and set up operations in Qom.

Both shrine cities have seen their share of political turmoil. Mehdi Khalaji, a former seminarian who was born in Qom, said Qom has tended to be more political and has "always had a special relationship with political authority" in a Shiite-ruled state. Traditionally, senior Shiite clerics reserved the right to criticize government policies as un-Islamic while not demanding the right to rule themselves. That changed with the Iranian revolution. Khomeini, while in exile in Iraq, invented the concept of *Velayat-e Faqih,* or rule by the jurisprudent— under which a senior cleric gives guidance to all institutions of government. With the shah's overthrow in 1979, Qom reached its apogee, as Khomeini returned to the city and Iranian politicians and visiting dignitaries traveled to Qom to pay court to the black-turbaned new leader. The new Islamic republic plowed money into Qom and paid for scholarships for Shiite seminarians from around the world. After U.S. forces toppled Saddam Hussein in 2003 and a Shiite-dominated government took power in Iraq, it was thought that Najaf would become more prominent, but the chaos that engulfed Iraq after the U.S. invasion— and the growing regional power of Iran—insured that Qom remained the key center for Shiite scholarship and politics.

Qom's importance for Shiite theological studies, along with Iran's oil

wealth and revolutionary ideology, has given the Islamic republic considerable soft power as it seeks to extend its influence in the Middle
East and beyond. Qom is home to dozens of seminaries, including several for women, which attract more than fifty thousand students from
seventy countries.[1] Its traditional religious education follows a
centuries-old pattern. Father George McLean, a professor emeritus of
philosophy at Catholic University who taught in Qom for a month in
2000, said the curriculum reminded him of the University of Paris during the time of Thomas Aquinas. At the same time, Iranians have
founded universities in Qom to teach Western philosophy, and insured
that the seminaries are technologically up to date. Qom's libraries and
computer centers are unmatched in the Shiite world, so well regarded
that Ayatollah Sistani, the Iranian-born cleric with perhaps the widest
following among the world's Shiites, has based his Internet operations
in Qom even though he lives in Najaf.[2]

Such a large population of students, primarily male, has made Qom
a city known for more than spiritual contemplation. The courtyard of
the gold-domed Fatemeh shrine is a well-known place for arranging
sigheh, or temporary marriage, a practice condoned in Shiite Islam that
sometimes resembles legalized prostitution. Temporary marriage, Shiites believe, was sanctioned by the prophet Mohammed to provide sol-
ace to the widows of Muslim warriors. Sunnis later banned the practice
as applicable only to Islam's early days, but Shiite clerics have a more
tolerant attitude toward sex and see temporary marriage as a way of
satisfying normal desires as well as legalizing the offspring of liaisons
outside regular marriage. According to Nasr, any Muslim man can perform a marriage of another Muslim man and woman. Middle-class
Iranians tend to look down on *sigheh* but clerics have been among its
strongest proponents. "Qom is mysterious and mystical with many
strata," said Khalaji, who studied in Qom for ten years. "For me, it's
not a town but a state of mind. In Qom, everyone has his own world."
Qom, Khalaji said, is also a city of contradictions. "The most radical
atheist I ever met was a cleric living in Qom. It is a city of sexual suppression and homosexuality and prostitution, a city of religion, in-
trigue, and politics."

Of some thirty senior clerics in Shiite Islam, known as grand ayatollahs, about ten live in Qom. The distinction is subjective and reflects
both Iranian politics and the inherent populism within the faith. In tra-

ditional Shiism, clerics' living expenses are paid from the contributions of their followers. Devout Shiites give 5 percent of their annual income to the cleric they have chosen as a mentor or *marja-e taqlid,* literally source of emulation. The more followers a senior cleric amasses, the more resources he has to pay the stipends of seminarians, who in turn seek to attract more supporters for their spiritual leader. Under the Islamic republic, however, the government has become a major source of funds for its favored clerics, and this has distorted the traditional process of clerical advancement. Khalaji dismissed several of the so-called grand ayatollahs of Qom as "political ayatollahs," elevated more for their acquiescence in the Iranian form of government than for their religious authority.

The path to ayatollahdom begins with studying Arabic, the language of the Koran, followed by Islamic law, philosophy, and logic. It may take fifteen to twenty years for a seminarian to reach the level of *hojatoislam,* or "proof of Islam," the title given to those considered qualified to interpret Islamic law. Those who develop a reputation for erudition—or sometimes in Islamic Iran, political correctness—become known as "ayatollahs," or "signs of God." Ahmad Iravani, a Qom-trained ayatollah who has taught Islamic law for several years at Catholic University in Washington, said that becoming an ayatollah "is like getting your license as a physician. Your prominence depends on how many patients you have, how many referrals you get." Ayatollahs concentrate on learning how to minister to their patients' spiritual needs through interpretation, or *ijtihad,* of the Koran, the life and traditions of the prophet Mohammed, and of the Shiite *imams.* "The goal is to give an opinion that is as close to what God or the prophet or the *imams* would have delivered," Iravani said. This is a complicated business; Irvani gave an example. Suppose you had a dream in which God told you to give one hundred dollars to a certain person when you saw him. Would that mean that you did not owe the money unless you saw the person? That you had to seek out the person to pay him? Or that the debt would have to be paid even if you did not see the person for many years? Such questioning gets at the nature of *ijtihad.* "It may take you three months of study just to learn how to treat a conditional phrase," Iravani said.

Shiite scholars, much like students of the Jewish Talmud, are taught to learn by questioning. Seminarians are encouraged to challenge their teachers and to review their lessons by quizzing fellow students. Roy Mottahedeh, a professor of Islamic history at Harvard University, describes clerical education in his book *The Mantle of the Prophet*. He quotes a teacher at the Faiziyeh telling a class, "You are here to learn to reason, not just to learn to read."[3] He compares gaining knowledge about the Shiite faith to the growth of a tree, and religious commentaries by various experts to branches and leaves. "If you don't ask, my lessons themselves will dry up and wither," the teacher tells his pupils.[4] Mohammad Mahallati, a Shiite cleric and son and grandson of senior ayatollahs, said, "Critical thinking is built into Shiite jurisprudence. You must convince your audience, not just tell them this is what God said." The added filter of the Shiite *imams* also encourages a more flexible interpretation of the Koran and the traditions of the prophet Mohammed, Mahallati said. Sunnis do not recognize the *imams*.

In comparison to Sunnism, whose adherents tend to accept authoritarian government, Shiites seem more willing to challenge those in power and instinctively to identify with the underdog. The faith began as a revolt against temporal authority—the great seventh-century schism in Islam that led to the division between Sunnis and Shiites—and Shiites remain a minority, perhaps 10–15 percent of the world's 1.3 billion Muslims. Sunni clerics were government employees who owed allegiance to the ruler, while Shiites were seen as guardians of their communities. Nasr compares mullahs to the rabbis of Central and Eastern Europe in the Middle Ages, spiritual advisers to often beleaguered minority groups.

Shiite clerics have a long history of political activism and factionalism. Senior clergy, among the few Iranians who were literate at the time, led the first revolt against the Iranian monarchy in the late nineteenth century, the boycott of tobacco products after a money-hungry shah sold a monopoly of tobacco sales to a British company. Mirza Hassan Shirazi, the leading *marja* of the time, issued a fatwa banning tobacco use, and the shah was forced to rescind the concession after much of the population, including his own family, obeyed Shirazi.[5] Clerics also played a major role in the 1906 constitutional revolution. Protests escalated after the death of a seminary student in a demonstration in Tehran, and a crowd of fourteen thousand, most of them clerics, sought sanctuary on the grounds of the British embassy for a month.[6] The shah agreed to a constitution making himself subservient to a popularly elected assembly, a first in the Middle East and South Asia. The title of ayatollah was coined to laud those clerics who signed the constitution.[7] However, the religious establishment split after an elected assembly took office and a group of clergymen argued that in the absence of the hidden or twelfth *imam,* the best government did not have to be elected, merely to rule according to Islamic law.[8]

A number of senior clerics acquiesced when Reza Khan, the Russian-trained military officer, declared himself king in 1925. Seeking to consolidate a new dynasty, Reza was deferential at first to the ayatollahs and visited them in their homes in Qom. In 1928, however, his wife scandalized the religious establishment by appearing unveiled at the Fatemeh shrine.[9] The shah went on to forbid the veil, and to further undermine the power of the clerics by ending their monopoly over education, the administration of justice, and the drawing up of legal documents. Forced to abdicate by Western powers in 1941 because of alleged pro-German sympathies, the shah was replaced by his son. The senior ayatollah at the time, Mohammad Borujerdi, preached that the clergy should stay out of politics, but that did not prevent clerics from taking sides for and against Mossadegh, the popular prime minister who nationalized Iran's oil in 1951 and was deposed two years later by a CIA-backed coup. One ayatollah, Abolqassem Kashani, first supported then opposed Mossadegh, earning the nickname, the "CIA ayatollah."

Khomeini did not play a prominent role in the Mossadegh affair. Still relatively junior, he became politically active only after Borujerdi died in 1961. Increasingly infuriated by the shah's campaign to modernize and Westernize Iran, which included giving women the right to vote, Khomeini gave a blistering speech in Qom in 1963 challenging the shah's reform program. Khomeini accused the shah of being an agent of Israel and suggested that the monarch would be forced to abdicate like his father. The ayatollah was arrested and jailed for ten months. Upon his release he again criticized the shah for legislation giving immunity from prosecution to Americans working in Iran. "If someone runs over a dog belonging to an American, he will be prosecuted," Khomeini told a large crowd at his home in Qom who had traveled there to hear his first speech after his release from jail. "Even if the shah himself were to run over a dog belonging to an American, he would be prosecuted. But if an American cook runs over the shah, the head of state, no one will have the right to interfere with him."[10]

Khomeini was arrested and exiled following the speech, but Qom remained a hotbed of resistance to the government. His disciples created a clerical underground that distributed tapes of Khomeini's sermons and agitated against the throne. A January 1978 newspaper article orchestrated by the government that harshly criticized Khomeini's character led to riots by seminary students in Qom in which at least six demonstrators were killed by security forces.[11] Their deaths set off a chain of protests that led to bigger and bigger demonstrations around the country, more bloodshed, and eventually the overthrow of the monarchy.

DISSIDENCE IN QOM

News of the shah's fall in 1979 produced jubilation throughout Iran, perhaps nowhere more than in Qom. Mottahedeh describes a scene at the Fatemeh shrine in which clerical students, "who usually labored so hard to seem dignified, were actually jumping in the air and waving their hands, almost as if they were dancing, an activity so repugnant to mullahs and their students that the students would have fled in terror if their teachers had suggested the possible resemblance."[12] Policemen who only days before had been cracking turbaned heads at protest demonstrations were bowing to the same turbans and accepting the authority of Khomeini's top representative in Iran, Ayatollah Hossein Ali Montazeri. Khomeini soon implemented his new system of *Velayat-e Faqih,* and employment opportunities expanded considerably for Qom's human products. Where before the revolution most clerics faced a future as a village mullah or a singer of songs mourning the death of the *imams,* under the new system there were thousands of new government-paid positions. Khomeini appointed so-called Friday prayer leaders for Iran's major towns and cities who would explain government policies in weekly sermons. Before the revolution the idea of such prayer leaders was considered heretical in the absence of the prophet or his *imams.* According to Iravani, there are now five hundred to six hundred Friday prayer leaders as well as scores of clerics who serve as professors of Islamic studies, chaplains in the military, judges, and representatives of the supreme leader in various government ministries and departments. As a result, religious education has become a growth industry in Iran; Iravani estimates that there may be two hundred thousand mullahs in Iran today, one for every thirty-five Iranians. Other estimates are even higher.

However, the system created by Khomeini was controversial from the start, and several senior ayatollahs expressed concern that it would harm traditional religious beliefs. One revered cleric, Grand Ayatollah Kazem Shariatmadari, sparked an open revolt in his home province of Azerbaijan when he was criticized by the regime for pointing out the central contradiction in the Islamic republic's new constitution: One article said sovereignty came from the people, while another gave ultimate power to the supreme jurisprudent. Shariatmadari was put under house arrest. Accused of supporting an abortive coup in 1982, he was essentially defrocked by the religious establishment and buried without public ceremony when he died four years later, betrayals of tradition that shocked the Shiite world.[13]

Many Iranians I met said that the clergy as a whole has lost prestige since the revolution because of its entanglement with government. Iranians blame the clerics for the inefficient economy, the channeling of oil money to foreign Arab causes, and cultural restrictions that have backfired and turned many young Iranians against their faith. Outside Qom taxi drivers often refuse to stop for clerics in the street and mullahs have been known to remove their turbans and put on civilian clothes to avoid becoming the objects of verbal or other abuse. I was struck during my first visit to Iran, in 1996, by the lack of overt piety among Iranians compared to the citizens of a U.S.-allied Muslim country, Egypt. In Cairo, it seemed, everybody prayed, nobody drank, and many people disliked U.S. policies; in Tehran, it was the reverse. Iranians celebrated pre-Islamic holidays, such as their new year, *Noruz,* or even a holiday marking the winter solstice, *Yelda,* or the longest night, with much more fervor than Islamic ones, including Ramadan, the month in which the Koran was revealed and the high point of religious observance for Sunni Muslims. Ashura, the Shiite holiday that appalls Sunnis, is the exception. The devotion to Persian as opposed to Islamic culture is a form of protest against the regime. Khalaji said an Iranian survey in 1999 showed that 70 percent of Iranians under the age of thirty do not pray or give money to a source of emulation. As a result, he said, the government has increasingly had to step in to support the clerical establishment, contributing further to its loss of popular esteem.

Concerned at the clergy's diminishing status as an independent moral voice, some clerics have become vociferous critics of the system. As of this writing, the chief clerical opponent to Khamenei is Khomeini's prerevolutionary representative in Iran, Montazeri. Long close to Khomeini, Montazeri was named in 1985 to succeed the supreme leader but was cast aside in 1989 when he objected to the summary execution of thousands of political prisoners at the end of the Iran-Iraq war. Khomeini disregarded private letters from Montazeri appealing for an end to the executions, so in early 1989, Montazeri went public with his indictment of the government. In a speech in Qom marking the tenth anniversary of the revolution, he said:

> Let us see what slogans we have used over the past ten years that have made us so isolated in the world and made the people pessimistic about this. . . . Let us see what happened to all the unity, co-ordination, devotion . . . that we enjoyed at the beginning of the revolution. . . . On many occasions, we showed obstinacy, shouted slogans and frightened the people of the world who thought our only task here in Iran was to kill. We should not stop at making promises about freedom of speech and freedom for political parties. Our behavior and actions should be such that all devoted revolutionaries who have ideals can state them. . . . without fear of persecution.[14]

Khomeini died a few months later without designating another successor and the Assembly of Experts, the elected body of clerics, named Khamenei to succeed the great revolutionary leader. The decision proved extremely controversial. Khamenei, while respected for his devotion to the revolution, was only a *hojatolislam,* and as such, unqualified to serve as a source of emulation, let alone be the leader of the largest Shiite nation. His hasty elevation by the Assembly of Experts to ayatollah, and a change in the constitution no longer requiring the supreme leader to be a grand ayatollah, convinced few of his qualifications to take Khomeini's place. As a result, according to German scholar Wilfried Buchta, "Qom is today one of the strongest bulwarks of resistance to Ayatollah Khamenei's claim to religious autocracy."[15]

According to Buchta, senior clerics in Qom and elsewhere have repeatedly rebuffed Khamenei's efforts to bribe or intimidate them into openly supporting his leadership. Rebellious clergy have suffered as a result. A special clerical court has executed more than six hundred clerics and students since 1988, stripped two thousand clerics of their religious titles, and punished four thousand others with fines, beatings, and jail terms.[16] Mohsen Kadivar, a *hojatolislam* and a prominent reformer, spent eighteen months in prison in 1999–2000 for suggesting in public that the ruling clerics had become as tyrannical as the kings they replaced. "I believe in a religious democratic state," he said. "But a religious state is possible only when it is elected and governed by the people."[17]

Within Qom, Khamenei's ascension was rejected by Montazeri and several other grand ayatollahs, including Mohammad Shirazi, who died in 2001. Both spent periods under house arrest in an effort by the government to undermine their popular support by cutting their ties to seminarians. Montazeri was punished for his dissidence by having his seminary closed; the doors and windows were even welded shut. Freed from five years of house arrest in 2003, he remained outspoken. "All these court summonses, newspaper closings, and prosecutions of dissidents are wrong," he said. "These are the same things that were done under the shah."[18]

In 2005, I visited Montazeri's son, Ahmad, a *hojatolislam,* in a small whitewashed house on a narrow street next to his father's home and around the corner from the shuttered seminary. Ahmad, a tall middle-aged man with imposing eyebrows and piercing, deep-set eyes that resembled those of Khomeini, had studied in Tehran to be an engineer before the revolution, but took on the clerical mantle after Montazeri's elder son, Mohammad, died in a terrorist bombing in 1981. "I am really sorry to say that at the beginning, people took to the streets so that government would be at the service of religion but now religion is at the service of the government," Ahmad Montazeri told me. "Our attitude today will force people away from Islam and religion." Montazeri criticized the appointment to senior government positions of clerics not qualified to serve and said the dualism of the Iranian system was its greatest failing. "The worst situation in Iran is where the supreme leader has power but the president has responsibilities," he said.

One of the biggest public relations blows to the regime came in 2002 with the resignation of Ayatollah Jalaluddin Taheri, who had been the prayer leader for thirty years in Isfahan. Taheri announced his decision in a blistering letter that was reprinted in Iranian reformist newspapers:

> [I can no longer tolerate the] chaotic situation [and the] general-ized corruption of religious power in Iran. Deception, unemploy-ment, inflation . . . the diabolic gap between the rich and poor, bribery, cheating, the growing drug consumption, the incompe-tence of authorities and the failure of the political structure are no longer bearable. . . . The ideas that we put forth in our revolution in 1979 have been rejected. . . . They made a thousand promises and kept not one.[19]

Another harsh critic of the system is Grand Ayatollah Yusef al-Sa'nei. Sa'nei, named as a member of the Council of Guardians after the revolution and a former prosecutor general, retreated to Qom in 1985 out of disappointment with the new regime. He has argued that Iran should have a real democracy, and has issued fatwas banning sui-cide bombing and discrimination against women in the workplace.[20] In 2003, Sa'nei told the *Philadelphia Inquirer*'s Trudy Rubin that Iran's leader should be popularly elected and that no person is infallible.[21] In April 2006, the ayatollah gave an interview to an Italian newspaper in which he said that Iran should hold a referendum on whether the country should make the development of nuclear power a priority. He also criticized President Ahmadinejad's threats against Israel and his denial of the Holocaust. "Iran has no need of these debates," the aya-tollah said. "It is far more important and urgent today to devote oneself to the problems of the young and of the unemployed, avoiding putting the rest of the world in a position to attack us." The cleric also warned the country's leaders that unless they stopped disqualifying candidates for elected office, the "indifference [of Iranians] will grow." And he re-jected censorship of newspapers and forcing women to wear the veil.[22]

The regime also has its supporters among the Qom clergy; for exam-ple, Ayatollah Taghi Mesbah Yazdi. Said to be Ahmadinejad's mentor, Yazdi is a fascistic figure who questions the right of people to participate in elections and believes that the supreme leader's word should be law. In a sermon at Tehran University in 2005, Yazdi said that an Islamic government should combat foreign ideas as akin to the virus that causes AIDS.[23] Nicknamed "Professor Crocodile" for his harsh looks, Yazdi has defended suicide bombing, public floggings, and executions, and runs a major seminary in Qom named for Khomeini that has about one thousand students. Yazdi supporters disrupted a speech by Rafsanjani in Qom in June 2006 in what was viewed as an attempt to hurt Rafsanjani's chances in elections for the Assembly of Experts, the body which selects Iran's supreme leader. Mesbah Yazdi appears to have hoped that he might increase his support in the assembly and have a chance of becoming the next supreme leader. However, Khamenei moved against Yazdi in late 2006, prodding the Guardian Council, which vets candidates for elective office, to disqualify Mesbah Yazdi's son and several other supporters from running in the assembly elections. The council also forbade a number of prominent reformers from participating and Rafsanjani was the overwhelming victor, laying the ground for him to choose Khamenei's successor.

Many senior clerics have tried to steer clear of politics and confined themselves to religious matters. Khalaji, a reformer who turned away from organized religion and left Iran in 2000, said none of the so-called grand ayatollahs of Qom really merited the title *marja,* and that the most revered figure for Shiites inside and outside Iran was Sistani, the Iranian-born senior cleric in Najaf. Sistani rejects the Iranian system and believes that clerics should not take positions in government. He espouses an approach known as "quietism," a term that is a bit deceptive. "Traditionalism" is a better word, according to Nasr. "Traditional ayatollahs see themselves as guardians of the community in the absence of the twelfth *imam,*" Nasr said. "They will speak up to protect the community and issue fatwas, but they don't believe there can be a perfect government and don't claim to have the blueprint for one." In a clear rebuke to the favored clerics of the Islamic regime, a majority of the bazaar merchants of Qom are said to pay their religious taxes to Sistani, Nasr said. According to Khalaji, Sistani is the richest major cleric in the Shiite world, with more than two thousand representatives worldwide, an annual income of between $500 million and $700 million, and assets of more than $3 billion.[24] Khalaji worries, however, that Sistani will be last true *marja,* that Iraq will not stabilize sufficiently to

produce a successor, and that after Sistani's death the Iranian government will move to politicize religion completely. He forsees an emascu-
lated system of government-controlled clerics with a few key clergy
ruling in collaboration with increasingly powerful members and veterans of military institutions, especially the Revolutionary Guards.

Iravani said most clerics in Qom support the Iranian system but
would like to see changes to eliminate the power of the Council of
Guardians to disqualify candidates and to make elections more democratic. He believes that Shiism contains within it the ingredients for reform, much as it fueled the revolution against the shah.

Iravani's intellectual journey mirrors that of many other devout Iranians who have become associated with Iran's reform movement. Born
in 1961 in Ali Abad, a small town in northern Iran near the Caspian
Sea, Iravani intended to become a medical doctor and planned to study
in the United States. But the revolution intervened and Iravani said he
decided instead to become "a spiritual doctor." Among his most cher-
ished memories is his annointing as a cleric by Khomeini in the early
1980s. Khomeini placed a turban upon Iravani's head and gave him
1,000 tomans (about $100 at the time)—inside a Koran in a ceremony at
the ayatollah's home in Tehran. "It was a dream for me," Iravani said,
his warm brown eyes moistening at the memory. "He told me, 'I hope,
my son, in the rest of your life you will be a pious person and obey
God.'"

During the Iran-Iraq war Iravani went frequently to the front to
minister to the soldiers while continuing his studies in Qom. His
brother-in-law, also a cleric, accompanied him and was killed by Iraqi
fire. In 1990, Iravani realized his old goal of coming to the United
States and visited thirty cities in forty-five days, using a special airline
ticket and often sleeping on planes or in airports. He went from Dis-
neyland to Dallas, Chicago to San Francisco, he said, staying with Iranian immigrants and broadening his outlook considerably beyond the
bookish confines of Qom. Returning to Iran, Iravani moved to Tehran
to teach at Tehran University and study for a bachelor's degree in
Western philosophy. He returned to Qom to serve as dean of the fac-
ulty of philosophy at Mofid University, one of several institutions of
higher learning established in Qom in the 1980s to augment traditional
religious education. In 2000, Iravani decided to run for parliament
from his Caspian district but was initially disqualified by the Council

of Guardians, which sought to boost the chances of more conservative figures. "They disqualified me on grounds that I was not a Muslim and not a believer in the Islamic republic," Iravani said—an astonishing charge to level against an ayatollah. He was permitted to run at the last minute but lost the election and decided to accept an invitation to attend a conference at Catholic University. When I met him in 2006 he was teaching Islamic law and planning a doctoral dissertation about a twentieth-century French Catholic philosopher, Jacques Maritain. Short and a bit plump, with a pleasant round face and a neatly trimmed beard, Iravani said he believes that "whatever political changes will happen in Iran will have to come from within the clerical system." Globalization and the Internet, he said, are opening the eyes of the clergy to Western ideas and will produce a new synthesis appropriate for an Islamic country that has struggled for over a century to become a democracy without losing its religious traditions. In Qom, he says, "there are thousands of discussions going on to try to find a new identity and a better way."

NINE

THE OPPOSITION

SHORT AND SLIGHT, WITH an impish smile, Akbar Ganji is an unlikely looking dissident. Yet this middle-aged journalist with thinning hair and a salt-and-pepper beard has done more than any other Iranian in recent years to expose the brutal underside of the Islamic republic. Ganji was jailed in Tehran from 2000 to 2006 for crusading articles that exposed the regime's complicity in the murder of intellectuals and opposition figures in the mid-1990s and he nearly died during an 80-day hunger strike in 2005 when he dropped from 155 to barely 100 pounds. On a trip to the United States a few months after his release from prison in March 2006, he said he was confident that Iran would eventually shed its authoritarian system but admitted that the road ahead would be hard. "We have a very large and widespread democratic movement in Iran," he said, "but this movement has two weaknesses: It's not organized ... [and] we still don't have a leader" like India's Gandhi, Czechoslovakia's Vaclav Havel, or South Africa's Nelson Mandela.

Three decades after the Iranian revolution, the Islamic government faces opposition from a mosaic of forces: intellectuals like Ganji; dissident clerics; student, feminist, and labor groups; ethnic and religious minorities; a militant exile organization; and a sprinkling of monarchists. So far, however, they have not coalesced into a unified force, and the regime appears to have succeeded in marginalizing its most outspoken critics.

As is so often the case with revolutions, many of these dissidents began as ardent supporters of the antimonarchist movement, which they
hoped would end the injustices of the Pahlavi era. Ganji, who was
raised in a poor district of southern Tehran and was twenty in 1979,
said that he and other youngsters caught up in the struggle against the
shah "wanted to build a paradise and we created hell." Ganji served
during the Iran-Iraq war in the paramilitary Revolutionary Guards
and in the ministry of culture and Islamic guidance, in charge of li-
censing newspapers and books. Increasingly unhappy with the authoritarian direction the system was taking under Ayatollah Khomeini and
his successor, Ganji came under the influence of dissident religious intellectuals such as Abdulkarim Soroush. Ganji stepped over the regime's
red lines in the late 1990s and 2000, publishing investigative articles—
later collected in books such as *The Dungeon of Ghosts* and *The Red
Eminence, The Grey Eminences*—that blamed Iran's senior leadership,
including former president Rafsanjani, for the murder of dozens of intellectuals and regime opponents. The books have been compared to
the work of Russian author Alexander Solzhenitsyn in terms of the
impact they had on the Iranian intelligentsia. Like Solzhenitsyn, Ganji
paid a heavy price for his investigative work. He was jailed after taking
part in a conference in Berlin on Iranian political and economic reform, but kept up his dissident activity from prison, penning a manifesto calling for a democratic republic. Like many other dissidents, he
backs a referendum on changing the constitution, and has urged Iranians to boycott all elections until such a referendum is held. "In a political system that forbids women and the Sunnis from becoming
president, where one man holds all the powers and is above the Constitution . . . and the Council of Guardians . . . has the right to reject any
candidates, there is no point for the people to go to the polls," Ganji
wrote in his "manifesto for republicanism."[1]

During his 2006 visit to the United States, Ganji outlined his vision
for revamping the Iranian government. "My project is transition from
the Islamic republic," he explained. "We cannot cooperate or collabo-
rate with any despotic regime. In this project we can work only with
those who believe in human rights and equality." Ganji said he favors a
massive program of civil disobedience and eschews violence or mone-
tary support from any foreign government. While in the United States
he refused to meet any officials of the Bush administration for fear of

looking like he was beholden to the United States. He also rejected the notion that U.S. military action would advance the cause of democracy in Iran. "If our infrastructure is attacked by missiles, our country will be destroyed and it will not bear any fruit for democracy," he said. "Iraq is a very good example for us." During his U.S. stay, Ganji took part in a three-day hunger strike to dramatize the plight of political prisoners in Iran and accepted an award from the National Press Club. But asked if he could become the leader of Iran's opposition forces, Ganji demurred. "I am a critic, a dissident intellectual," he said. "Even in a democratic society, I would be a critic."

Ganji's path from regime supporter to jailed dissident has been trod by many others, among them, Mohsen Sazegara. The activist who was on Khomeini's "victory flight" to Tehran from Paris in 1979, and who helped found the Revolutionary Guards, Sazegara held several important posts in the regime in the 1980s, including vice minister of planning and the budget. Like Ganji, he began to turn against the system during the Iran-Iraq war. He quit his government job and became a publisher of reform newspapers during Khatami's first term, and in 2001 tried to run for president against Khatami but was disqualified by the Council of Guardians. Arrested several times in the early 2000s, Sazegara went on two hunger strikes that damaged his eyesight, and was allowed to leave Iran and seek medical treatment in Britain. He came to the United States in 2005 as a fellow at the Washington Institute for Near East Policy, a prominent think tank, and pursued an Internet petition campaign promoting a referendum on the Iranian constitution. The following year Sazegara wrote an open letter to Iranian president Ahmadinejad meant to respond to Ahmadinejad's letter to Bush of May 2006. Sazegara followed Ahmadinejad's pattern by posing a series of questions about Iran's human rights abuses, assistance to Palestinian extremists, favoritism toward members of the Revolutionary Guards, and what he alleged was the waste of billions of dollars in Iranian oil revenues on outdated nuclear technology from Pakistan. "Instead of writing prescriptions for others . . . you should think of our own people," Sazegara wrote. "Mind your own business and put aside this infantile behavior. Your image in the world has been reduced to something like that of Idi Amin," the former Ugandan dictator.[2]

Sazegara believes that there is no way for the regime to evolve without eliminating the post of supreme leader and the clerical bodies the leader controls. "All the powers are concentrated in the hands of the leader," he told me. "Even if you appoint me as leader, I may behave like Khamenei because you have [control over] the radio and television, the army, the Revolutionary Guards, the money, the propaganda, the intelligence services, the police, the judiciary, the Council of Guardians, which can control any election including the Assembly of Experts. Sometimes I say, the leader of Iran is like a satellite: When you send it outside the atmosphere, nobody can bring it down." Like Ganji, Sazegara advocates civil disobedience, strikes, and demonstrations that can mobilize Iranians for a referendum on the constitution. "The experience of the reform movement showed us there is no other way," he said.

In recent years, however, the Iranian opposition has had great difficulty organizing and sustaining public protests. In June 2006, for example, many of those who planned to take part in a rally for women's rights were called by police three days in advance and warned not to attend. Those who did turn up faced Iran's version of Hitler's brown shirts: scores of men in white shirts and dark trousers from *Ansar e-Hezbollahi,* the vigilante organization loyal to Khamenei. One of the women who was to attend the June 12 demonstration told me she turned away at the last minute when she saw the "white shirts." Government bullyboys and police outnumbered the demonstrators in Tehran's downtown Haftatir Square. Of about one hundred people who did attend, many were beaten with batons and sprayed with pepper gas; seventy were arrested. "It was over before you knew it, very, very fast," she said. "They were taken to a prison for drug addicts and then to Evin prison and released." A reformist newspaper questioned the need for such methods. "Now that women held their unauthorized gathering, would it have been against God's command if the law and order forces had tolerated them for a few minutes and then dispersed them gently?" asked the paper, *E'temad e Melli.* "Was it necessary to arrest 70 people and use violence?"[3] Police and *Hezbollahi* broke up a similar demonstration in 2006 on March 8, International Women's Day, a protest in February by Sufi Muslims in Qom trying to protect their mosque from demolition, and a rally by striking Tehran bus drivers in January.[4] Authorities used the same tactics against women protesters in March 2007.

The regime has also been efficient in suppressing student protests.

The crackdown began under the Khatami presidency, in 1999, when police and vigilantes brutally attacked students protesting new antipress laws and the closure of a reformist newspaper. About fifteen hundred students were arrested during rioting that followed a police attack on a student dormitory at Tehran University, and four alleged ringleaders were sentenced to death, later commuted to long prison terms. The protests "were spontaneous but lacked leadership and coordination between various student associations involved," according to Ali Akbar Mahdi, a professor of sociology at Ohio Wesleyan University.[5] One of those jailed after the riots, Amir Abbas Fakhravar, said after his release in 2006 that he was subjected to "white torture," which consisted of being put in a completely "color-free environment 24 hours a day." Not only were the walls of his cell painted white and his prison garb white, but even the food he received—rice—was all white, he said, and the psychological impact was one of complete disorientation.

Student activists such as Fakhravar have joined Ganji and Sazegara in calling for a referendum on the constitution and a boycott of all elections until one is held. In a letter he wrote from prison in 2003, Fakhravar said that "violence has absolutely no place in our struggle. Our goal is to reveal the unmasked face of the Islamic Republic and for the whole world to see the level of its unpopularity among Iranians. We are of the belief that with the pure grace of Almighty God and support of international public opinion, the evil of theocracy will be brought to its knees."[6]

Three years later Fakhravar continued his appeal for foreign support but admitted that Iranian authorities had stepped up surveillance and repression of student activists. A slight young man with sad green eyes, he said that the Ahmadinejad administration had beefed up offices in universities representing the supreme leader and turned universities into "a combination military camp and religious school." Students who attempt to organize against the government are suspended, expelled, or jailed. "The people of Iran are ready for a big movement but need confidence that the world will support them," he told a small group of reporters in Washington at a luncheon arranged by the American Enterprise Institute (AEI), a neoconservative think tank. Fakhravar's ability to influence Iran from abroad was doubtful, however, and he appeared to have discredited himself among many Iranians by accepting the patronage of men such as AEI's Richard Perle and

Michael Ledeen, who strongly supported the U.S. invasion of Iraq and promoted Ahmad Chalabi, a controversial Iraqi exile, as a replacement for Saddam Hussein. Around the same time that Fakhravar visited Washington, Abdollah Momeni, leader of Iran's main student group, the Office for Consolidation of Unity, told the *Philadelphia Inquirer's* Trudy Rubin that the student movement had split and "there isn't a new coalition yet."[7] In another blow, Akbar Mohammadi, one of the students arrested in the 1999 protests whose death sentence had been commuted to fifteen years, died in Tehran's Evin prison following a hunger strike.[8] In December 2006 a handful of students did succeed in staging a protest against President Ahmadinejad at Tehran's Amirkabir University, once a hotbed of revolutionary upheaval against the shah. Enraged when they saw busloads of the president's supporters entering the university auditorium in advance of a speech, students spontaneously began chanting "Death to the dictator" and held posters of Ahmadinejad upside down. The president cut short his speech and the demonstrators fled.[9] Many were later arrested.

Iranian authorities have marginalized dissidents such as Fakhravar, Ganji, and Sazegara by jailing them, then allowing them to leave the country. The regime has also calibrated its brutality to avoid massive casualties of the sort that were the catalyst for the 1978–79 revolution. In the lead-up to the overthrow of the shah, Iranian police and soldiers killed scores of protesters, triggering a cycle of violence that followed the rhythm of Shiite Muslim rituals in which new demonstrations occurred on the fortieth day of mourning for previous deaths, producing new casualties and new protests forty days later. Meanwhile, the network of devout Muslims who turned out for these mass protests has attenuated as the government has co-opted religious observance. "After the revolution, this network was confiscated by the government and it has been destroyed," said Mehdi Khalaji, the former seminary student who left Iran in 2000. "In the absence of these means, you cannot do anything, neither reform nor another revolution."

ETHNIC UNREST

Taking no chances, police have been especially careful not to cause massive bloodshed in Tehran, where images of repression would be sent quickly around the country and the world via the Internet. Police and *Hezbollahi* have been less restrained in putting down protests far from Tehran in Iran's ethnic minority regions, a growing source of opposition to the Islamic republic.

Like the old Soviet Union, Iran is still in many ways an empire. Ethnic Persians account for only 50 percent of the population, and there are substantial minorities of Azeris, Kurds, Arabs, and Baluch, as well as hundreds of smaller ethnic and tribal groups overlapping Iran's borders with Iraq, Turkey, Azerbaijan, Afghanistan, and Pakistan. Most of these regions enjoyed considerable autonomy until the rise of the Pahlavi dynasty in the early part of the twentieth century. Reza Shah acquired power in large part as a result of his success in conquering ethnic domains, and he sought to centralize authority in Tehran. His son, Mohammad Reza, continued the pattern and glorified Persian nationalism, Iran's pre-Islamic history, and its "Aryan" identity. As a result, ethnic minority activists avidly joined the revolution, only to be bitterly disappointed after 1979, when the new Islamic government continued the same policies of Persian chauvinism and repression.

Among the poorest and most deprived segment of society are ethnic Arabs, who are concentrated in the western province of Khuzestan, where most of Iran's oil is located. According to Amnesty International, Iranian Arabs, who make up between 3 and 8 percent of the population, lag behind ethnic Persians in terms of education, access to running water, and electricity.[10] Water is frequently diverted from the Karoun River in Khuzestan's capital of Ahvaz to the ethnic Persian cities of Isfahan and Sanandaj. Karim Abdian, director of a U.S.-based foundation that promotes Iranian Arab rights, said that Khuzestan ranks twenty-sixth out of Iran's twenty-nine provinces in terms of poverty, and that only 10 percent of jobs in the oil industry go to ethnic Arabs. Despite its championing of Arab causes elsewhere, such as the Palestinian issue, the Iranian government has appointed Persians to all senior positions in Khuzestan and is trying to displace Arabs and transfer more Persians into the province to dilute its ethnic character. Ab-

dian said that the Tehran government had launched a program of ethnic cleansing that aimed to reduce the Arab population of Khuzestan
from 70 percent to no more than one third over ten years. Riots broke
out in 2005 after the leak of a government document authorizing the
population transfer, and there have been a series of attacks on Iranian
oil installations and bombings in Khuzestan. The Tehran government
has blamed the unrest on British troops across the border in Iraq but
presented no evidence to back up its claims.

Repression has worsened since the June 2005 election of Ahmadinejad, Abdian said. At least under the Khatami government Arabs were
allowed to form their own political party—*Al Wafagh* (Solidarity)—to
run in municipal elections and to publish a newspaper in Arabic. "Ahmadinejad came and all of that ended," said Abdian, a U.S.-educated
aerospace engineer who keeps up ties with activists at home. *Al Wafagh,*
which seeks a federal system in Iran, was forced to go underground,
and thousands of activists have been arrested, but that has not suppressed unrest. On January 23, 2006, two bombs went off in Ahvaz just
before the Iranian president was to visit the city. He canceled his trip,
citing bad weather.[11]

There were also reports in late December 2005 that Ahmadinejad
survived an assassination attempt in the southeast province of Sistan-
Baluchistan across the border from Pakistan. Iranian officials acknowledged that a driver and a Revolutionary Guardsman who were part of
an advance security contingent for a presidential visit were killed, but
blamed the deaths on drug smugglers common in the region.[12] Baluch,
who make up about 2 percent of Iran's population, are Sunni Muslims
with ties to members of the same ethnic group in Afghanistan and
Pakistan. Iranian Baluch have joined several militant organizations, including the so-called Armed Sunni Opposition, headquartered in Pe-
shawar, Pakistan. Founded in the mid-1980s during the Pakistani- and
U.S.-backed Afghan rebellion against Soviet occupation, the group
maintained a training camp for Iranian Sunnis in the frontier region at
the intersection of Afghanistan, Pakistan, and Iran.[13] Another militant
group called Jondollah has skirmished with the Iranian army and
seized hostages to dramatize the plight of the Baluch. The commander
of Jondollah, Abol-Malek Rigi, accused the Tehran government of
killing Baluch Sunni clerics, branding them as foreign agents, and arresting and torturing others who spoke out in favor of civil rights.[14]

"We realized that there is no other way than to take up arms," he said in a 2006 interview posted on an Iranian expatriate Web site. He denied, however, that his group sought to break the province away from Iran and join it to Pakistan's Baluchistan region. "We are Iranians," he said. "We do not want to destroy the national unity and the territorial integrity of the country."[15]

The Baluch are among Iran's Sunni Muslim minority, which comprises about 9 percent of the population and complains bitterly of religious discrimination. Article 12 of the Iranian constitution establishes so-called Twelver Shiism as the state religion of Iran and puts Sunnis in the same category as Zoroastrians, followers of Iran's pre-Islamic faith, Christians, and Jews. In fact, Sunnis often face worse treatment than non-Muslims. Although there are numerous churches in Tehran, for example, there is not a single Sunni mosque in the Iranian capital. In 1994, the local government in the Shiite shrine city of Mashhad destroyed a major Sunni mosque, triggering riots and bombings in Mashhad and Zahedan, capitals of two eastern border provinces that have Sunni majorities.[16]

Sunnis also predominate in Iranian Kurdistan, one of the nation's most restive areas. Kurds, who live primarily in mountainous regions in Iran, Iraq, Syria, and Turkey, are the world's largest ethnic group without their own country—about 30 million people, of whom about 6 million live in Iran. The Kurds have had difficulty with the governments of all the countries in which they live. Iraqi Kurds were in near constant rebellion against Saddam's Iraq before they achieved autonomy thanks to U.S. intervention in 1991 at the end of the first Gulf war. Kurdish dissidents have been blamed for bombings in the Syrian capital, Damascus. Turkey has long battled a violent Kurdish insurgency and claims that Kurdish terrorists are using northern Iraq as a safe haven. Iran also accuses its Kurdish dissidents of using autonomous Iraqi Kurdistan as a base for opposition to the Iranian government.

Kurdish grievances against Iran go back to the nineteenth century, when Iranian monarchs suppressed uprisings in the Kurds' mountainous homeland. The Kurds have also been pawns in disputes between neighboring states. In the early 1970s, the shah—with the assistance of the CIA—backed Iraqi Kurds in their insurgency against Baghdad, then abandoned the Kurds in 1975 after he reached an agreement with Saddam that gave Iran territorial concessions in the Shatt al-Arab waterway that leads into the Persian Gulf. After the shah was overthrown in 1979, Kurdish groups staged a bloody rebellion that was crushed in 1981 by a combined force of the Iranian army and the Revolutionary Guards.[17] The conflict continued between the Iranian regime and Kurds in exile; Iranian intelligence agents are alleged to have assassinated Iranian Kurdish opposition leaders in Vienna and Berlin in 1989 and 1992.

Like other ethnic minorities in Iran, Kurds complain that they are neglected when it comes to government spending on housing, water, electricity, and education.[18] Protests broke out following Ahmadinejad's election in 2005 and triggered weeks of rioting after Iranian police shot and killed Shivan Qaderi, a Kurdish dissident leader, and dragged his body through the streets of Mahabad in northwestern Iran. As many as twenty other people were killed.[19] Iranian security forces have also sustained casualties in clashes with Kurds. A group called the Kurdistan Independent Life Party, affiliated with an anti-Turkish Kurdish guerilla organization, has staged attacks in Iran since 2004, killing more than one hundred members of the Iranian security services.[20] The Bush administration has shown some interest in encouraging ethnic opposition to the Iranian government. The leaders of two parties, the Kurdish Democratic Party of Iran and the Komala (Kurdish Workers' Socialist) Party of Iran, sent their leaders to a conference of Iranian ethnic dissidents in Washington in May 2006. Abdullah Muhtadi, the leader of the Komala Party, called for autonomy for Iranian Kurdistan and the creation of a "broad democratic coalition that fights for democracy, secularism, human rights, women's rights and nationalities' rights."[21]

The largest and most assimilated ethnic minority in Iran is the Azeris—Turkish-speaking residents of the Iranian province of Azerbaijan adjacent to the former Soviet republic of the same name. Russia conquered northern Azerbaijan in the nineteenth century and the two parts were briefly united under Soviet control during World War II; Moscow was forced by the United States and Britain to relinquish the southern portion in 1946. Comprising about a quarter of the Iranian population, Azeris are Shiite Muslims and are relatively well integrated into society. Supreme leader Khamenei is of Azeri origin, for example. A small minority of Iranian Azeris favors union with the independent republic of Azerbaijan; most would settle for greater autonomy and official support for education in the Azeri Turkish language. Azeris would also like an end to what they regard as patronizing treatment by ethnic Persians who make Azeris the butt of jokes—rather like Polish-Americans used to be treated in the United States. The phrase *"Torki kar"*—"Turkish donkey"—is a common pejorative among Persians, and when Iranian movies want to depict people of lesser intelligence, they are shown speaking Turkish.[22] In May 2006, publication of a cartoon in an Iranian official newspaper showing a cockroach speaking Azeri sparked demonstrations in Tabriz, the provincial capital, and other Azeri cities. Iranian security forces responded brutally, killing at least four people, injuring more than forty, and arresting hundreds.[23] The Iranian government apologized for the offensive cartoon, suspended publication of the paper, *Iran,* and jailed the cartoonist and an editor.

U.S. opponents of the Iranian government, such as Michael Ledeen, have suggested that these minorities may be the key to overturning the regime. Others doubt that ethnic unrest alone would trigger regime change. "The government has done a really good job of pissing off the Azeris, the Baluch, and the Kurds," said Patrick Clawson, of the Washington Institute for Near East Policy. "But the demands are much more for civil and religious rights than to break away. It takes real incompetence to make this a threat. This should not be a problem."

Abdian, the Arab activist, said ethnic minorities were the only opposition groups that could bring tens of thousands of supporters into the streets. He was skeptical, however, about the ability of ethnic Persian regime opponents to work with minorities and said that these groups, having been betrayed after the Islamic revolution, would not allow themselves to be used again. "This experience will prevent us from participating in any coalition unless the platform for federalism is clear. Anything else will end up with the disintegration of Iran or another dictatorship," he said. That has not kept the Bush administration from seeking to use Iranian minorities to pressure the Tehran regime, or ethnic groups from asking for help from Washington. Abdian said he had applied for U.S. government funds to broadcast in Arabic into Khuzestan. U.S. officials have met frequently with Iranian Kurdish dissidents in Iraqi Kurdistan and are said to be encouraging them to step up insurgent activities on the Iranian border.[24] ABC News reported in April 2007 that the Bush administration had been secretly aiding the Baluch dissident group, Jondollah, laundering funds through Europe.[25]

THE MUJAHEDIN

If words alone could bring down a government, Mohammad Mohadessin would be in Tehran celebrating the end of the Islamic republic. Instead, Mohadessin spends his time in a Paris suburb, Auvers-sur-Oise, that serves as headquarters for the National Council of Resistance, the political wing of the Mujahedin e-Khalq (MEK), or People's Holy Warriors. The MEK is on the State Department's terrorism list for bombings and assassinations carried out in Iran and attacks that killed six Americans in Tehran in the 1970s, but the Bush administration has had an ambigious attitude toward the group. Mohadessin's mission is to get the MEK off the terrorism list so that it can openly solicit support for its campaign against the Iranian regime.

I met Mohadessin in Paris in the winter of 2005. I was flying to Tehran the next day and wanted to make sure that I got the MEK's side of the story before I heard Iran's views about the controversial group. We talked for more than four hours over tea in my hotel and dinner at a nearby restaurant, and if I had not pleaded exhaustion from jet lag, Mohadessin would have continued for another four hours. By keeping the MEK on the terrorist list, "the message you give is that you prefer the current regime," he said. With his dark suit, white shirt and blue tie, neat mustache, and thinning hair he looked like any middle-aged businessman. Only his determined stare and the almost desperate way in which he pressed his case gave him the aura of a zealot. I had heard that the MEK requires its members to be celibate. Mohadessin acknowledged that he had separated from his wife and two sons in 1990. The MEK obliges its members to live apart from their families and forbids young recruits from marrying or having children to facilitate the struggle against the Iranian government, he said. "Looking from the outside, it may look strange," he told me. "It was not a simple decision for us to make."

Critics of the organization say it breaks up families to facilitate mind control and a personality cult around the leaders of the group—Massoud Rajavi, whose whereabouts are unknown, and his wife, Maryam, who lives in Auvers-sur-Oise. When Maryam Rajavi was briefly detained by French authorities in 2003, two young women belonging to the group burned themselves to death to show their devotion to the cause. The English Web site of the National Council of

Resistance refers to Maryam Rajavi as the "president-elect of the Iranian resistance" and lists a fourteen-point program for Iran, including an end to discrimination against women and ethnic minorities, autonomy for Kurds, and renunciation of weapons of mass destruction.[26] Should the MEK take power in Iran, Mohadessin said, it would set up a provisional government headed by Maryam Rajavi for "no more than six months" and then hold free and fair elections. Many Iranians I have interviewed doubt the MEK would prove more democratic than the current regime.

The MEK remains the best organized Iranian opposition movement abroad, with hundreds if not thousands of supporters in Europe and the United States, and several thousand under U.S. protection and supervision at Camp Ashraf, a military base north of Baghdad. At least until Saddam's overthrow in 2003, the group occasionally managed to carry out bombings and assassinations in Iran from bases in Iraq. Its most spectacular hit came in 1999, when MEK assassins disguised as garbagemen shot and killed Ali Shirazi, the deputy commander of the general staff of the Iranian armed forces and a former commander of Iranian grounds forces in the Iran-Iraq war. The assailants ambushed him outside his home in northern Tehran.[27] In 1998, the MEK killed an elderly bazaar merchant, Asadollah Lajevardi, who had presided over Tehran prisons a decade earlier, when the regime had summarily executed thousands of MEK prisoners.[28] Relatives of those executed appear to form a large portion of the group's base of sympathy and funds. In 2005, a few hundred supporters attended a conference in Washington at the Daughters of the American Revolution Constitution Hall. The room was arranged to look like a U.S. political convention, with signs on poles from various states. The conference was broadcast on satellite television accessible to Iranians and filmed in such a way that it looked as though the cavernous hall was filled when, in fact, it was two-thirds empty.

For years U.S. officials had little interest in the organization. That changed in August 2002, when the MEK revealed the existence of the two key nuclear sites that Iran had hidden from the International Atomic Energy Agency, including the large uranium enrichment facility at Natanz south of Tehran. Mohadessin and his U.S. supporters argue that for intelligence reasons alone, the Bush administration should take the MEK off the terrorism list and enlist the services of its members. "The enemy of my enemy is my friend," said Neil Livingstone, a terrorism expert, at a news conference in Washington in February 2005, announcing the formation of a U.S. lobbying group, the Iran Policy Committee, that advocates removing the MEK from the terrorism list. So far, the Bush administration has not done so, but it has also refused to extradite MEK leaders to Iran and rumors persist, despite official denials, that the Pentagon and CIA have recruited MEK members in Iraq to carry out covert activities against the Iranian regime.

Founded in 1965, the MEK had a major role in overthrowing the shah and is a classic example of a revolutionary organization that lost out in the postrevolutionary struggle for power. Its original ideology— a pastiche of Islam, Marxism, and nationalism—attracted thousands of young Iranians from middle-class Shiite Muslim families who saw joining the MEK as an easier leap than becoming communists. The organization's platform was heavily influenced by Ali Shariati, an Iranian intellectual educated in France who reinterpreted traditional Shiite Islam as a revolutionary movement based on class struggle and martyrdom. The MEK was also intensely anti-American—a common stance among Third World revolutionaries at a time when U.S. soldiers were fighting in Vietnam and the U.S. government supported dictators such as the shah. In the 1970s, the MEK killed six Americans—three military officers serving as advisers to the shah's government and three civilian contractors working on an electronic surveillance system.[29] In our interview Mohadessin insisted that the MEK assassins had been arrested and executed by the shah before the 1979 revolution. Mohadessin also claimed that the MEK had not taken part in the 1979–81 seizure of U.S. Embassy hostages. This despite the fact that when the hostages were released, the MEK condemned the decision as a "retreat" and a "surrender" to the United States.[30]

What is not in dispute is that the organization broke with Ayatollah Khomeini and his supporters in 1980 when they forbade Massoud Rajavi from running for president and began to consolidate clerical rule. The MEK fought back violently, staging massive demonstrations in Tehran and carrying out a series of bombings that killed scores of senior regime figures, including a giant explosion in June 1981 at the headquarters of the ruling Islamic Republican Party that killed seventy-four people, and another bombing in August of that year that killed both Iran's president and prime minister. Massoud Rajavi fled to

Paris in July 1981, but was expelled from France five years later and found refuge in Iraq. His decision to accept Saddam's hospitality and to fight on Iraq's side against Iran in the Iran-Iraq war turned most Iranians against the organization.

Particularly damaging was an MEK offensive carried out after Iran had agreed to a cease-fire with Iraq in 1988. The invaders got only about eighty miles into Iran and were defeated in two days; the regime used the offensive as a pretext to execute several thousand MEK prisoners who had been languishing for years in Iranians jails, some of them arrested as teenagers for merely handing out leaflets.[31] Despite lingering popular outrage over the executions, in six visits to Iran over ten years I have met only one person who praised the group—a taxi driver who said he liked the MEK because it had managed to kill so many proregime clerics. Other Iranians compared the MEK to Pol Pot's murderous Khmer Rouge in Cambodia or to the Branch Davidians, a Christian doomsday cult that literally went up in flames when the U.S. Bureau of Alcohol, Tobacco, and Firearms raided the group's compound in Waco, Texas, in 1993. "I don't know anyone who likes them," Mahnaz, forty-two, a gynecologist's assistant, said of the MEK when I spoke to her in the Jam-e Jam food court in upscale northern Tehran. "They helped Saddam during the war."

Despite the group's unpopularity, the Iranian government appears to regard the MEK as a serious security threat. The regime paid Iraqi bounty hunters four hundred dollars a head to try to capture MEK members after Saddam's ouster, according to U.S. military authorities in Iraq. The Tehran government also tried in 2003 to get the Bush administration to trade MEK members at Camp Ashraf for a half-dozen members of al-Qaeda detained in Iran, among them a son of Osama bin Laden. The Bush administration has refused to forcibly repatriate any of the Iranians. Meanwhile, Iranian officials are incensed that MEK front organizations continue to operate freely in the United States. "Why terrorists who have committed crimes in Iran are not returned here?" Rafsanjani, Iran's former president, asked me to ask President Bush in 2005. "Worse yet, they are permitted to enter your Congress, the UN, and have lobbying and political activities."

When I visited Iran in 2005 the foreign ministry produced six former MEK members who, not surprisingly, described the organization in the most unfavorable terms. It is possible they were exaggerating.

However, their accounts jibed with stories by other former members at liberty in the United States and Europe and were corroborated in one case by relatives. Among the tales I heard, Arash Sametipour's was the saddest. Tall and handsome, Sametipour was born in 1975 and moved with his family to northern Virginia in the midnineties. While attending a community college there, he said he met an attractive Iranian girl named Elham who became "a sort of a girlfriend" and began persuading him to think positively about the MEK. She gave him a free ticket to France to watch Iran play the United States in a qualifying match for soccer's World Cup in 1998, and then convinced him to go to Iraq. Once there, "they took my passport and told me my father had died," he said. They indoctrinated him in the group's ideology and "little by little, pulled me in. There is a saying in Persian: 'Although it's night, some people can convince you it's day,'" he said. After a few months Sametipour was told that he had been selected to carry out a mission and was sent to a military base in Basra in southern Iraq to train. Informed that he was to assassinate a former Tehran police chief, he was given an AK-47 and bullets hidden in a computer bag and sent into Iran through Iraqi Kurdistan. Sametipour was arrested before he could carry out the assassination and tried to commit suicide by swallowing cyanide pills. The pills had lost their potency, so he detonated a grenade, accidentally blowing off his right hand. When I met him in a Tehran hotel he had a plastic prosthetic hand and had just completed serving four years in prison. He was working for an Iranian organization, the *Nejad* (Salvation) Society, that helps former MEK members readjust to life in Tehran. Sametipour was no lover of the regime and said he wished he could return to northern Virginia, where his mother and brother still live. "I had a green card; in a few years I could have gotten my U.S. citizenship," he told me, his young face consumed with anguish. "I ruined my life, but I don't want others to do so."

Other former MEK members described similar tales of brainwashing and sacrifice. Ali Mouradi, then forty-five, said he joined the MEK as the condition for being released as a prisoner of war in Iraq and found "myself in a trap that I couldn't get out of." He said he was moved from camp to camp, forbidden to listen to any radio station but the MEK's, and could not phone or send letters to relatives in Iran. "They told us that whoever goes back to Iran would be tortured and executed," he said.

Ronak Dashti, then twenty, said she had been abducted while in Turkey in 2001 trying to get a visa to go to Italy to study medicine. She wound up at Camp Ashraf, where she said she was forced by MEK officials to sign documents promising not to contact her family, and she lived in a barracks with twenty other girls to a room. She and another former MEK member, Hora Shalchi, described long days of menial labor and guard duty, plus nightly self-criticism sessions that sounded like something out of China's Cultural Revolution. "Every evening from 7 to 7:30 you write a daily report on what you have done that day and what you thought while doing it," Shalchi said. "After dinner, you read the reports before the group and criticize yourself harshly, and then the whole group joins in." Dashti said most of the women she met at the camp were there against their will. "The Red Cross should go inside and talk to them one by one, not in a group," she said. She managed to get out after the U.S. invasion, when her brother, who knew what had happened to her, contacted U.S. military authorities, she said. The Red Cross has repatriated several hundred former MEK members to Iran, and a few thousand remain at Camp Ashraf. Clawson, of the Washington Institute for Near East Policy, said the Swedish Communist Party was also attempting to find asylum for MEK members but without great success.

SON OF THE SHAH

I found few Iranians eager to see Maryam Rajavi rule their country but some support, especially among working-class Iranians too young to remember the monarchy, for Reza Pahlavi, the middle-aged son of Iran's late shah. Pahlavi, who was eighteen at the time of the 1979 revolution, lives in exile in the United States in a Maryland suburb outside Washington. In 2001, he excited considerable interest in Iran when he appeared on Persian-language television stations based in Los Angeles that are accessible in Iran. His appearances coincided with the riots following Iran's loss to Bahrain in a World Cup qualifying match. Young Iranians poured into the streets, chanting, "Reza Pahlavi is our spiritual leader," a taunting reference to Iran's unpopular supreme leader.[32] When I visited Iran a month later the shah's son was still in vogue in some quarters. He "will give us back our rights," said Farshid Jabari,

then a nineteen-year-old student, whom I met on the slopes of the Alborz mountains. Others called Pahlavi an opportunist. "He's sitting
over there enjoying himself and pushing us to the front," said a
nineteen-year-old electrician named Fahid who was jailed for two
weeks after participating in the soccer riots.

Pahlavi told me that he wanted to be a "catalyst" for change, not necessarily to retake the throne, and he has joined others, such as Sazegara
and Ganji, in calling for an internationally monitored referendum on
the constitution and a democratic government based on a separation of
mosque and state. "I've called for people to be patient and be aware that
this will be a complex campaign," he told me in 2001. He added that he
had received surprising support from members of the clergy upset by
their loss in popularity since the Islamic revolution. "The dynamics of
change are just as strong if not stronger than in the 1970s," he said.
"This regime is far less merciful in terms of letting people express their
point of view."

The Bush administration has offered verbal and financial encouragement to a variety of Iranian opposition groups. In 2006, the administration asked Congress for $85 million to promote democracy within
Iran, of which $76 million was approved. However, key figures in the
opposition movement, from Ganji to Reza Pahlavi, have rejected U.S.
money, and several U.S. democracy promotion organizations, such as
the National Democratic Institute, have refused to accept government
funds for fear of tainting themselves and their recipients. "Our way of
operating is to be very open and work with small 'd' democrats around
the world," Les Campbell, director of Middle East programs for NDI,
told me. "If a program comes across as attempting to foster regime
change, that's counterproductive." Most of the U.S. democracy funding
is going to the Voice of America and other U.S. media outlets that
broadcast to Iran, but that has not kept the Iranian government from
accusing its opponents of taking American money in an effort to mar-
ginalize them. Even those who refuse the funds have been the target of
such accusations. "We have a saying in Persian: 'Not having eaten the
soup, my mouth is burned,'" Ganji said.

The U.S. campaign has also been hampered by the absence of U.S.
diplomats in the country, the climate of confrontation over Iran's nuclear program, and the chaotic and violent results of U.S. democracy
promotion efforts in Iraq, the Palestinian territories, Lebanon, and Af-

ghanistan. Where in 2001, Iranians appeared eager for U.S. intervention, and whimsically called for U.S. air strikes to get rid of their "Taliban," referring to the Islamic fundamentalist movement that had ruled in Afghanistan, by 2006, no one I met in Tehran wanted such assistance. A U.S. attack on Iran, instead of helping the opposition, would likely consolidate support for an otherwise unpopular regime.

Iranian dissidents recognize that they have a difficult route ahead of them. The Iranian government has intensified repression of even the most seemingly innocuous groups. In February 2006, the government arrested fifty Iranians who had attended a workshop on nonviolent change a year earlier in Dubai and held two of them in solitary confinement for three weeks. Those arrested had participated in a conference organized by the International Center on Nonviolent Conflict, a Washington-based group that, according to its founder, Peter Ackerman, accepts no U.S. or other government funds. The timing of the arrests appeared linked to Secretary of State Condoleezza Rice's announcement that the administration was requesting additional funds to promote democracy in Iran.

In May 2006, authorities arrested Ramin Jahanbegloo, a mild-mannered political philosopher barely known outside intellectual circles who had visited the United States and other foreign countries, and who had been quoted in an Indian newspaper as criticizing Ahmadinejad's comments about the Holocaust. A hard-line Iranian newspaper accused Jahanbegloo of working for the CIA and the Israeli Mossad, and of trying to promote a Czech-style "velvet revolution" in Iran.[33] He was released four months later. In return for his freedom he gave an interview to an Iranian news agency in which he "confessed" that he had inadvertently become the tool of American think tanks out to overthrow the Iranian regime. He was also forced to post his house and that of his mother as bail.[34] In May 2007, my dear friend and mentor, Haleh Esfandiari, was jailed on similar bogus charges.

So far, the regime has succeeded in repressing its opponents through such tactics. This is not to say that the possibility for abrupt change does not exist. Iranian politics have surprised so-called experts time and again and will likely do so in the future. But absent a dramatic catalyst or the emergence of a new charismatic leader, "the reality is that Iran has a stable authoritarian regime and there is no obvious way to dislodge it," says Vali Nasr of the Naval Postgraduate School.[35] Oil revenues keep a

welfare economy afloat, and Iranians have vivid memories of the revolution, the Iran-Iraq war, and Iraq's "liberation" to dissuade them from
risking their lives to challenge the status quo. Ganji and other activists
say the best way to help the Iranian opposition is by publicizing the
regime's human rights abuses through media that is accessible in Iran.
"We need the help of foreign media to get our message to the Iranian
people," he said. Progress is likely to be slow and to depend on the continued bravery of individuals as well as the modest openings presented
by Iran's restricted electoral system. In 2006, Ganji said he planned to
return to Iran. But a year later, he was still outside, intimidated by a
mounting regime crackdown on its opponents.

TEN

_____

OUT OF SYNC:
IRAN AND THE UNITED STATES

O N A B L U S T E R Y S T. Patrick's Day 2000, an audience of Iranian-Americans, U.S. and foreign diplomats, and Iran policy advocates gathered at Washington's Shoreham Hotel in an atmosphere of excitement and anticipation. Three years earlier, Mohammad Khatami had stunned Iranian and foreign pundits by winning a landslide victory for president. He had called for a "dialogue of civilizations" with the United States, and now, a U.S. secretary of state was making a major attempt to turn that dialogue into a true reconciliation. Madeleine Albright, speaking four days before the Persian New Year, wished Iranians everywhere a happy holiday. Spring "is the season of hope and renewal," she said. It was time for the United States and Iran to put aside their differences and "plant the seeds now for a new and better relationship in years to come."[1]

A year earlier the Clinton administration had softened sanctions on Iran and other so-called rogue states to permit them to buy U.S. food, medicine, and medical equipment. Albright announced a further easing, saying that Americans could now legally import Iranian carpets and pistachios. Much more significant from the Iranian point of view, she publicly apologized for the CIA role in overthrowing Prime Minister Mossadegh in 1953, and for reinstalling the shah who, she said, brought economic progress to Iran but also "brutally repressed political dissent." U.S. support for Iraqi dictator Saddam Hussein, whose 1980 invasion of Iran began a war that killed or injured nearly a million Iranians, had been "regrettably short-sighted," she said, and the United States still had "cordial relations with a number of countries that are less democratic than Iran." Albright went on to list areas of mutual U.S.-Iran interest and potentially greater cooperation, especially Afghanistan, a source of refugees and narcotics that were a huge burden for Iran and, although no one knew it at the time, the breeding ground for the 9/11 attacks. Albright mentioned U.S. grievances with Iran as well, beginning with the seizure of U.S. Embassy hostages during the 1979 revolution. The question, she said, was whether "to allow the past to freeze the future" or to strive for a new relationship. "Certainly, in our view, there are no obstacles that wise and competent leadership cannot remove," she said.[2]

To celebrate the hoped-for breakthrough, a former Iranian diplomat in the audience had worn a sports jacket and knitted tie—a Western style of dress barred to Iranian officials after the Islamic revolution. The diplomat, who had worked for years to try to renew U.S.-Iranian ties, was so elated after Albright's speech that he grabbed my hand and shook it warmly—another Western custom forbidden by hard-line Islamicists at home. Others in the audience were also delighted and believed that Albright's speech marked a major shift in U.S. policy that would be reciprocated by the Iranians. But the reconciliation was not to be. As so often in the past, and perhaps the future, Americans and Iranians were out of sync. By the time the Clinton administration had decided to intensify its outreach to Iran, Iranian reformers were in retreat. Hard-liners controlling the judiciary and police had broken up student demonstrations, banned newspapers, and killed intellectuals, suppressing a Tehran spring the previous year. Only a few days before Albright spoke, rogue members of Iran's intelligence establishment had shot one of Khatami's top advisers, gravely wounding him, and the judiciary announced that thirteen Iranian Jews arrested for allegedly spying for Israel would go on trial the following month. Iranians knew full well the impact the case would have on U.S. popular opinion.

Iranian officials acknowledged positive aspects of Albright's remarks but singled out the negative, especially her comment that despite democratic trends in Iran, "control over the military, judiciary, courts, and police remains in unelected hands." Even though Albright did not mention him by name, her clear reference was to Iran's supreme leader, Ayatollah Khamenei, chosen by a body of clerics who were themselves elected but with limited public influence in the choice of candidates. Two years later, then Iranian foreign minister Kharrazi singled out Albright's remark when asked whether he regretted that Iran had not tried harder to restore relations while Clinton was in office. "I regret that Clinton failed to do better to finish the job," Kharrazi said. "They had some efforts and took some positive positions but mixed those positions with some negative elements. They talked about elected and nonelected elements.... That was considered an intervention in our internal affairs and backfired in Iran."

The phrase had clearly antagonized Khamenei, but the Iranian complaint was more pretext than cause. Iran and the United States are like a once happily married couple that has gone through a bitter divorce. Harsh words have been exchanged—husband and wife have even come to blows and employed others to inflict more punishment. Apologizing is hard and changing behavior even harder. The relationship is unequal, with one side or the other feeling more vulnerable at any given time and afraid that the other will take advantage of concessions. Attempts to reconcile have come to naught, well-intentioned intermediaries have suffered, and unsavory go-betweens profited at the couple's expense. Relatives and friends on each side have argued for and against reconciliation, each wanting credit for restoring the marriage or for convincing the two that they are better off apart.

Ayatollah Khomeini, the leader of the revolution, and many of his supporters clearly preferred that the divorce stay final. Khomeini saw the United States as a Great Satan that had encouraged the shah to repress his people and their Shiite Islamic faith. Relations with the United States would oblige Iran to end its efforts to export the Islamic system, Khomeini believed, and seduce Iranians into resuming decadent Western ways. Still, among the revolution's top officials there were always pragmatic figures who saw reconciliation with the United States as the ultimate guarantee of regime survival. Rafsanjani was paramount among them. He had toured twenty American states in 1974, driving cross-country to visit his brother studying at Berkeley. Rafsanjani told me years later that he was impressed by what he saw. "I found the States a large, developed, and rich country, he said.

Rafsanjani began reaching out to the United States in the mid-1980s, during the Iran-Iraq war, when Iran was desperate for spare parts for its U.S. weapon systems. In his efforts to re-establish contact with Washington, Rafsanjani was aided by an eclectic cast of characters, including intelligence operatives from Israel—which at that time saw Iraq as the greater threat—ambitious and naïve U.S. officials, and crooked arms dealers of uncertain loyalties. The result was Iran-Contra—the scandal in which the United States agreed to trade weapons for American hostages held by Iran-backed militants in Lebanon, and then used the profits to fund anticommunist guerillas in Nicaragua. The convoluted scheme worked in the sense that several hostages were freed, but failed because others were taken to replace them. The story leaked to a Lebanese newspaper, causing huge embarrassment to U.S. diplomats and U.S. allies in the Middle East and innoculating many U.S. officials against dealing with Iran or putting faith in so-called moderates there.

The scandal nearly brought down the second Reagan administration. Among the American officials whose careers were destroyed or derailed by Iran-Contra were Reagan's national security adviser, Robert "Bud" McFarlane and a jug-eared Marine lieutenant colonel named Oliver North. Elliott Abrams, an American neoconservative later pardoned by President George H. W. Bush, pled guilty to withholding information from Congress. In charge of Latin American affairs under the Reagan administration, he was given top positions dealing with the Middle East, including Iran, on the National Security Council of Bush's son. There he argued, for a long while successfully, against offering direct talks with the Iranians. Iranian officials fared better after Iran-Contra, although one individual, a member of the Revolutionary Guards, was arrested and executed for leaking details of the arms transaction.[3] Those who orchestrated the deal emerged unscathed. Speaker of Iran's parliament at the time of the scandal, Rafsanjani became president of Iran in 1989 after helping to arrange then president Khamenei's succession to Khomeini.

IRAN AND THE FIRST BUSH ADMINISTRATION

Rafsanjani's top priority was reconstructing Iran's shattered infrastructure after the carnage of the revolution and the Iran-Iraq war. For this he knew Iran needed investment from the West, and in particular, from the United States. He had great hopes for the first president Bush, who promised Iran in his 1989 inaugural address that "goodwill begets goodwill," an indication that Iranian help in freeing remaining U.S. hostages in Lebanon would be rewarded. Despite sanctions in effect since the hostage crisis barring the sale of U.S. arms and items with potential military use, U.S. trade with Iran in other areas was substantial. U.S. oil companies had become the largest buyers of Iranian oil, a half-million barrels a day, sold by U.S. subsidiaries in Europe.

Brent Scowcroft, national security adviser to the first president Bush, said the administration "had a positive view toward expanding the relationship with Iran," and tried to get talks going. "Businessmen came back saying the Iranians wanted a dialogue, and I said, 'We're happy to do it. We could have it official, public or private citizen to private citizen, any way you want it,'" he told me in 2006. At one point in 1990, he said, the two sides got as far as agreeing to meet in Switzerland, "but at the last minute, the Iranians pulled the plug. There was this reaching around, feeling around, but they were never willing to consummate it. My judgment at the time was that the situation in Iran was delicate enough that nobody was prepared to stick his neck out and actually have a conversation with the Great Satan."

U.S. eagerness for a dialogue caught Bush in an embarrassing diplomatic hoax. In early 1990, a man called the White House saying he wanted to arrange a conversation between the president and Rafsanjani about the U.S. hostages in Lebanon. A date and time for the call were set, and Bush spoke for more than thirty minutes through an interpreter to a man he thought was his Iranian counterpart. The Iranian promised to broadcast a special message on Iranian state radio to prove his desire for a better relationship, but the message was never aired, and Bush realized he had been tricked.[4]

Iran and the United States had skirmished during the latter part of the Iran-Iraq war, after the Reagan administration offered protection against Iranian mines and gunboats to Kuwaiti oil tankers traversing the Persian Gulf. Iran, however, was quietly cooperative during the 1991 Gulf War, watching with appreciation while a U.S.-led coalition of truly willing nations expelled Saddam Hussein's invading army from Kuwait. As his military was pounded by U.S. bombers and missiles, Saddam grew so desperate that he ordered his air force to fly surviving warplanes into the territory of his former foe in hopes he might get them back at the end of the war. But Iran "let us know that the planes would be interned," Scowcroft said. The United States had feared that Iran might use the planes to attack Saudi oil fields.

The success of the United States and its allies in expelling Iraqi forces from Kuwait sparked uprisings against Saddam's rule in the Kurdish north and Shiite south, and Iran allowed members of the Badr Brigade—the Iraqi Shiite militia trained in Iran—to cross the border to support the uprising. The Bush administration also hoped that Saddam would fall, but did not intervene to help the Shiites in part out of fear that the Iraqi central government would collapse, and that Iranian-backed Shiites would create a pro-Iran statelet in the south. This president Bush wanted a weakened Iraq but one with enough military punch to still keep Iran's ambitions for regional power in check. Iran, meanwhile, engineered the release of the remaining U.S. hostages in Lebanon in return for a U.S.-backed UN Security Council resolution blaming Iraq for starting the Iran-Iraq war. But it had taken the Iranians so long to free the captives that Tehran did not get the credit it had expected from the United States.

A spate of Iran-backed terrorist attacks abroad also complicated efforts to improve U.S.-Iranian relations. Iranian agents murdered the shah's last prime minister, Shapour Bakhtiar, in Paris and killed other regime opponents in Vienna and Berlin. One of Khomenei's last acts before his death in 1989 was to issue a fatwa, or religious ruling, calling for the death of Salman Rushdie, the Muslim-born author of a blasphemous (in the view of Khomeini and many Muslims) book called *The Satanic Verses*. No Iranian hit men were ever dispatched, but the fatwa encouraged other Muslims to try to kill Rushdie and sparked outrage in the West.

Bruce Riedel, who served the first Bush administration as director for Persian affairs on the National Security Council, said Scowcroft "engaged in a long process of indirect negotiations with Iran using the United Nations" and came up with the idea of the resolution blaming Iraq for the Iran-Iraq war as a quid pro quo for the release of U.S. hostages in Lebanon. "Afterward the President and Brent very much wanted to do more to open the door to the Iranians and they asked me for options," Riedel told me. Then came the assassinations in Paris, Vienna, and Berlin. It was clear that Iranian intelligence officials "were embarked on a policy of liquidating regime opponents and doing so in a very blatant way so as to intimidate other potential enemies," Riedel said. "I was told to put the options paper on hold. It never got off the ground again."

DUAL CONTAINMENT

U.S. relations with Iran hit new lows and highs under the Clinton administration. In his first term President Clinton imposed a total embargo on economic dealings with Iran, then eased the sanctions in his second term in what turned out to be a futile attempt to restore relations. Before tightening sanctions, Clinton began by ordering a review of U.S. policy toward Iran, and devised a strategy that Martin Indyk, then top Middle East adviser on the White House National Security Council, dubbed "dual containment."[5] Meant to deal with threats from both Iraq and Iran, the policy did not advocate overthrowing the government of Iran but increased economic pressure to convince it to stop sponsoring terrorism, trying to disrupt the Arab-Israeli peace process, and seeking nuclear weapons and ballistic missiles. Indyk, who unveiled the strategy in a 1993 speech before the Washington Institute for Near East Policy, said the United States rightfully considered Iran's regime as hostile. Clinton's first national security adviser, Tony Lake, went on to label Iran a "rogue state," and the State Department for the first time branded Iran as the country most actively sponsoring terrorism.[6]

Then assistant secretary of state Edward Djerejian argued that it was a mistake to lump Iran and Iraq into the same category given the important differences between the two countries. Iraq, after all, had invaded two of its neighbors—Iran and Kuwait—and was ruled by a totalitarian dictator of truly Stalinesque proportions. Iran was repressive but far more pluralistic. " 'Dual containment' was a rhetorical flourish that confused more than clarified," Djerejian told me. "Saddam Hussein was a bad actor who had been a threat to his own people and his neighbors. With Iran, we also had very serious concerns, but there was always the possibility of an opening." Djerejian went so far as to take the "dual containment" phrase out of the speech when it came to the State Department for clearance, but when Indyk delivered it, Djerejian said, "the damn thing was back in."

Indyk said the administration did see a distinction between Iraq and

Iran and was willing to talk to Iran, provided that the discussions were conducted by officials with clear authorization, not shady go-betweens such as Manucher Gorbanifar, an Iranian arms dealer who helped concoct Iran-Contra (and remained a favorite of U.S. neoconservatives). In the first Clinton term, Indyk said, "we never had any direct contact with the Iranians because they didn't want it." Admittedly, he said, the U.S. didn't try very hard. Warren Christopher, Clinton's first secretary of state, had developed a deep distaste for Tehran when he was the top U.S. negotiator for the Carter administration during the 1979–81 hostage crisis. His focus under Clinton was the Arab-Israeli peace process and giving Israel the strategic space it needed to trade land for peace. Israel was particularly worried about Iran's ballistic missile program and suspected that Iran was also trying to develop nuclear weapons. The Clinton administration made strenuous efforts to stop other countries, especially the Russians, from providing nuclear and missile technology to Iran, and tried to persuade the Europeans to limit trade with it unless it stopped supporting terrorist groups.

Iran retaliated for U.S. efforts at containment by redoubling its efforts to sabotage the peace process. Iran gave support to Palestinian militants and seemed determined to prevent Israel and Syria from reaching a peace agreement—at the time the top foreign policy priority of both Israel and the United States. A Syrian-Israeli peace deal would have left Iran without an ally in the region; Syria, ruled by a rival faction of the Baath Party that controlled Iraq, was the only country that came to Iran's defense during the Iran-Iraq war. Syria also provided safe passage for Iranian operatives, funds, and weapons to Shiite factions in Lebanon, in particular Hezbollah. To disrupt Israeli-Syrian peace talks, Iran encouraged Hezbollah to fire rockets at Israel's northern towns. Iranian efforts to wreck the peace process got an unexpected boost when a right-wing Israeli zealot assassinated Israeli prime minister Yitzhak Rabin in November 1995. Iran increased support for both Hezbollah and Palestinian militants, who conducted a wave of suicide bombings in Israel that destroyed the electoral chances of Rabin's dovish successor, Shimon Peres, in 1996.

It was in this dismal climate for peacemaking that the first Clinton administration imposed a total embargo on U.S.-Iran trade and investment, and tried to force other countries to curtail economic ties. It was also reacting to domestic pressures. Republicans had taken control of the House of Representatives in 1994 for the first time in forty years and saw Iran as an issue they could use to batter the administration. Newt Gingrich, the vocal House speaker, pushed for an additional $18 million to be appropriated for the CIA to use to undermine the Iranian government. The money had little appreciable impact on Iran apart from becoming a propaganda bonanza for the Iranian regime and another excuse to crack down on Iranians promoting better ties with the United States. Meanwhile, the American Israel Public Affairs Committee (AIPAC), the powerful pro-Israeli interest group, lobbied to tighten sanctions on Iran, and for legislation that called for punishing other countries if they invested in Iran's petroleum industry.

The Iranians inadvertently helped the sanctions campaigners. In an exquisitely ill-timed move in March 1995, the Rafsanjani government offered a billion-dollar contract to a U.S. oil company, Conoco, to develop two offshore oil fields. The contract was meant to improve U.S.-Iran ties; instead it drew U.S. and world attention to the fact that U.S. companies were still doing business with the Islamic regime at a time when the United States was urging other countries to curtail their own financial interests in Iran. Clinton signed an executive order banning U.S. investment in the Iranian oil industry on March 15, 1995. On May 6, he barred all trade and economic dealings with the country. The following year, Clinton signed into law the Iran-Libya Sanctions Act (ILSA), which called for the U.S. government to penalize foreign companies that invested more than $20 million in the Iranian oil industry.

The second set of sanctions was illegal under international law and caused a huge row with the Europeans. "We ended up with these supersanctions, which were a disaster," Indyk said. "They were the worst kind of policy, because for our containment effort to succeed, we had to have the Europeans onboard." By that time, however, there was little left to lose. Rabin was dead, Peres had lost the Israeli elections, and Saudi terrorists with suspected ties to Iran had blown up the U.S. Air Force barracks at Khobar Towers, Saudi Arabia, killing nineteen Americans and wounding nearly four hundred. U.S. peace efforts in the Middle East had bottomed out, and so had the prospects for U.S.-Iran reconciliation.

THE SMILING MULLAH

When Rafsanjani's second four-year term as president was due to end, the Iranian political establishment chose parliament speaker Nateq Nouri to replace him. To provide an appearance of democratic choice, the Council of Guardians allowed three other candidates to run, including Khatami. His revolutionary credentials were stellar. He wore the black turban of a *seyyid,* or descendant, of the prophet Mohammed. But the way he presented himself during the campaign suggested that Khatami would bring a new dimension to Iranian politics. Handsome and well groomed, in finely tailored tunics and cloaks, he smiled frequently and with genuine feeling. The Iranian electorate, particularly the women and young people who represent a majority of voters, collectively swooned—and chose Khatami in a landslide of 69 percent.

For Americans as well as Iranians Khatami symbolized the possibility of a new beginning. In his inaugural address, he said that Iran was willing to have "relations with any state which respects our independence," and he called for a "dialogue of civilizations" with all nations.[7] He repeated the phrase and explained what he meant by it in his landmark interview with CNN in early 1998. Khatami expressed many standard Iranian government views, for example, calling Israel a "racist, terrorist regime" that oppresses Palestinians, and saying that Iran was not yet ready for direct negotiations with the United States. But he began by sending greetings to "all the followers of Jesus Christ . . . particularly to the American people." He also expressed regret that Americans' feelings had been hurt by the hostage crisis—the closest any Iranian official had come to apologizing for the seizure of U.S. diplomats in 1979. Khatami praised the Puritans who landed on Plymouth Rock as visionary, and called Abraham Lincoln "a strong and fair-minded president." Iran, Khatami asserted, had an "intellectual affinity with the essence of American civilization" because it had been trying for over a century to construct a system based on the same pillars of "religiosity, liberty, and justice." Although Iran was not yet ready for its diplomats to meet American officials, Khatami proposed an exchange of "professors, writers, scholars, artists, journalists, and tourists" to chip at the "bulky wall of mistrust between us and the U.S. administration."[8]

A delighted Clinton swiftly embraced Khatami's idea. In an attempt to replicate the "ping-pong" diplomacy that preceded U.S. rapprochement with China in the 1970s, the administration encouraged five U.S. wrestlers and their coaches to fly to Tehran and take part in an international competition there a month after Khatami spoke. The trip had been in the works before the CNN interview and "suddenly became a mainstream activity sanctioned by both governments," said John Marks, president of Search for Common Ground, a nongovernmental group that facilitated the visit. Nervous at first, the wrestlers—the first Americans officially representing their country to go to Iran since the hostage crisis—were soon bowled over by Iranian hospitality and pent-up admiration. Hundreds of reporters and well-wishers greeted them at the airport when they arrived in the middle of the night on a connecting flight from Germany. During the opening ceremony of the wrestling competition in Tehran's Freedom stadium, the standing-room-only audience of more than twelve thousand cheered and clapped more for the Americans than any team but their own. One of the wrestlers, Kevin Jackson, said he felt like another Jackson (namely Michael, at that time still popular) in terms of the unprecedented attention he and his teammates received. A U.S. flag hung prominently in the stadium, the first time it had been properly displayed in Iran in a quarter century, and not burned in an anti-U.S. demonstration. "I'm the most paranoid of the group, and I've felt more than safe here," wrestler Zeke Jones said afterward. He had brought two sets of singlets—the uniforms wrestlers wear—one plain and the other covered with American flags. After the opening ceremony, he told me, "I'm wearing the one with the flags."

Wrestling is a hugely popular sport in Iran, and the atmosphere in the stadium was like that of a heavyweight boxing championship combined with baseball's World Series. The Iranians had permitted foreign women journalists to cover the competition, overruling a regulation banning women from watching male athletes in their skimpy dress. Iranian fans greeted us warmly and cheered and whistled every time American wrestlers competed. They even cheered when American Shawn Charles defeated one of their own, Mehdi Kaveh. "The people like wrestling very much, and you see it is easy for the Americans here," said Atar Behmanesh, an Iranian wrestling official and sports commentator. When the athletes returned home, Clinton invited them to the Oval Office, to reinforce the message that contacts with Iran were now welcome. The administration also dragged its feet about implementing the Iran-Libya Sanctions Act, which should have been triggered by a $20 million deal signed by French, Russian, and Malaysian oil companies the previous September. "The law permits the administration to examine this decision as long as is necessary," Riedel, promoted by Clinton to top Middle East staffer on the National Security Council, deadpanned at the time. The Clinton administration never enforced the law.

The Iranians made concrete gestures, too. They quietly stopped helping Iraq smuggle oil in violation of UN sanctions, and toned down anti-Israel rhetoric, saying that they would accept whatever decision the Palestinian leadership made about a settlement with Israel. In September 1998, Khatami visited the United States for the first time, and at a news conference essentially rescinded the Khomeini fatwa against Rushdie. "We should consider the Salman Rushdie matter as completely finished," he said. Earlier, at a breakfast for a dozen reporters and editors, he praised Clinton for a speech to the United Nations in which the U.S. leader said those who believe a clash between Western and Muslim nations was inevitable were "terribly wrong." Khatami praised the "industriousness, innovation, and creativity" of Americans, and expressed regret that his visit was short.

The charm offensive had its limits. Albright had hoped to meet her Iranian counterpart, Kharrazi, at a meeting at the United Nations of the so-called Six plus Two. The forum, involving Afghanistan's neighbors—China, Iran, Pakistan, Tajikistan, Turkmenistan, and Uzbekistan—plus Russia and the United States, had been started in 1997 to deal with the growing crisis caused by the ultrafundamentalist Sunni Muslim Taliban movement, which was consolidating control over Afghanistan and imposing a particularly repressive version of Islamic law. Iran had nearly gone to war with the Taliban after the faction captured the northern Afghan city of Mazar-e-Sharif in August 1998, and massacred Iranian diplomats along with scores of Afghan Shiite residents. Two million Afghans had fled to Iran as refugees, and the country was awash in Afghan drugs, compounding a growing drug addiction problem among the young. Rick Inderfurth, then an assistant secretary of state dealing with Afghanistan, said the United States often found itself arguing on the same side as Iran against Pakistan and

Turkmenistan, which were backing the Taliban. "We were working together and for the right reasons," he said. But the Iranians were not yet ready to take the cooperation to a higher level. Then UN secretary-general Kofi Annan scheduled a meeting of the Six plus Two at the foreign ministers' level, hoping to engineer a meeting between Albright and Kharrazi.[9] Albright found herself sitting across a conference table from an important-looking Iranian who she and Inderfurth at first thought was Kharrazi. It was not—it was a deputy foreign minister. "Madame Secretary was not pleased," Inderfurth told me later. The two finally met at the Afghan forum as the administration was leaving office in 2000.

The Clinton administration sought official contact with Iran on other levels and in other settings. Besides the Six plus Two talks, it sent midlevel State Department officials to conferences that Iranian officials were also attending in New York and foreign cities to discuss issues including chemical weapons and narcotics. It gave visas to Iranian film-makers and university professors and permission to Iranian officials to travel in the United States beyond the twenty-five-mile limit outside the United Nations allotted to foreign nationals whose governments lack formal diplomatic relations with the United States. William Miller, a former U.S. diplomat in Iran who worked with Search for Common Ground to arrange many of the exchanges, said the Clinton administration missed opportunities for higher level encounters with Kharrazi and his deputy, Mohammad Javad Zarif. The two traveled frequently to New York for conferences. (Zarif, a fluent English speaker educated at the University of Denver and San Francisco State, was later named Iran's UN ambassador.) Iranians, meanwhile, demanded that the United States take a dramatic practical step, such as ending sanctions on oil investment or unfreezing Iranian assets in the United States, before they would authorize a high-level dialogue. "Khatami expected something concrete and bold," said Hadi Semati, the professor of political science at Tehran University. "He had to be able to sell it to his friends, his enemies, and the supreme leader."

The Clinton administration, mindful of its predecessors' experience with Iran, was wary of offering too much in advance. "My view was 'no,'" Indyk said. "If we can find a way to talk to them, we can work it all out, so if we do something big they'll respond. But we cannot be in the business of making concession after concession after concession

and they keep moving the goalposts, because then we're suckers."
There was a short window in which Khatami might have been able to
act, and it was closing.

KHOBAR TOWERS AND A PRESIDENTIAL LETTER

The Clinton administration faced domestic pressures, too. A major ob-
stacle to any dramatic move by the United States toward Iran was the
1996 bombing of the U.S. Air Force housing complex of Khobar Towers. Steven Simon, the terrorism expert on Clinton's National Security
Council, said Iran was an early suspect, because for several years members of the Revolutionary Guards had been casing U.S. embassies and
other facilities around the world in an aggressive manner that suggested Iran was preparing an attack. The Iranian actions followed
Clinton's cancellation of the Conoco oil deal, the embargo on U.S.
trade and investment, and the passage of ILSA. "From the Iranian perspective, we were at war with them and they were looking for ways to
hit back when the time was right," Simon said. "They got it done in a
way intended not only to kill Americans but to embarrass the Saudis
and drive a wedge between the Saudis and the United States."

Iran-backed Saudi Shiites, members of a group called Saudi Hezbollah, were believed to have carried out the bombing, but the Clinton administration had trouble getting Saudi Arabia to share information
about the investigation. The Saudis and Iranians had patched up their
own diplomatic relations, and the Saudi government was worried that
the United States would retaliate massively if it got proof that Iran was
involved in the attack. The Saudi ambassador to the United States at
the time, Bandar bin Sultan, played a game, Indyk said. "He said, 'You
tell us what you're going to do and we'll tell you what we've got.' We
told them, 'We can't tell you what we're going to do until you tell us
what you've got.' So we were in this absurd argument."

By the spring of 1998, the Saudis had provided enough information
for the Clinton administration to probe more deeply for the identity of
the parties responsible for Khobar Towers and to test Iran's desire for a
new relationship with the United States. In May 1998, according to
Riedel, Vice President Al Gore went to the Middle East and saw then
Saudi crown prince (and acting ruler) Abdullah and relayed a proposal

from Clinton to Khatami to open a direct dialogue. Abdullah delivered the message, but Khatami did not reply. Riedel told me that the Clinton administration also sent a message through the Swiss embassy in Tehran, which represents U.S. interests in Iran, that the United States was ready to talk. It named Riedel, then undersecretary of state Tom Pickering, and David Welch, another senior State Department official, as the team that would represent the United States. Again, there was silence from Tehran.

Clinton did not give up. In the summer of 1999 he wrote a letter to Khatami, the first by a U.S. president to an Iranian leader in two decades, asking for his help in solving the Khobar Towers investigation and opening the door to cooperation. It said that Iran, an ancient nation, and the United States should work together, as two great civilizations, to fight common threats such as terrorism. The letter was delivered by Indyk and Riedel to Sultan Qaboos of Oman at his estate outside Paris. The Omani foreign minister, Yousef Bin Alawi, took it on to Tehran. His instructions, Indyk said, were to hand the letter to Khatami and Khatami alone. But Foreign Minister Kharrazi, who had close ties to Rafsanjani and supreme leader Khamenei, turned up at Khatami's office and was present when the handover was made. When the story of the letter became public the following month, the Iranians denied any knowledge of or responsibility for the attack. A federal grand jury two years later indicted thirteen Saudis and a Lebanese on charges of taking part. At the time, three of the suspects were at-large in Iran, according to Vince Cannistraro, former head of counterterrorism for the CIA.

After much agonizing internal debate, the administration decided not to punish Iran for the bombing. The administration was afraid that the damage would be to Khatami, who had no responsibility for the crime and who had cracked down on the least savory members of Iran's intelligence establishment. Israel also opposed U.S. retaliation for fear that Iran would respond by increasing support for Arab terrorists who would target Israel. Clinton was distracted by his own domestic political problems (he had just survived impeachment for lying about a relationship with a White House aide, Monica Lewinsky) and by the on again–off again U.S. confrontation with the other target of dual containment, Iraq. The administration had already retaliated quietly for Khobar with something it called Operation Sapphire. The CIA outed

scores of Iranian intelligence officers abroad, leading some to be expelled and others to feel threatened. Anti-U.S. terrorism stopped
abruptly after the operation was launched. Years later Indyk conceded
that the Clinton administration had erred in trying to single out
Khatami and somehow separate him from the rest of the regime but
said Americans couldn't deal with officials whom it believed had U.S.
blood on their hands. "Khatami proved to be a false dawn for them and
for us," Indyk said. "When we were ready, they weren't, and when they
were ready, we weren't." Khatami told me that both Iran and the
United States "were a bit too cautious" and should have moved faster to
restore relations while relatively dovish governments were in power in
both countries.

Meanwhile, Khatami and his followers had antagonized Khamenei
and Rafsanjani by pushing too far too fast in opening Iranian society.
Critical newspaper articles accusing the regime of domestic terrorism
were hitting too close to the regime's repressive core. The Iranian establishment had fought back and the issue of U.S.-Iran relations paled
in importance to the new crackdown against just expanded freedoms
of speech and assembly. Relations with the United States became a
nonpriority for Khatami, Semati said. "Both Khatami and Clinton
were prisoners of domestic politics."

A certain momentum had been established, however, and exchanges
between the two countries continued. In August 2000, five Iranian
members of parliament, including the then speaker, Mehdi Karroubi,
met with four U.S. members of Congress—Senator Arlen Spector
(R-PA), and Representatives Gary Ackerman and Eliot Engel (both
D-NY) and Bob Ney (R-OH)—at a reception for an Iranian art exhibit
at the Metropolitan Museum of Art in New York. The Iranians
claimed later that they didn't know the Americans would be there, but
the encounter—the first between U.S. and Iranian legislators since the
revolution—had been carefully prepared in advance.

At the United Nations a month later, UN officials arranged—at U.S.
request—to have Khatami speak soon after Clinton, and the U.S. president stayed in his seat to listen to the Iranian, a clear sign of respect.
Riedel said the U.S. hope was to set up a meeting between the two
presidents, but the Iranians balked. "Clinton was always pushing to
find some way to open a dialogue with Khatami," Riedel said. "He saw

an opening with Iran like getting a deal with the Palestinians or Syria; it would be a major breakthrough to a more stable Middle East."

In a speech eleven months after she left office, Albright said she was sorry that the efforts made during the second Clinton administration had failed to "bring down the wall of distrust" between the two countries.[10] In the aftermath of the September 11 attacks, whose victims, she noted, included five Iranians, she suggested that Iran and the United States could still unite against terrorism, agreeing that "whatever the alleged motive, it is terrorism and wrong to engage in lethal attacks against innocent people." The two countries, which were already taking part in talks about forming a post-Taliban government in Afghanistan, could consider establishing diplomatic relations at a level below ambassador to begin to deal with the many disputes between them, she said. By the time she spoke, however, another administration was in power in Washington, and Albright had joined the swelling ranks of former officials trying to influence U.S. policies from the outside. Iranian officials praised her speech but said it was too little, too late.

ELEVEN

THE WAR ON TERRORISM AND
THE AXIS OF EVIL

Two months and a day after the September 11 attacks, an American Airlines plane bound for the Dominican Republic crashed and burned just after takeoff from Kennedy Airport, killing all 260 people onboard. New York City was already on high alert after the September tragedy, and extra security was in place for the delayed opening of the United Nations General Assembly. In the basement of the UN headquarters on the East River, a meeting was under way of the Six plus Two—top officials from Afghanistan's neighbors plus the United States and Russia—to discuss how to confront the fundamentalist regime that had harbored the 9/11 plotters. The new plane crash had led officials to lock down the UN's iconic headquarters on the East River, and the assembled diplomats feared that terrorists might strike again. Kamal Kharrazi, Iran's foreign minister, handwrote onto his prepared remarks a statement of condolences to the United States and handed it to an aide, who passed it to a member of the U.S. delegation, headed by Secretary of State Colin Powell. "The United States should know that the Iranian people and the Iranian government stand with the United States in its time of need and absolutely condemn these vicious terrorist attacks," Kharrazi had written, according to a U.S. diplomat who saw the document.

Earlier that morning Iranian president Khatami also had condemned the 9/11 attacks, at a breakfast with reporters. "I hope this bitter event will be the last we will have, and that terrorism and hate will be replaced by coexistence, empathy, logic, and dialogue," Khatami said. He praised former president Clinton for taking "a positive step" toward Iran the previous year by slightly easing sanctions and having his secretary of state acknowledge the U.S. role in the 1953 coup that restored the shah to the throne. "It was relatively brave to say that the United States had done some wrong," Khatami said. "This could be the beginning of a new and positive relationship if accompanied by practical steps. In this administration we see the same hostile policies continue. We hope they will change. The change in one policy can completely change the situation. If practical steps are taken, we will have a more positive framework to move in."

According to a U.S. diplomat who worked on preparations for the Six plus Two meeting, the Iranians had let it be known that Khatami would be coming to New York with an unusually large delegation, including Iranian intelligence and Revolutionary Guards experts on the Taliban and al-Qaeda. These people would be prepared to open a counterterrorism dialogue with the United States, the U.S. diplomat was told. But senior State Department officials were unwilling to push for such discussions, the diplomat said. Khatami's request to visit the still smoldering ruins of the World Trade Center to pay tribute to the victims and say a prayer was also turned down as potentially offensive because of Iran's record of support for other terrorist groups.

These rebuffs were among a series of missed opportunities by the Bush administration to build a new relationship with Iran, a rising power in the Persian Gulf whose influence increased in large part due to Bush's own actions. Bruce Riedel, the Middle East expert who remained in the National Security Council for the first year of Bush's presidency, said, "The irony is that Clinton pressed so hard to begin a dialogue and got nothing. Bush 43 [George W. Bush] has had opportunities to talk, and even talks themselves, but didn't want them."

Bitterly divided over foreign policy, the administration struggled in its first term to put together a coherent strategy toward Iran, and seemed to lurch between calling for regime change and demanding that Iran assist the United States in its military actions, or at least remain neutral. The argument was never resolved, and the stalemate favored the status quo of isolation backed by administration hard-liners led by Vice President Cheney. It is impossible to know how the future would have turned out had the Bush administration taken a different course. Iran's own political divisions could well have defeated any U.S. initiatives. Still, efforts at reconciliation could have boosted Iran's reform movement, preventing a consolidation of power by hard-line conservatives. Mahmoud Ahmadinejad might not have been elected president in 2005, and Iran might not be as close to achieving the capacity to build nuclear weapons. The United States could have acquired a strategically situated Muslim ally against al-Qaeda, or at least lessened Iran's motivation to play the spoiler in Iraq, Lebanon, and the Palestinian territories.

Ironically, given the focus the Bush administration placed on confronting Iran in its second term, Iran did not surface as a U.S. priority before 9/11. An article by soon-to-be national security adviser Condoleezza Rice in the magazine *Foreign Affairs,* published during the 2000 presidential campaign, concentrated on the need to defend U.S. national interests by building relationships with Russia and China and avoiding "humanitarian intervention" that would deplete U.S. military strength. The article devoted only three paragraphs to Iran, which was listed last—after Iraq and North Korea—in a final section on rogue regimes. While Iran sought to spread fundamentalist Islam, Rice wrote, "fortunately the Iranians do not have the kind of reach and power that the Soviet Union enjoyed in trying to promote its socialist alternative." Rice also saw Iran in the context of the Republican campaign platform calling for a shift from negotiating international arms-control agreements to building systems that could intercept incoming ballistic missiles. Iran, Rice conceded, posed a problem for moderate Arab states, and especially for Israel, "so defense cooperation with the United States—particularly in the area of ballistic missile defense—is critical." She also noted some positive political trends in Iran after the election of Khatami as president but dismissed the idea of any change in U.S. policy barring unspecified "changes in Iranian behavior."[1]

Powell also barely mentioned Iran at his confirmation hearings before the Senate Foreign Relations Committee. The only reference in his opening remarks was conciliatory, however, and came in the context of the U.S. desire to shore up flagging international sanctions against Iran's old rival, Iraq. "We see a weakened Iraq that utters threats and pursues horrible weapons to terrorize its neighbors," Powell said. "We have seen what they will do, and have done in the past in Tehran" and Kuwait.[2] Under questioning, Powell acknowledged positive political changes in Iran, and said that the United States would try to encourage reform by showing Iranians that they "are not our enemies, that we are trying to make life better for them. . . . I think it serves our interests and the interests of the region."[3] There was no early move, however, to devise a new approach toward Tehran. Asked in 2006 about U.S. policy toward Iran, Ned Walker, who served as assistant secretary of state for the Near East and South Asia until March 2001, said, "What Iran policy? It didn't come up."

In fact, Powell was open to new approaches with Iran but found himself stymied from the start in his efforts to implement a traditional Republican realist policy toward so-called rogue states. He had his head handed to him in March 2001 when he promised "to pick up where President Clinton left off" on engagement with North Korea and resume negotiations on that country's missile program. The White House forced Powell to recant his conciliatory comments the next day, humiliating both Powell and visiting South Korean president Kim Dae Jung. Lawrence Wilkerson, Powell's chief of staff, said the State Department tried to build a proactive policy toward Iran but faced "ferocious" opposition from Cheney, then defense secretary Donald Rumsfeld, and his deputies, particularly Paul Wolfowitz. "The press missed how vicious the fight was in the internal decision-making process. You always got the feeling that Cheney was sitting in the background laughing his ass off because he had succeeded in stopping the statutory process, and what he wanted was no talks with 'evil,'" Wilkerson said. Richard Armitage, Powell's deputy, said Iran was less of a bureaucratic battleground than other issues, such as North Korea, Iraq, and the Arab-Israeli dispute. "We had other problems to worry about, and Iran was such a third rail," he recalled.

One high-ranking diplomat in the State Department lobbied to send a few positive signals to Tehran at the beginning of Bush's first term. Richard Haass, a Middle East expert under Bush's father who became Powell's director of policy planning, led an effort in the summer of 2001 to limit to two years the renewal of the Iran Libya Sanctions Act, which sought to penalize foreign companies for investing in Iran's oil industry. The administration backed him but lost out to the Republican-led Congress, which overwhelmingly backed a five-year extension. Haass also argued unsuccessfully for the administration to drop its longtime opposition to Iran applying to join the World Trade

Organization. "I was looking for modest things that could send positive signals," Haass told me in 2006. "I tried to sell it inside and outside the administration. My argument was that if your goal is regime modification, this is one way to bring it about." Haass said that WTO accession talks would be a "Trojan horse," assisting Iranian reformers in their efforts to integrate Iran into the world economy and to combat economic corruption and inefficiency. "There was sympathy for my position at the upper levels of the State Department, but it was not shared elsewhere in the administration," Haass said. "They looked at me a little like I was Don Quixote. Most people saw this as a loser, to use the technical phrase. I did not make the sale."

Then came September 11. While many Arabs thought the United States had the attacks coming for its long support of Israel and perceived indifference to Arab suffering, thousands of Iranians held candlelit vigils in Tehran in a spontaneous show of support for the United States. President Bush declared a war on terrorism and sought as many allies as possible in its first installment—the battle to topple the Taliban regime that had harbored Osama bin Laden. In an address to Congress on September 20, Bush noted that citizens of eighty other countries had died at the World Trade Center, and mentioned eight by name, among them, surprisingly, Iran.

If the remark was meant as a signal to Tehran, it fell on receptive ears. The Iranian government, which had nearly gone to war with the Taliban three years earlier, saw an opportunity to serve Iranian national interests, be seen around the world as a responsible power, and build on the warming trend with the United States that had started under the Clinton administration. "The general impression was that this was a national tragedy for the United States and that success in addressing that national tragedy was extremely important for the U.S. public in general and the administration in particular," said a high-ranking Iranian diplomat. "There was not another moment in U.S. history when there was more of a psychological need for success on the U.S. part. That is why we consciously decided not to qualify our cooperation on Afghanistan or make it contingent upon a change in U.S. policy, believing, erroneously, that the impact would be of such magnitude that it would automatically have altered the nature of Iran-U.S. relations."

Iran, which, after Pakistan, had the longest border with Afghanistan, brought considerable resources to the table. Beyond allowing U.S.

pilots in distress to land on Iranian soil if necessary, the Tehran government had provided refuge to two million Afghan refugees and had
close ties with leaders of most of the anti-Taliban factions. It was a major supporter of the group that was to become the chief U.S. ally in
Afghanistan—the Northern Alliance, an amalgam of fighters from
groups other than the Taliban's ethnic Pushtun faction, including
Tajik Shiite Muslims. The alliance had lost considerable ground to the
Sunni fundamentalist Taliban in the civil war that followed the ouster
of Soviet troops at the end of the 1980s, but still held 5 percent of Afghanistan's territory in 2001. James Dobbins, who served as the Bush
administration's special envoy for Afghanistan, said that while Russia
and India were also helping the Northern Alliance, "Iran was the most
active."

Iran played an equally if not more supportive role in the diplomatic
arena, helping to craft a broad-based government to replace the ousted
Taliban regime. Dobbins, who represented the Bush administration at
a conference in Bonn, Germany, after the fall of Kabul, said that the
Iranians had been the most helpful delegation and were the ones to
suggest that the draft communiqué call for democracy in Afghanistan
and declare that the new government should not harbor terrorists.[4] A
senior Iranian diplomat who attended the conference said that Iran was
"the only country with very similar views on the outcome" as the
United States, and that they convinced the Northern Alliance to com-
promise and accept fewer ministerial jobs to support the new government of President Hamid Karzai. Iran persuaded two key Afghan
leaders—former president Burhanuddin Rabbani and warlord Abdul
Rabb Rasoul Sayyaf—to stay out of the new government and agree not
to use force against it, said a U.S. diplomat involved in the discussions.
The diplomat said that Iran kept a particularly nasty former anti-Soviet
guerrilla, Gulbuddin Hekmatyar in Tehran, out of Afghanistan, and
used its influence with another warlord, Ismail Khan, to gain his support for the Karzai presidency.

POTATO CHIP DIPLOMACY

Meanwhile, the Six plus Two process that had begun in 1997 to try to
bring peace to Afghanistan's warring factions had been transformed

discreetly into One on One. More than a dozen meetings were held between a handful of U.S. and Iranian diplomats from 2001 through May 2003, alternating between Geneva and Paris. For cover purposes, the sessions were preceded by a meeting under UN auspices at UN offices in Geneva or the Paris apartment of Lakhdar Brahimi, UN Secretary-General Kofi Annan's special envoy on Afghanistan. Then the U.S. and Iranian diplomats would adjourn to the Intercontinental Hotel in Geneva or one of several hotels in Paris, including the Marriott, to chat over nonalcoholic drinks and potato chips. Usually, the meetings took place in the hotel bar, although several encounters were in rooms booked by the delegation leaders, according to a U.S. diplomat who took part in most of the sessions. The meetings were cordial and professional, the diplomat said, and the initial focus remained Afghanistan. At one meeting in November 2001, an Iranian diplomat took out a map of Afghanistan and "actually pointed out where the United States should be bombing," the U.S. diplomat said. The map was sent to U.S. Central Command headquarters in Tampa, Florida, but it is unclear whether U.S. forces took the Iranians' advice.

As allied forces consolidated their victory over the Taliban, the U.S. emphasis in the talks with Iran shifted to al-Qaeda fugitives. In December 2001, Ryan Crocker, a veteran U.S. diplomat who led the U.S. delegation, gave the Iranians a list of five names of al-Qaeda leaders who had disappeared on the battlefield and who might have sought refuge in Iran. According to the U.S. diplomat, the Iranians deported two of them to Afghanistan, and in January 2002, delivered to the United Nations copies of two hundred passports of Arabs caught fleeing Afghanistan whom the Iranians had deported or said they would deport to their home countries.

The talks continued through May 2003 on a monthly basis, with one exception. The Iranians canceled the meeting scheduled for February 2002 in a huff after Bush's State of the Union speech in which he referred to Iran as a member of "an axis of evil." The comment followed the Israeli capture of the ship, the *Karine A*, that the Israelis said was carrying Iranian weapons to the Palestinian Authority. An Iranian diplomat said his government sent a message to the Bush administration through the Swiss embassy in Tehran asserting that the allegations were baseless and that the Iranian government had no knowledge of the arms shipment. However, it is also likely that the Iranian Foreign

Ministry had not been informed of the deal, which appears to have been carried out by Iran's Revolutionary Guards.

Whether the shipment merited Iran's inclusion in the axis of evil is questionable. The Bush administration might not like Iranian support for the Palestinian intifada, but the stated U.S. priority at the time was defeating al-Qaeda, and Iran had provided significant help and was in a position to provide more. David Frum, a White House speechwriter, said he had suggested the notion of an axis but did not know who decided that Iran, which holds regular if flawed elections, should be lumped in the same category as totalitarian Iraq and North Korea. Michael Gerson, who took the word "axis" and added "of evil," said that then national security adviser Rice or her deputy Stephen Hadley provided the list of axis members. Haass said the State Department never approved the inclusion of Iran. However, Armitage said that he and Powell did not object to the phrase. "We removed a lot of things" from the State of the Union speech but " 'axis of evil' was not one that bit me on the ass," said Armitage in his characteristically colorful way.

Rice also saw little significance in the phrase. "I went down to brief [reporters] before the State of the Union. It was our first effort to talk about democracy in the Middle East and to imply that our friends were not doing enough. That's what I thought was going to be the headline of the speech," she told me four years later. "The idea that it was some kind of conscious phrase that was supposed to describe a policy shift is just not right." Rice said she had no idea what impact the remark would have in Iran. "I didn't know what impact it would have in the United States."

Bush defended the wording, saying it would encourage reformers in Iran; instead, it had the opposite effect. Iranian officials had stuck out their necks by publicly calling for dialogue with the United States, and now they looked naïve and foolish. Some saw the remark as proof that no good deed goes unpunished. "It is very strange for us, and shocked everyone, why Americans after all this cooperation in Afghanistan came up with this notion of the 'axis of evil,' " Foreign Minister Kharrazi said in an interview at the United Nations the following September.

A U.S. diplomat who took part in Iran policy formation said that neoconservatives in the Bush administration, such as Elliott Abrams, didn't care if the comment undercut Iranian reformers, because the neocons did not want to do anything to shore up the Islamic system and saw little distinction between Iranian political factions. The remark also served as another rebuke to the State Department in the unending war of attrition between administration hawks and doves in Bush's first term. Only a month before the speech Powell had told reporters accompanying him to Moscow that on Iran, "I am open to explore opportunities." Without revealing the secret talks in Europe, he said, "We have been in discussions with the Iranians on a variety of levels and in some new ways since September 11 . . . there are a number of things going on and . . . we are open to exploring opportunities without having any Vaseline in our eyes with respect to the nature of the government or the history of the past twenty-two years."[5]

The Iranians—no strangers to demonizing rhetoric—swallowed their irritation and resumed the talks with the Americans in March. In the summer of 2002 the U.S. delegation presented the Iranians with a new list of al-Qaeda people believed to have escaped from Afghanistan into Iran. The Iranians promised to do their best, and continued to extradite al-Qaeda suspects to their home countries. Kharrazi told me in September 2002 that "with the long border we have with Afghanistan and Pakistan [that] after the removal of the Taliban, it was very natural for them [al-Qaeda] to look for safe haven. But as soon as we found them, we have arrested them and sent them back to their countries of origin."

The U.S. list was fragmentary and often contained only surnames common among Arabs, according to the U.S. diplomat who took part in the talks. Some of the fugitives were in Iranian Baluchistan, a lawless area along the Afghan border notorious for drug trafficking and other criminal activity. Wilkerson said the Iranians "took care of some" of the suspects but held onto others as potential bargaining chips. Some analysts also believe Iran wanted to hold some al-Qaeda figures hostage to dissuade the terrorist group from attacking Iranian interests.[6] An Iranian diplomat acknowledged that the detention often consisted of "hotel arrest," and that some al-Qaeda figures did not suffer from their stay in Iran. It is not clear how many al-Qaeda members remain in the country or under what circumstances.

The focus of the U.S.-Iran talks shifted again as it became clear that the Bush administration intended to widen the war by invading Iraq. In the fall of 2002, a Pentagon official told me that "preliminary feelers" had taken place between the United States and Iran about dealing with military emergencies during a U.S. war in Iraq. "They made it clear that if one of our pilots went down in Iran, and we came to pick him up, they wouldn't interfere," Armitage said.

In January 2003, the Iranian delegation got a new leader for what turned out to be the final three meetings: Mohammad Javad Zarif, then a deputy foreign minister but soon to be Iran's top UN envoy. According to the U.S. diplomat who participated in the talks, Zarif expressed support for a U.S. attack on Iraq so long as it was not intended as a launching pad against Iran. He also warned that Iraqi military commanders had been instructed to use chemical weapons against U.S. troops. Zarif spoke about the problems the Americans would encounter once they entered Iraq. Zarif talked "about Iraqi society, how the United States was unfamiliar with that society and unprepared for what would happen," an Iranian diplomat who took part in the meetings said. Zarif warned against trying to install a new government in Baghdad, and cautioned that "Iraqis will take matters into their own hands. This will happen and you will accuse Iran of being behind it."

Zalmay Khalilzad, a senior member of the White House National Security Council who later served as U.S. ambassador to Afghanistan, Iraq, and the United Nations, headed the U.S. side for the final two sessions. Khalilzad, in an interview in 2006, gave a similar account of the discussions, but added, "Sometimes people who plan to cause difficulties warn you about it in advance" to deflect the blame. Khalilzad summarized the Iranian view, as presented to him, of U.S. plans to invade Iraq: "On the one hand, we don't support the use of force; on the other hand, we would welcome the overthrow of Saddam's regime."

The final meeting was on May 3, 2003, in Geneva, and by then what Zarif had warned would happen had started to take place. A Sunni insurgency had begun against the U.S. occupation, and U.S. forces failed to bring order to Baghdad and other Iraqi cities. The Americans and Iranians also discussed the Mujahedin e-Khalq (MEK), the antiregime Iranian group that had been given refuge by Saddam Hussein. In earlier meetings the U.S. diplomats had promised Iran that the several thousand MEK fighters in Iraq would be treated as enemy combatants; Iran was furious when the U.S. military signed a truce with the MEK instead and put its members under U.S. protection. The Bush administration was slow to disarm the MEK fighters. Defense Secretary "Rumsfeld's answer was that he didn't have enough troops" to deal with the MEK, Wilkerson said. Khalilzad, in his interview with me, conceded that the U.S. had promised "to do the right thing with" the MEK, but complained that the Iranians had not dealt properly with important al-Qaeda detainees by turning them over to the United States, Afghanistan, or Arab governments. He acknowledged that the administration was not willing to swap MEK leaders for al-Qaeda members—a deal that the Iranians wanted and had expected.

EXPOSURE

According to the U.S. diplomat who participated in most of the Geneva/Paris discussions, the Americans who took part did not take notes or prepare written cables on the talks because "the Bush administration was paranoid about leaks." Cheney's office and the civilian leadership of the Defense Department were vehemently opposed to the meetings, the diplomat said. The attitude was, "We didn't need the Iranians; we can do it alone. It was important in the post-9/11 environment to demonstrate that we were tough and invincible. To work with a terrorist state would be a victory for al-Qaeda." The diplomat added that the Bush administration "didn't want to be in a position where we were grateful to the Iranians or owed them anything," or appeared to be recognizing the legitimacy of the Iranian government. Indeed, the administration appeared embarrassed when the story broke in *USA Today*. Top officials such as Rice went out of their way to downplay the talks; Powell, traveling in the Middle East at the time, said, "The issue of diplomatic relations is not on the table right now for either side." Queried later, Powell said that the Six plus Two "was a useful format" and "should have been restarted." However, an event that took place the night after the talks were revealed gave new ammunition to those in the administration who had opposed the contacts all along. Hours before Powell was due to visit Saudi Arabia, al-Qaeda terrorists carried out bombings in the Saudi capital, Riyadh, targeting compounds where Americans and other foreigners lived, killing thirty-four people, including eight Americans. U.S. officials charged that there had been communications between the Riyadh bombers and al-Qaeda members in Iran, including Saif al-Adel, once the organization's number three.

At the May 3 meeting between the United States and Iran, Khalilzad had told the Iranians that U.S. intelligence was picking up indications that a terrorist attack would occur somewhere in the Persian Gulf. According to the Iranian diplomat who took part in the talks, Khalilzad did not suggest that the attack was imminent or give any other specific details. (Khalilzad said he didn't remember everything he had said, but that the Iranian account sounded "plausible.") The Iranians passed on the information to their government, but Tehran was unable to disrupt the plot. The Iranian diplomat added that as far as Iran knew, the only communication that occurred between those responsible for the terrorism and al-Qaeda figures under Iranian surveillance was "a telephone call from Riyadh saying, 'We succeeded.'"

Paul Pillar, the former chief Middle East expert on the National Intelligence Council, the senior body comprised mostly of veteran CIA analysts that prepares estimates on key intelligence matters, said, "There is a lot we don't know about the nature of possible cooperation between al-Qaeda types and Iranian authorities." However, he said there was no proof of Iranian complicity in the Riyadh bombings. Pillar pointed out that other terrorists have managed to order attacks while in custody—for example, Israel's longtime Palestinian detainee, Marwan Barghouti, who from his prison cell orchestrated suicide bombings in the West Bank. Whatever the nature of the link between Iran and al-Qaeda members in Iranian hands, both the Bush administration and the Iranians decided to cancel their next meeting, which had been scheduled for May 25.

A GRAND BARGAIN?

The Riyadh bombings also undermined the prospects for a far more ambitious initiative, which has been described to me by diplomats from the United States and Iran. An agenda for comprehensive talks between the two countries, it was prepared by Iran's then ambassador to France, Sadegh Kharrazi, in consulation with the then Swiss ambassador in Tehran, Tim Guldimann, who traveled frequently to Washington and was well briefed on U.S. concerns. A preliminary document was refined by Zarif. Following normal diplomatic procedure for passing messages between the United States and Iran, the final proposal was faxed from the Swiss embassy in Tehran to the Swiss embassy in

Washington and hand-delivered by the Swiss to the State Department in early May. It listed Iranian and U.S. aims for negotiations, including all the issues of major importance to the two sides. The Iranians agreed to put on the table their nuclear program, their policy toward Iraq, and their support for Palestinian militant groups, as well as the possibility of accepting an Arab League declaration offering Israel recognition in return for its withdrawal to its pre-1967 war borders. The United States, for its part, would accept "a dialogue in mutual respect" about Iran's concerns, among them a halt in "hostile behavior" toward Iran, the end of U.S. economic sanctions, access to peaceful nuclear technology, a clampdown on the MEK, and "recognition of Iran's legitimate security interests in the region." The paper also outlined how the negotiations would begin, with "simultaneous statements" on the two sides' readiness for a dialogue and a meeting aimed at establishing several working groups, including a U.S.-Iran forum on how to stabilize Iraq.[7]

Kharrazi, nephew of Iran's then foreign minister and brother-in-law of the son of the country's supreme leader, said the proposal had the support of supreme leader Khamenei. "The American government missed a golden opportunity," he told me in 2006.

It appears that the offer was never seriously considered at the highest levels of the Bush administration. A senior U.S. diplomat dealing with the Middle East at the time called the proposal "a very intriguing set of possibilities which some people have termed 'a grand bargain.' " But he said there was no "battle royale" over the initiative within the administration. "It may well be that it was worth taking it another step and testing the proposition, but I don't think anyone could have had their hopes up," he said. "People wanted to see performance on al-Qaeda as a test of Iranian intentions." Asked about the offer three years later, Rice told me, "I honestly don't remember seeing it."

Iranian officials put forward the agenda in part out of nervousness about Iraq and concern that Iran might be the next target of the United States. At the beginning of the Iraq invasion, "Iranians were completely in awe to see that the war they fought for eight years without winning, the Americans completed in three weeks," said Trita Parsi, a scholar who heads the National Iranian American Council, a group that lobbies for Iranian Americans and advocates better relations between Iran and the United States. That sense of awe began to dissipate

as U.S. forces failed to restore law and order to the streets of Baghdad
and other Iraqi cities, and Iraqi Sunnis rose up against the American
occupation. Another U.S. diplomat involved in Iran matters said that
the State Department's Bureau of Near East Affairs lobbied throughout the summer of 2003 for talks with the Iranians on Iraq but faced
opposition elsewhere in the administration. "There was a worry that
we would be manuevered into a grand bargain, that the Iranians were
sneaky and liars and couldn't be trusted. They were seen as the source
of the problem," he said.

The Bush administration also rejected Iranian offers to swap their
al-Qaeda detainees for MEK officers in Iraq. Iranian diplomats complained bitterly in the summer of 2003 that the organization, despite
being branded as terrorist by the State Department, was allowed to
broadcast propaganda into Iran, and to keep light weapons. Armitage
confirmed that there was a battle within the administration over the
MEK. "Some of us took the view that the MEK was a terrorist organization, and others, in the Pentagon, wanted to use the MEK against
Iran," he said. Rice was among those who regarded the MEK as terrorist. Armitage said Deputy Secretary of Defense Paul Wolfowitz and a
top Wolfowitz aide, Douglas Feith, thought the MEK could prove useful against Iran.

Armitage, a barrel-chested, salty-tongued Navy veteran, did his best
to convey to the Iranians that the Bush administration was not out to
topple their government. Asked during testimony in 2003 before the
Senate Foreign Relations Committee by Senator Chuck Hagel (R-NE)
whether "regime change" was U.S. policy toward Iran, he replied in a
booming voice, "No, sir!" The Bush administration hoped to influence
Iran to change its behavior, but "meaningful change has to come from
within," he said. In fact, the White House and Pentagon leadership
were divided about trying to overthrow the Iranian regime, and Armitage admitted to me later that he was "freelancing" when he said
that regime change was not U.S. policy.

HUMANITARIAN HELP

Armitage also reached out to the Iranians, this time with the full approval of the administration, after a devastating earthquake leveled the

ancient Iranian city of Bam in December 2003. He called Zarif in Tehran at 2 A.M., catching Iran's UN ambassador just as he arrived from New York, and offered U.S. humanitarian assistance. Zarif told Armitage it might take him a while to get back to him but returned the call within an hour, Armitage said, and gratefully accepted relief supplies flown in by the U.S. military—the first time such flights had landed in Iran since the failed U.S. effort to rescue U.S. diplomatic hostages in 1980. The Americans were greeted enthusiastically, and the Bush administration tried to build on the gesture by sending a delegation, including Bush's sister, Doro, and Senator Elizabeth Dole (R-NC), the former head of the American Red Cross, but the Iranians refused.[8]

John F. Kennedy once said that success has a thousand fathers while failure is an orphan. In the case of U.S.-Iran relations, it may be the other way around. Scores of people—Iranian and American, European and Middle Eastern, inside government and outside—have tried to bring the two countries together, so far with little to show for their efforts. Former U.S. diplomats, think tank experts, and academics have taken part in endless so-called track two meetings with Iranian counterparts from Greece to Sweden. Among those who tried to persuade President Bush and his top advisers to talk to the Iranians was Brent Scowcroft, national security adviser to Bush's father. An Iranian diplomat told me that the first president Bush also lobbied his son to change policy on Iran, although the former president, in keeping with his standard practice when asked about his relationship with his son, refused to confirm or deny giving such advice.

Armitage concedes that the Bush administration, in its first term, "could have left Iran policy in a better place," but doubts much more could have been accomplished given the cleavage within the administration between hawks and doves. "I would suggest that the demands on the U.S. side, because of the divisions in the administration, were so excessive that I don't think we would have been able to make the compromises necessary," he said. Armitage, who served as a U.S. military adviser in Iran before the revolution, said Iranians then and Iranians now want a relationship with the United States, but not a close embrace. "The shah may have had a smiling face but Iran at heart was a very ethnocentric and hegemonistic country, and I don't think that has changed," he said. "The grin is not so wide now, but their desire is still for a correct or proper relationship with the United States."

Haass, who left the administration in June 2003 to assume the presidency of the Council on Foreign Relations, a prestigious think tank, said he wanted to explore the May 2003 offer but was by then exhausted from losing so many policy battles with the White House and Defense Department. He wasn't sure that the proposal had the full backing of Iran's bifurcated government, and the Riyadh bombings "reinforced the sense that Iran's commitment to terrorism was greater than anything else." Still, Haass nurses many regrets about the administration's unwillingness to test Iranian intentions by continuing and broadening the dialogue at a time when the United States was relatively strong and Iran was nervous about the outcome in Iraq. "This wasn't like laying down a great bottle of vintage French wine and you come back after a couple of years and it was even better to drink," he said. "Left alone, the regime wasn't going to fall. They would have more time to do what they were doing on the nuclear front. It wasn't clear to me that a policy of neglect would prove to be benign."

TWELVE

UNINTENDED CONSEQUENCES AND WHAT LIES AHEAD

CONDOLEEZZA RICE WAS IN a triumphal mood. Baghdad had just fallen and the then White House national security adviser had summoned the top members of the National Intelligence Council to a meeting in the wood-paneled Situation Room in the basement of the West Wing. About 18 people attended the meeting, mostly CIA veterans, together with Rice, her deputy Stephen Hadley, and several other senior White House staffers. Rice, who sat closest to the door at an oblong table that nearly filled the 20-by-14-foot room, opened the meeting with a confident and emphatic prediction. "We're going to fix the Middle East just the way we fixed Europe after World War II," she said.

One of the participants, who recounted this story, said the intelligence officers in the room gasped inwardly, but no one challenged Rice. Rice's belief—and that of President Bush and Vice President Cheney—in the rightness of the Iraq war and the beneficial impact it would have on the rest of the Middle East led the Bush administration to miss or mishandle repeated opportunities to reach out to Iran. Better relations could have boosted the chances to stabilize Iraq and the rest of the region and assisted in the war against the main threat to U.S. security—suicidal Sunni fundamentalist terrorism. By the time the administration offered in May 2006 to talk to Iran about its nuclear program—provided Iran suspended uranium enrichment and the talks included other nations—Iran had been so emboldened by other U.S. policies that it felt little pressure or inclination to accept.

Rice seems to have a habit of forgetting meetings that others consider important. Asked about the session with the National Intelligence Council three years later, Rice said she didn't remember it. The comment attributed to her, she said, conveyed a sense of "chutzpah" and sounded "a bit nuts." She went on, however, despite the benefit of hindsight, to defend the basic premise that underlay the administration's wishful thinking about Iraq and Iran. "To say that this was an opportunity, that Iraq would play the same role or a similar role as a democratic Germany or a democratic Japan [after World War II], that doesn't seem far-fetched," she said.

Many journalists, myself among them, have written about the lack of U.S. planning for the aftermath of overthrowing Saddam Hussein. Not only did the White House and Pentagon not anticipate the utter collapse of law and order within Iraq; they also failed to foresee the beneficial impact Saddam's removal could have on Tehran. This was despite the fact that for decades U.S. policy toward the Persian Gulf had been based on the notion of balancing Iran's Islamic regime against Saddam's Baathist dictatorship. "The whole strategy of the United States after the fall of the shah was to maintain stability in the region by balancing Iran and Iraq off against each other," said Brent Scowcroft, national security adviser to the first president Bush. That was one of the main reasons, he said, why the first Bush administration did not try to remove Saddam during the 1991 Gulf War, out of concern that Iraq would splinter along ethnic and religious lines, and that Iran would be the chief beneficiary.

The second president Bush was so confident that all would turn out well in Iraq that he and his advisers never even asked the U.S. intelligence community to produce an assessment of the likely impact of the Iraq invasion on the region. Paul Pillar, the chief Middle East analyst on the National Intelligence Council at the time, said he initiated such an assessment himself in early 2003 because "nobody asked—there were no requests at all for reports on the region" from the White House. The analysis Pillar presented in January 2003 "threw cold water on the democratic domino theory, that if we had an exemplar in Iraq, it would spread everywhere else." He said the report did suggest that there might be a beneficial impact on reform efforts in Iran if Iraq's Shiite majority was successful in forming a democratic alternative to Iran's clerically guided system. "This judgment was based on a positive outcome in Iraq, and there wasn't one," Pillar said.

At the State Department, Colin Powell, less optimistic about the upcoming invasion, asked Assistant Secretary William Burns and Ryan Crocker, who had led talks with Iran in the aftermath of 9/11, to draft a memo on what could go wrong following a military victory in Iraq. The so-called Perfect Storm memo suggested Iran, Syria, and Saudi Arabia would try to influence the new Iraq, and pointed out the personal connections many leading Iraqi Shiites had with Iran, but also said that did not mean Iraqi Shiites would blindly follow Iran's lead. As was so often the case during the first Bush term, the White House and Pentagon paid little heed to the State Department's warnings. Powell doesn't remember how widely the memo was distributed. Rice told me in 2006 that she recalled "discussions of the potential effect on Iran of Najaf [the Iraqi Shiite holy city] becoming dominant over Qom," its Iranian counterpart, but no conversation about the consequences of failure. Richard Armitage, then deputy secretary of state, said much of the administration viewed Iran through the prism of a successful war in Iraq. Pentagon hawks such as Deputy Defense Secretary Wolfowitz and Undersecretary Feith believed victory in Iraq would weaken Iran's theocratic government, and that the United States "could use Iraqi bases to pressurize Iran," Armitage said.

Indications that the reverse was happening—that Iran was growing stronger due to the turmoil in Iraq—were apparent within months of the U.S. invasion. Iranian intelligence agents and Revolutionary Guards entered the country through ill-defended borders, and thousands of Iraqis who during Saddam's reign had been given refuge—and military training—in Iran returned home. More nimble than the Americans, better able to blend in with the locals, and with much more intimate knowledge of Iraq's political and physical geography, Iranians provided weapons and funds to a variety of Shiite factions, and reconstruction aid and social services from Basra in southern Iraq to the Kurdish north. Iran's goal appeared to be to prevent Iraq from completely collapsing but to encourage just enough violence to keep U.S. forces pinned down—goals it quickly achieved. U.S. officials began complaining early in the war about the Iranian influx but lacked the troops to do much about it, just as they lacked the manpower initially to

disarm the MEK. The head of the U.S. occupation authority, Paul Bre-
mer, had decided to disband the Iraqi army, the only force that could
have guarded Iraq's eight-hundred-mile border with Iran. By 2004, a
report by Britain's Royal Institute of International Affairs had already
concluded that "the real long-term geopolitical winner of the 'War on
Terror' could be Iran."

Meanwhile, Iran's nuclear program was accelerating, in keeping
with one prediction by the National Intelligence Council that turned
out to be correct—that both Iran and North Korea would hasten to become nuclear powers after witnessing the fate of the one country on the
axis of evil that did not possess nuclear arms. The Bush administration,
having ignored the Iranian offer of a broad dialogue in May 2003, left
nuclear diplomacy to Britain, France, and Germany from 2003 to 2005.
After the revelation of Iran's enrichment plant at Natanz in 2002 by the
MEK, the three European countries began a negotiating process to attempt to delay Iran from going nuclear and avoid a third Middle East
war. The talks were the Europeans' idea, Powell said. The White
House and Pentagon were skeptical about the value of the negotiations,
but Powell persuaded his bureaucratic rivals to let the Europeans try.
Armitage said Bush agreed with Powell, but "didn't like it—it
smacked of weakness; you're talking to these guys."

Philip Gordon, a European analyst at the Brookings Institution, a
Washington think tank, called the initial U.S. attitude toward the European negotiating effort one of "malevolent neglect." By not joining
the Europeans, he said, the Bush administration could say " 'I told you
so,' if they fail, while the Europeans could say the talks failed because
the United States did not join them." Coordination was not helped by
the fact that the Europeans' point of contact in Washington was then
undersecretary for arms control and international security John Bolton,
an arch conservative who showed his low regard for European efforts
by once falling asleep—or pretending to—during a meeting in Washington to which *he* had summoned European negotiators. A European
diplomat who took part in the meeting with Bolton, in the fall of 2004,
recalls that the American read a brief prepared statement but otherwise
stayed silent while the Europeans discussed how negotiations with Iran
should proceed. "There was no support from the U.S. government,"
the diplomat said. "They thought our effort would fail and that we
should push for referral to the U.N. Security Council."

Iranian negotiators saw the talks with the Europeans as a useful means of reducing pressure on them and staving off possible new economic sanctions. There are differences of opinion over how serious the Iranians were about reaching a deal. Hossein Mousavian, the former Iranian ambassador to Germany who was one of the top negotiators from 2003 to 2005, saw the discussions as a prelude to broader negotiations that might include the United States and produce economic and political incentives sufficient to compensate Iran for accepting close monitoring of its nuclear program. However, no Iranian official I have interviewed said Iran would be willing to relinquish what it saw as its right to make nuclear fuel. Iran's often expressed view was that it had been double-crossed repeatedly by foreign suppliers, and that it would be foolhardy to accept outside assurances of a guaranteed supply of enriched uranium. Iran did agree to suspend the uranium program while it negotiated with the Europeans, but it continued its research and development work. In what was meant to be a secret speech in 2006, Hassan Rowhani, Iran's chief nuclear negotiator from 2003 to 2005, said Iran had gotten the better of the Europeans by continuing to install equipment at a plant in Isfahan to produce yellowcake, the first step in the process of enriching uranium as a fuel for power plants or bombs.[1] Rowhani was responding to criticism from Iranian conservatives that his negotiators had been too conciliatory toward the Europeans. The Iranian pattern appeared to be one of agreeing to suspend uranium enrichment while trying to master the next technological phase in the enrichment process, then ending talks when Iranian scientists needed to test what they had done.

The Europeans struggled to come up with a package that included sufficient incentives and penalties to have a chance of convincing Iran to restrain its nuclear program for a long period. The European effort got a belated boost from the Bush administration after Bush was reelected in 2004. On his first foreign trip after his second inauguration, Bush traveled to Europe in 2005 and held extensive talks with then German chancellor Gerhard Schroeder and French president Jacques Chirac. With the United States failing to bring peace to Iraq, Bush hoped to mend U.S.-European relations. He realized that U.S. policy toward Iran was isolating the United States instead of Tehran's theocratic government. At the urging of European leaders, Bush agreed in March 2005 that the United States would lift its long-standing objec-

tion to Iran applying for membership in the World Trade Organization, and would allow the Iranians to buy spare parts for its aging fleet
of American planes, if Iran agreed to give up its efforts to make nuclear
fuel. Rice, in announcing the decision, emphasized that the main motive was to patch up U.S. ties to Europe, not to reach out to Tehran.
"This is most assuredly giving the Europeans a stronger hand, not re-
warding the Iranians," she said.[2] The reader may recall that Iran had
been seeking an end to the U.S. veto on its application to the WTO
since before 9/11. In offering the gesture with preconditions, the Bush
administration appeared to be following the Clinton pattern of responding with too little, too late.

At the same time, the contradictions of the administration's first-
term approach to Iran persisted. While demanding that Iran restrain its
nuclear ambitions, Bush continued to make provocative statements in
support of overturning Iran's cleric-dominated system. He had begun
the regime change talk in his first term with the axis of evil speech, as
well as with a statement in July 2002 in support of freedom for Iranians
on the third anniversary of Iran's 1999 student uprising. In his second
inaugural and State of the Union address in 2005, Bush was more ex-
plicit. His presidency, he said, was all about advancing freedom and
combating tyranny; he told Iranians that his administration would help
them achieve that goal. "As you stand for your own liberty, America
stands with you," Bush said.

In April 2005, just after the White House agreed to contribute incentives to the European effort to halt Iran's nuclear program, the State
Department for the first time solicited proposals from "educational institutions, humanitarian groups, non-government organizations and
individuals inside Iran to support the advancement of democracy and
human rights." Iran's UN ambassador Zarif angrily rejected the move
as violating the 1981 accord that freed U.S. diplomatic hostages and
promised that the United States would not "intervene directly or indirectly, politically or militarily, in Iran's internal affairs." The amount
allocated by the United States, $3 million initially, was increased the
following year to $10 million, followed by another $66 million, primarily for U.S. broadcasting into Iran. It infuriated Iran's government
while tainting Iran's struggling reformers—who largely rejected the
funds—as agents of the United States.

In the summer of 2005, the European negotiations with Iran faltered. The Europeans had waited to present a package of incentives until after the Iranian presidential elections in hopes that former president Rafsanjani would win. Rafsanjani had campaigned on a platform of reaching an accommodation on the nuclear issue, but lost to Ahmadinejad. Two days after Ahmadinejad took office, Iran resumed work at a facility in Isfahan, introducing raw uranium into machinery that converts the material into uranium hexafluoride gas.

Ahmadinejad was not the decision maker on nuclear policy; strategy was set by the national security council dominated by representatives of Khamenei and the military. However, Ahmadinejad's ascension coincided with rising optimism in Tehran about Iran's strategic position. Despite successful Iraqi elections in 2005, Iraq was no closer to political stability, and Iran was feeling increasingly confident that it did not have to fear meaningful economic sanctions or a U.S. attack. Iran swiftly rejected the European offer, which called for a ten-year suspension of enrichment efforts in return for vague promises of an external source of fuel and improved economic and diplomatic ties with European states. International reaction was relatively weak, and Iran continued to move forward in the nuclear program, trying to make up for lost time. In January 2006, Iran introduced uranium gas into a pilot centrifuge facility at Natanz, ending a suspension on centrifuge work that had lasted more than two years. The Europeans declared negotiations over and joined with the Bush administration to persuade the board of the International Atomic Energy Agency to refer Iran to the UN Security Council.

I was in Iran when the thirty-five-member IAEA board voted in Vienna, and was struck by Iran's temporary loss of self-confidence. Iranian reporters grilled their government's spokesmen after only Syria, Cuba, and Venezuela sided with Iran at the IAEA, and countries Iran had counted on—including Russia, China, and India—voted for Security Council referral. Even Yemen, a Muslim nation, abstained. Iranian officials responded with indignation to the IAEA vote and cut back their cooperation with the UN watchdog agency, barring short-notice inspections that they had allowed for two and a half years as part of their negotiating process with the Europeans. At the same time, they accelerated new efforts to reach out to the United States.

The outreach had resumed in the fall of 2005 as the Bush administration sought to devise a more flexible approach to Iran, and Iranian officials settled into new jobs following their presidential elections. Rice, recalling the talks with Iran that had followed the 9/11 attacks and focused initially on Afghanistan, authorized the new U.S. ambassador to Iraq, Zalmay Khalilzad—veteran of past talks with Iran—to reopen narrow discussions about stabilizing Iraq. A meeting was scheduled in late 2005, through the mediation of Jalal Talabani, Iraq's Kurdish president. Khalilzad told me he traveled to Dokkan, a resort in Iraqi Kurdistan that Talabani used as a meeting place—a sort of Kurdish Camp David—but the Iranians did not show up. They told the Kurds, who told Khalilzad, that they were spooked when Rice mentioned in congressional testimony the possibility of an Iran-U.S. meeting and the authority she had given to Khalilzad. The Iranians denied the story, however, and in our interview in 2006, Rice made it sound as though the Bush administration had canceled the talks because the Iranians wanted to expand the discussions beyond Iraq. "Word came back that they were prepared to do it, and they wanted to do it, but they wanted a big delegation" to begin a broad-based dialogue, she told me. "That's what derailed it. It was turning into something that was not intended."

The Bush administration, cornered by its regime change rhetoric about Iran and worried about reaction from its domestic critics on the right, shied away from broad talks at yet another moment when they might have borne fruit. In the winter of 2005 to 2006, a consensus appeared to have emerged from the right to the left of the Iranian political spectrum that the time was right for talks, with Iran in a position of relative strength because of high oil prices and U.S. forces mired in Iraq. Following Ahmadinejad's election in June 2005, conservatives controlled all the levers of power and reformers would no longer be in a position to claim credit for a diplomatic breakthrough. Rumors swept Tehran that talks with the United States had already begun in secret. Saeed Laylaz, the reformer and former deputy interior minister, said in February 2006 that Tehran bus drivers had told him that they had seen Khalilzad on the streets of the Iranian capital. "I believe this government is ready to negotiate with the United States, but I'm not sure the United States is ready," Laylaz said.

The high-level interviews I was granted on my trip to Iran also seemed to convey a diplomatic message. If the U.S. administration would not engage, how better to appeal over its head to the American people than through the pages of *USA Today,* America's largest circulation newspaper? My request for an interview with Iran's new top nuclear negotiator was granted in only a few days. Ali Larijani, a bespectacled conservative intellectual with reddish hair and a fondness for European suits who fancies himself the Iranian Henry Kissinger, had succeeded Hassan Rowhani as national security adviser. In our interview he spouted the usual anti-U.S. rhetoric, but also told me there was "no limitation on our side" to negotiating with Americans. "Any country that does not intend on aggressing our rights, we are prepared to talk to them," he said with a wide smile.

I had learned that Larijani was a student of Western philosophy and had written a doctoral dissertation about the eighteenth-century German philosopher Immanuel Kant. I asked him what modern Western thinkers he admired, and out of the blue, he replied, "Hadley." I wasn't sure who he meant at first; when pronounced with a Persian accent, Hadley sounded more like *hedly.* "Do you mean Stephen Hadley, President Bush's national security adviser?" I asked. He nodded and said, "What is really important is his logical thinking." For an Iranian, particularly one who has studied philosophy, calling someone "logical" is as good as it gets, although Hadley did not appreciate the compliment; he joked later that "it almost cost me my job."[3]

Larijani also said that Iran would consider allowing U.S. diplomats to return to Iran for the first time in twenty-six years to process visas for Iranians if Bush would respond favorably to a request in January by Ahmadinejad for direct flights between New York and Tehran. This would have been an enormous help to Iranians, who otherwise had to travel first to Turkey or the United Arab Emirates to obtain U.S. visas, a time-consuming and expensive process. Even Ahmadinejad, in my interview with him, said Iran was prepared to talk to the United States provided the U.S. adopted a more humble attitude toward Tehran. And the Iranian president asked me why there had been no reply to his request for direct flights.

Larijani's aide, former Revolutionary Guards officer Mohammad Javad Jaffari, reinforced the conciliatory message privately, and said that Iran wanted talks with Hadley or a designated emissary at a place and time of the Bush administration's choosing to prepare the ground for broad-based negotiations. The Iranians, it appeared, did not particularly like or trust Khalilzad, a Sunni Muslim born in Afghanistan, and knew he was not authorized to discuss anything other than Iraq. I passed on the message to U.S. officials when I returned to Washington in the middle of February. Other Americans visiting Iran that winter told me they received similar approaches and informed the White House and State Department. So did foreign diplomats. "We were getting pinged in a lot of places," Rice told me later, from the United Nations to Baghdad and the Afghan capital, Kabul, with messages saying the Iranians wanted to talk.

When the Bush administration did not respond, Larijani in March publicly accepted the U.S. offer from the previous fall to talk to Iran about the situation in Iraq. Larijani claimed that he was acting on behalf of Iran's Iraqi ally, the Supreme Council for the Islamic Revolution in Iraq, the Iraqi Shiite party organized in Iran in the early 1980s. Still, it was the first time an Iranian official had agreed openly to direct negotiations with Washington since 1980, when the United States broke diplomatic relations with Iran in the midst of the hostage crisis. Even more significantly, Ayatollah Khamenei publicly blessed the idea of talks a week later—a dramatic step for someone who had up until then threatened Iranians with treason charges just for calling for such contacts. Another of Larijani's deputies, Mohammad Nahavandian, a U.S. green card holder who needed no visa to enter the United States, traveled to Washington in April in hopes of meeting with administration officials but got no appointments.[4] At the same time, the Iranians put together a high-level delegation to go to Baghdad to meet with Khalilzad; the Iranian Web site, *Baztab,* announced that talks would begin April 9. The Bush administration, which had proposed the Iraq conversation to begin with, suddenly got cold feet. U.S. officials said they wanted to wait until Iraq formed a new government and did not want Iraqis—especially unhappy Sunnis—to think the United States and Iran were deciding the country's political future over their heads. Administration spokesmen said they also feared that Iran wanted to use the talks to stave off international pressure over its nuclear program. Iranian friends told me that the public U.S. rejection embarrassed Larijani and weakened those supporting dialogue within the Iranian government. The chief beneficiary: Larijani's rival, Ahmadinejad.

A former Swiss ambassador to Tehran once told me that "Americans play football; Iranians play chess." By that he meant that Americans think only in terms of the next play, while Iranians are planning many moves ahead. Awkwardly for the Bush administration, Larijani announced Iran's willingness to talk to the United States on the same day that the Bush administration unveiled a new White House national security strategy, the administration's first in four years, that reaffirmed Bush's willingness to take preemptive action against rogue states. The White House strategy document put Iran at the top of the list of U.S. adversaries. "We may face no greater challenge from a single country than from Iran," it said. Diplomatic efforts to halt Iran's nuclear program "must succeed if confrontation is to be avoided," the booklet added ominously. It did not specify what would happen if diplomacy failed.

Hadley, asked repeatedly at a press conference at which he unveiled the new strategy whether the United States would talk to Iran, sidestepped the questions. "I think when you talk about saying, well, let's have bilateral diplomatic contacts, you have to ask yourself whether that is going to serve the overall interests or is in fact going to break the international consensus and suggest to Iran that they have an alternative way, other than responding to the demands of the international community. . . . We are going to look at any kind of conversation . . . in the context of our overall strategy of trying to keep the international community together and get Iran to change its policy on the nuclear issue, on support for terror, and on its treatment of its own people. And we will make those kinds of tactical decisions in the context of whether it will advance our overall strategy."[5]

In fact, the administration was preparing to offer to talk about the nuclear program but wanted to couch this shift in a way that would not look like caving. The new security doctrine was part of an escalating rhetorical war against Iran in the spring of 2006. The chief warriors were Rice and Nicholas Burns, undersecretary of state for political affairs, who had replaced Bolton as the Europeans' point of contact on Iran. Rice had told me in an interview in November 2005 that while Khalilzad was authorized to talk to Iran about Iraq, the administration rejected broader negotiations that would "run the risk of granting legitimacy to a government that does not deserve" it. Following the new Iranian overtures in February, Rice announced the administration request for an additional $75 million to support democracy in Iran; Congress approved $66 million. The United States, she told the Senate Foreign Relations Committee, would "actively confront the aggressive

policies of this Iranian regime and at the same time . . . work to support the aspirations of the Iranian people for freedom in their own
country."[6] Burns, a smooth-talking professional diplomat who had
switched seamlessly from defending Clinton administration policy to
Bush's more hawkish views, went further in congressional testimony
the following month. Iran, he said, "is actively working against all that
the U.S. and our allies desire for the region—peace in Lebanon, peace
between Israel and the Palestinians, and an end to terrorism. In fact, no
country stands more resolutely opposed to our hope for peace and freedom in the Middle East than Iran."[7]

Burns gave more details about the democracy-promotion campaign
and said the administration would beef up its Iran desk in Washington
and put Farsi-speaking American diplomats in embassies near—but
outside—Iran. He compared the strategy to the posting of Soviet expert George Kennan to the Baltic republic of Latvia in the 1920s before
U.S. diplomatic recognition of the Soviet Union. What Burns did not
say: U.S. ability to influence the Soviet Union and ultimately bring
down its regime came only after decades of direct contact. Without
U.S. diplomats, students, and businessmen in Iran and Iranians in the
United States, Iran's unpopular theocratic system seemed likely to persist longer than it would otherwise.

Some State Department officials appeared to understand this. In the
fall of 2005, the department prepared a menu of options for Iran, including sending U.S. diplomats to staff an "interests section" in
Tehran.[8] Iranian and U.S. diplomats told me later that the leak of the
options paper to *The Wall Street Journal,* whose editorial page opposed
what it viewed as concessions to Iran, killed the idea. Burns said in the
fall of 2006 that the administration was not thinking about sending
Americans back to Iran. For one thing, he said, the State Department
lacked the appropriate personnel, with only one person still in the department who had served in Iran before the revolution. U.S. strategy,
Burns said, was to "rebuild the institutional capacity of the State Department," training Farsi speakers and stationing them on Iran's periphery to prepare them to "play for the long term."

In early May 2006, Iranian president Ahmadinejad added his flourish to the diplomatic dance: his cheeky eighteen-page letter to Bush.
U.S. officials dismissed the letter as another attempt by Iran to deflect
pressure over the nuclear issue, but others said the administration had

missed a chance to speak directly to the Iranian people. "The Iranians are always interested in talking when someone puts the squeeze on them," then U.S. ambassador to the United Nations Bolton said.

Ironically, Ahmadinejad's letter arrived on the very day that Bush decided privately to change the U.S. position on Iran and agree to talk about the nuclear issue, in company with others, if Iran would suspend its uranium program. Bush was swayed by his secretary of state and a parade of European officials and U.S. foreign policy veterans who lobbied vociferously for a change in the U.S. approach, if only to call Iran's bluff and solidify international opposition to Iran's nuclear work. The Germans were the most outspoken. Foreign Minister Frank-Walter Steinmeier asked why, if the United States was willing to talk to Iran about Iraq, would it not also talk about the nuclear issue. Chancellor Angela Merkel, a native East German who was developing a close relationship with Bush, may have clinched the decision when she met with Bush at the White House in early May 2006. Former secretaries of state Kissinger and Madeleine Albright and Republican senators John McCain, Richard Lugar, and Chuck Hagel also said publicly that the United States should agree to talk with Tehran.

A BIG DEAL

At home alone in her apartment in Washington's Watergate complex on Sunday, May 7, Rice drew a color-coded calendar charting the steps the administration would need to take before announcing the policy shift. The next morning, before flying to New York to raise the idea with European, Russian, and Chinese envoys, she met with Bush over breakfast and won his approval.

"It was a big deal," Burns told me, describing the decision and the way in which the administration orchestrated the announcement. "We thought long and hard about it, and there was a tremendous amount of internal introspection about whether we should do it." He said the administration came to the decision because "it became apparent to us that we were the real issue here, and the only way the Iranians would have an incentive to suspend and negotiate would be if we were part of the equation."

Rice announced the shift on May 31: The United States would take part in talks with Iran, along with Russia, China, Britain, France, and Germany, and augment the Europeans' previous offer of economic and diplomatic goodies, but only if Iran suspended its uranium enrichment program. At a formal press conference in the State Department's ornate Benjamin Franklin room, decorated with seventeenth- and eighteenth-century American antiques, Rice sought to portray the concession—as she had the previous year's turnaround on WTO and airplane spare parts—as less a gesture toward Iran than toward the other permanent members of the UN Security Council and Germany. I asked her whether the new U.S. position gave tacit recognition to the Iranian government and meant that the United States no longer sought to overturn the Iranian regime. "What's being provided legitimacy here is the negotiating process" not Iran's government, she replied. Rice said Iran could decide on "one of two paths": integration into the international community or "progressively stronger political and economic sanctions." She also tried to address the Iranian people over the heads of the Iranian regime, in a particularly convoluted fashion. "The United States looks forward to a new relationship between our peoples," she said. "We sincerely hope that the Iranian regime will choose to make that future possible."

A few days later European Union foreign affairs chief Javier Solana presented a package of incentives to Larijani in Tehran. Dubbed the "elements of a long-term agreement," the three-page document reaffirmed Iran's "right to develop nuclear energy for peaceful purposes" and promised that the parties would "commit to actively support the building of new light-water reactors in Iran through international joint projects." Iran was also promised nuclear fuel, including "a buffer stock to hold a reserve of up to five years' supply," improved "access to the international economy, markets and capital," the "possible removal of restrictions on U.S. and European manufacturers from exporting civil aircraft to Iran," and the "possible removal of relevant U.S. and other export restrictions" on modernizing Iranian telecommunications.

The offer did not include any assurances that the Bush administration would not attack Iran, only "support for a new conference to promote dialogue and cooperation on regional security issues." In return, Iran was to suspend all uranium enrichment activities, commit to answering all remaining questions from the IAEA, and permit the nuclear watchdog agency to resume short-notice inspections of Iranian facilities.[9] The Iranians replied quickly that the offer had positive aspects but postponed a formal answer. When it finally came, in August, it was ambiguous. Larijani said Iran would like to talk but would not suspend uranium enrichment as the price of admission. "We have already said that we would not accept any preconditions," he said.[10]

In agreeing to talk to Iran with preconditions and chaperones, the Bush administration was holding its nose while it stretched out a pinky toward Tehran—the same strategy that failed to stop North Korea's march toward becoming a nuclear weapons state. Rice defended the policy in 2006 in an interview conducted a week after North Korea had shown its contempt for U.S. and international opinion by exploding its first nuclear device. Seated behind a desk in her private cabin on an Air Force jet as we flew home from a five and a half day, round-the-world trip intended to bolster opposition to both Iran and North Korea, Rice said: "I continue to think the best chance for, the word that I hate, 'engagement,' continues to be on the nuclear issue, with the potential for a broader agenda."

That Rice, America's chief diplomat, could not use the word "engagement" in relation to Iran without disparaging it, speaks volumes about the administration's difficulty in meeting a fundamental requirement of negotiating success: showing a modicum of respect for your adversary. Rice seemed both disappointed and surprised that Tehran did not quickly take up her conditional offer of talks. She apparently had assumed that the Iranians would have been bowled over by the fact that a U.S. secretary of state was willing to sit down with them "anywhere, anyplace," as she put it. Iran's view all along, however, has been that the United States would gain as much or more from such contacts as Iran, and that U.S. officials needed to acknowledge this to give negotiations a chance to succeed.

Other seasoned U.S. diplomats found the administration's reluctance to engage Iran directly and without preconditions puzzling and self-defeating. "We should discuss the full range of our relationship with the Iranians, and should have enough confidence in our diplomacy to do so," said Armitage, the former deputy secretary of state. "Diplomacy is the art of letting the other guy have our way." Talks, he told me, "are more than just a matter of exchanging talking points. They are an intelligence-gathering mission, a way of probing each other's positions and exchanging information. They are not necessarily a sign of weakness."

The administration shift, albeit tactical and tentative, provoked fury among neoconservatives who had backed the Iraq war in hopes that it would be a prelude to regime change in Iran. "How is it that Bush, who vowed on his watch 'the worst weapons will not fall into the worst hands,' has chosen to beat such an ignominious retreat?" asked Richard Perle, a former Pentagon adviser.[11]

The war that broke out between Israel and Iran's Lebanese proxy, Hezbollah, in the summer of 2006 appeared to harden positions in Tehran and Washington even as it underlined the potential value of U.S.-Iran talks. The Bush administration accused Iran of instigating Hezbollah's capture of two Israeli soldiers, and the United States backed to the hilt Israel's bombing and ground campaign in Lebanon in what turned out to be an unsuccessful effort to destroy the Lebanese Shiite militia. Iranian media trumpeted Hezbollah's performance, and posters of militia leader Hassan Nasrallah were plastered all over Tehran. "The truth is that Hezbollah . . . proved to the world that the Zionist regime, which had been turned into an invincible giant by Western and Zionist media propaganda, is nothing but a paper tiger," wrote a reformist newspaper, *E' temad Melli*.[12]

There was no proof that Iran was behind the Hezbollah raid, although the timing was suspicious. The Lebanese militia acted on the very day, July 12, that the Bush administration had initially set as a deadline for Iran to respond to the U.S.-backed nuclear proposal. The Lebanon war showed the havoc Hezbollah could wreak on Israel if Israel or the United States attacked Iran. On the other hand, Israelis proved they could take the punishment, and some analysts argued that if Iran was trying to frighten the United States and Israel from bombing Iran's nuclear sites, Hezbollah had engaged in premature retaliation. Hezbollah was judged the winner, however, and appeared to recoup quickly, sending its fighters back into southern Lebanon well in advance of the Lebanese army or international peacekeepers. Nasrallah announced that he would provide homeless Shiites with ten thousand dollars per family each to rebuild, funds collected from wealthy Lebanese Shiite expatriates and, U.S. officials claimed, Iran. The Hezbollah leader also organized mass demonstrations in Beirut in December 2006 in a bid to increase the faction's power in the Lebanese government.

As Lebanon moved closer to a new civil war, Iraq was already awash in sectarian bloodletting. For the first time the Pentagon laid the blame squarely on the Iranian regime, not just elements within it, for Iraq's spiraling violence. In February 2007, unnamed U.S. military intelligence officials displayed an array of alleged Iranian weapons to U.S. reporters in Baghdad and claimed that the "highest levels" of the Iranian government were behind the supply of sophisticated bombs that had killed 170 American and allied troops.[13] President Bush told a news conference two days later, "I can say with certainty" that the elite Qods force of Iran's Revolutionary Guards provided the explosives.[14] While Bush and his new defense secretary, former CIA director Robert Gates, denied any intention to use military force, the Pentagon sent a second aircraft carrier to the Persian Gulf and U.S. troops arrested half a dozen Iranian officials in Iraq. One target—Deputy National Security Adviser Jaffari—eluded them. Rice and Gates suggested these actions were mostly a means of acquiring leverage for talks with Iran. But the administration appeared to be building a case for military action based on the same issues it had used against Saddam Hussein: weapons of mass destruction, support for terrorism, and repression of human rights.

In Washington, members of the foreign policy community nervously speculated about the chances for war with Iran before Bush leaves office. One State Department official told me after the Israel-Hezbollah war that the odds of a U.S. attack on Iran were 50-50. Richard Haass, the former policy planning chief in Bush's first term, put the chances at "2 or 3 out of 10. There is a strong strand in this president that he is willing to do what he believes is right and necessary, and he doesn't much care about the immediate political fallout. The more people say you can't do it or shouldn't do it, the more he's willing to buck the tide if he thinks it is right," Haass said.

The Democratic takeover of Congress in November 2006 and a bipartisan panel's recommendation that the Bush administration open talks with Iran led some Iranians and Americans to conclude that the chances of a military confrontation had diminished. U.S. diplomats finally sat down with Iranians—and representatives from a dozen other nations—in March 2007 at talks on stabilizing an increasingly chaotic Iraq. Ryan Crocker, by then U.S. ambassador to Iraq, met his Iranian counterpart in Baghdad in May and July. But the talks were limited to Iraq, and Iraqi officials were present throughout as chaperones. Meanwhile, financial sanctions imposed by the United States and the United Nations compounded Iran's economic problems and led some in Washington and Europe to argue that Iran could be pressured this way into suspending its nuclear program. Rice, her position strengthened after Bush fired Defense Secretary Donald Rumsfeld in 2006, gave signals that she hoped to emulate Henry Kissinger. Several of her aides compared Iran to China of the early 1970s, when Kissinger orchestrated a breakthrough in relations after two decades of hostility. China, however, was already a nuclear power when it reconciled with the United States. And Iran showed no signs of buckling to Western pressure.

Haass said he doubted Bush would be dissuaded from military strikes if he felt that Iran was getting close to becoming a nuclear power. Bruce Riedel, the former top official on the National Security Council, said Israel might strike Iran first, dragging the United States into a wider conflict. "Don't rule out stupid behavior because it seems idiotic," he told me. "In the Middle East, it is usually what happens."

As of this writing, the United States and Iran appear headed, at best, for a Cold War of nerves and sanctions; at worst, to a conflict that would destabilize what is left of the "old" Middle East. A nuclear Iran is not a pleasant prospect, but a preemptive U.S. attack on Iran might be even more costly. Beyond the impact on world oil supplies and prices, tensions in Iraq, Lebanon, and the Palestinian territories would rise even higher. Questions about the quality of U.S. intelligence would surface, given the failure to find a nuclear weapons program in Iraq. Even if some of Iran's neighbors privately felt relieved, few governments would praise the United States in public, and a new wave of anti-U.S. sentiment would crest around the world. The U.S. invasions of Afghanistan and Iraq already provoked anti-American hatred among the world's Sunni Muslims; air strikes on Iran would incite the Shiites as well. "If we attack a third Muslim country, there won't be a Muslim from Morocco to Manila that doesn't believe we are out to destroy their faith," said Ted Galen Carpenter, vice president of the Cato Institute, a libertarian think tank in Washington.

Flush with petro dollars and convinced that U.S. power is overstretched and on the decline, Iranian leaders may believe they can survive new sanctions or air strikes more easily than Americans can handle four dollars a gallon gas. But Iran would also lose from a confrontation. The price of gasoline and other petroleum products that Iran must import because of a lack of refineries would also soar. Badly needed foreign investment, already in short supply because of Ahmadinejad's reckless rhetoric and economic mismanagement, would dwindle further. While many Iranians would support their government, others would join a growing Iranian diaspora, setting back their country's chances to become a modern nation fully integrated into the global economy and the world of ideas.

In impoverished south Tehran, Mojde Robabei, shopping for buttons in a notions store, expressed the ambivalence many Iranians felt as they watched a gathering crisis beyond their control. "We have a special respect for Americans," the thirty-five-year-old mother of four told me. "When my children watch TV they always say the people of the U.S. are very good but their government is not good." Pulling her *chador* tighter around her, she said she would support relations with the United States if that was what her government decided, or war, if that was the supreme leader's choice. "I would sacrifice myself and my four kids for God," she said. "Bush and the United States should not force their ways on us." Then she added with a sad smile. "We don't want anything bad to happen. Pray for us. We always pray for you."

APPENDIX

IRAN'S 2003 OFFER TO THE UNITED STATES
(with final edits)

Iranian aims:

(The US accepts a dialogue **"in mutual respect"** and agrees that Iran puts the following aims on the agenda)

- ~~US refrains from supporting change of the political system by direct interference from outside~~ **Halt in US hostile behavior and rectification of status of Iran in the US:** (interference in internal or external relations, "axis of evil", terrorism list.)
- **Abolishment of all sanctions:** commercial sanctions, frozen assets, ~~refusal of access to WTO~~ judgments (FSIA), impediments in international trade and financial institutions
- **Iraq:** democratic and fully representative government in Iraq, ~~pursuit of MKO, support of repatriation of MKO members,~~ support of Iranian claims for Iraqi reparations, ~~no Turkish invasion in North Iraq,~~ respect for Iranian national interests in Iraq and religious links to Najaf/Karbala.
- Full ~~a~~**Access to peaceful nuclear technology, biotechnology and chemical technology**
- Recognition of **Iran's legitimate security interests** in the region with according defense capacity.
- **Terrorism:** pursuit of anti-Iranian terrorists, above all MKO and support for repatriation of their members in Iraq, decisive action against anti Iranian terrorists, above all MKO and affiliated organizations in the US

US aims:

(Iran <u>accepts a dialogue "in mutual respect" and</u> agrees that the US puts the following aims on the agenda)

- **WMD:** full transparency for security that there are no Iranian endeavors to develop or possess WMD, full cooperation with IAEA based on Iranian adoption of all relevant instruments (93+2 and all further IAEA protocols)
- **Terrorism:** decisive action against any terrorists (above all Al Qaida) on Iranian territory, full cooperation and exchange of all relevant information.
- **Iraq:** coordination of Iranian influence for activity supporting political stabilization and the establishment of democratic institutions and a non-religious government.
- **Middle East:**
  1) stop of any material support to Palestinian opposition groups (Hamas, Jihad etc.) from Iranian territory, pressure on these organizations to stop violent action against civilians within borders of 1967.
  2) action on Hizbollah to become a mere political organization within Lebanon
  3) acceptance of the Arab League Beirut declaration (Saudi initiative, two-states-approach)

Steps:

I. communication of **mutual agreement on the following procedure**

II. **mutual simultaneous statements** "We have always been ready for direct and authoritative talks with the US/with Iran <u>in good faith and</u> with the aim of discussing—in mutual respect—our common interests and our mutual concerns <u>based on merits and objective realities,</u> but we have always made it clear that, such talks can only be held, if genuine progress for a solution of our own concerns can be achieved."

III. **a first direct meeting** on the appropriate level (for instance in Paris) will be held **with the previously agreed aims**

    a. of a **decision on the first mutual steps**

        ■ **Iraq:** establishment of a common group, active Iranian support for Iraqi stabilization, ~~US commitment to resolve MKO problem in Iraq,~~ US-commitment to ~~take~~<u>actively support</u>

Iranian reparation claims within~~into~~ the discussions on Iraq foreign debts.

- **Terrorism:** US-commitment to disarm and remove MKO from Iraq and take action in accordance with SCR1373 against its leadership, Iranian commitment for enhanced action against Al Qaida members in Iran, agreement on cooperation and information exchange
- Iranian general statement "to support a peaceful solution in the **Middle East** involving the parties concerned"
- US general statement that "Iran did not belong to 'the axis of evil'"
- US-acceptance to halt its impediments against Iran in international financial and trade institutions ~~of Iranian access to WTO membership negotiations~~

b. **of the establishment of three parallel working groups** on disarmament, regional security and economic cooperation. Their **aim is an agreement on three parallel road maps,** for the discussions of these working groups, each side accepts that the other side's aims (see above) are put on the agenda:

   1) **Disarmament:** road map, which combines the mutual aims of, on the one side, full transparency by international commitments and guarantees to abstain from WMD with, on the other side, full access to western technology (in the three areas),

   2) **Terrorism and regional security:** road map for above mentioned aims on the Middle east and terrorism

   3) **Economic cooperation:** road map for the abolishment of the sanctions, rescinding of judgments, and ~~solution of frozen~~ un-freezing of assets

c. of agreement on a time-table for implementation

~~c.~~d.   and **of a public statement after this first meeting on the achieved agreements**

NOTES

1. "DEATH TO AMERICA" AND "CAN I HAVE YOUR AUTOGRAPH?"

1. Reuters, "Iran's Ahmadinejad Says No Need for U.S. Ties," Tehran, June 26, 2005.
2. Shaul Bakhash, *The Reign of the Ayatollahs* (New York: Basic Books, 1984), p. 21.
3. Ali Ansari, *Confronting Iran* (New York: Basic Books, 2006), p. 31.
4. Bakhash, *The Reign*, p. 34.
5. George Jahn, "Iran Threatens U.S. with 'Harm and Pain,'" Associated Press, Vienna, March 8, 2006.

2. IRAN AND THE BOMB

1. David Albright and Corey Hinderstein, "The Clock Is Ticking but How Fast" (brief, Institute for Science and International Security, Washington, D.C., March 27, 2006).
2. David Albright, interview with author, March 27, 2007.
3. John Negroponte, interview with BBC Radio "Today," June 2, 2006.
4. Oly Halpern, "New Estimates on Iranian Nukes," *Jerusalem Post,* Aug. 1, 2005.
5. Anthony Cordesman and Khalid Al-Rodhan, *Iran's Weapons of Mass Destruction* (Washington, D.C.: Center for Strategic and International Studies, 2006), p. 3.
6. Gil Hoffman and Sheera Claire Frenkel, "Sneh: IDF Must Be Ready to Stop Iran," *Jerusalem Post*, Nov. 10, 2006.
7. Patrick Lang, "Iran War Options" (presentation at the Nixon Center, March 22, 2006).
8. Judith S. Yaphe and Charles D. Lutes, *Reassessing the Implications of a Nuclear-Armed Iran*, appendix by David Albright (Washington, D.C.: Institute for National Strategic Studies, National Defense University, 2005), p. 49.

9. Mustafa Kibaroglu, "Good for the Shah, Banned for the Mullahs: The West and Iran's Quest for Nuclear Power," *The Middle East Journal,* vol. 60, no. 2 (Spring 2006), p. 215.

10. Ibid., p. 108.

11. Ibid.

12. Carlos Pascual, "The Trouble with Tehran" (presentation at the Brookings Institution, Washington, D.C., July 24, 2006).

13. Ibid.

14. IAEA Board of Governors report, Vienna, April 28, 2006.

15. Cordesman and Al-Rodhan, *Iran's Weapons,* p. 106.

16. Ibid., p. 107.

17. "Iran Must Not Give in to 'Threats and Bribes': Supreme Leader," Agence France Press, Tehran, June 4, 2006.

18. Ali Akbar Dareini, "Khatami: Iran Ready to Guarantee It Won't Make Nuclear Weapons," Associated Press, Tehran, Aug. 28, 2004.

19. Ali Akbar Dareini, "Iran Defies U.N. Nuke Curbs, Associated Press, Tehran, April 11, 2006.

20. Robert Einhorn, testimony, U.S. Senate Foreign Relations Committee, May 17, 2006.

21. *Shargh* newspaper as quoted by Mideast Mirror (a translation and news digest service based in London), April 12, 2006.

22. "Inside Iran," Reader's Digest/Zogby International poll, May–June 2006.

23. Jamie Glazov, "Iran: To Strike or Not to Strike?" FrontPageMagazine.com, May 19, 2006.

24. Lang at the Nixon Center, March 22, 2006.

25. Ibid.

26. Cordesman and Al-Rodhan, *Iran's Weapons,* p. 351.

27. Yaphe and Lutes, *Reassessing the Implications,* p. 10.

28. Cordesman and Al-Rodhan, *Iran's Weapons,* p. 157.

3. THE BLACKSMITH'S SON

1. Babak Dehghanpisheh and Christopher Dickey, "How Dangerous Is Iran," *Newsweek,* Feb. 13, 2006.

2. International Crisis Group, "Iran: What Does Ahmadi-Nejad's Victory Mean?" (update briefing, Tehran, Brussels, Aug. 4, 2005).

3. "'Street Sweeper' Ahmadinejad Promises New Era for Iran," Agence France-Presse, Tehran, June 24, 2005.

4. Scott Peterson, "Waiting for the Rapture in Iran," *Christian Science Monitor,* Dec. 21, 2005.

5. International Crisis Group briefing, Aug. 4, 2005.

6. Siamak Namazi, "The Iranian Presidential Elections: Who Voted, Why, How &

Does It Matter" (occasional paper series, Woodrow Wilson International Center for Scholars, Middle East Program, Summer 2005).

7. Nasser Karimi, "Iran's President Says Israel Should Be 'Wiped Off the Map,'" Associated Press, Tehran, Oct. 26, 2005.

8. Ali Akbar Dareini, "Iranian President Says Holocaust Is 'Myth' Europe Used to Create Israel," Associated Press, Tehran, Dec. 14, 2005.

9. Karl Vick, "A Man of the People's Needs and Wants," *Washington Post,* June 3, 2006.

10. Bijan Khajepour, "Iran Under President Ahmadnejad" (presentation at Woodrow Wilson International Center for Scholars, June 26, 2006).

11. Agence France Press, "Supreme Leader Vows Iran Will Not Attack Any Countries," Tehran, Nov. 4, 2005.

12. Gareth Smyth, "Iran's Intellectuals Left in Cold by Populist President," *Financial Times,* June 21, 2006.

13. Iran: Full text of President Ahmadinezhad's press conference, BBC monitoring, Jan. 14, 2006.

14. Ibid.

15. Stanley Renshon, "Mr. Ahmadinejad's Mindset: A Strategic Diagnosis." politicalpyschology.blogspot.com, May 10, 2006.

16. Speech by Mahmoud Ahmadinejad in Hamedan as carried by Islamic Republic of Iran News Network Television, June 21, 2006.

17. Ibid.

18. Text of speech by Mahmoud Ahmadinejad at the United Nations General Assembly, as released by the Permanent Mission to the United Nations of the Islamic Republic of Iran, Sept. 17, 2005.

19. Peterson, "Waiting," *Christian Science Monitor.*

20. Roozonline, as quoted by the International Crisis Group, June 30, 2005.

21. Nazila Fathi, "Israel Fading, Iran's Leader Tells Deniers of Holocaust," *New York Times,* Dec. 13, 2006, p. A10.

22. Stefan Aust, Gerhard Spörl, and Dieter Bednarz, "Spiegel Interview with Iran's President Ahmadinejad," *Der Spiegel* online, May 30, 2006.

23. President Mahmoud Ahmadinejad, interview with Mike Wallace, *60 Minutes,* CBS, Aug. 13, 2006.

4. IRANIAN SQUARE DANCE

1. Ali Gheissari and Vali Nasr, *Democracy in Iran* (New York: Oxford University Press, 2006), p. 80.

2. Shaul Bakhash, *The Reign of the Ayatollahs* (New York: Basic Books, 1984), pp. 55–70.

3. Ibid., p. 23.

4. Ibid., p. 38.

5. Nasser Karimi, "Iran's Supreme Leader Says He Approves of Talks with U.S. on Iraq," Associated Press, Tehran, March 22, 2006.

6. Editorial, "Preventing a Full-Blown Crisis," *Iran* newspaper, Feb. 5, 2006, p. 2.

7. Gareth Smyth, "Khamenei Appoints Body to Oversee Iran's Foreign Policy," *Financial Times,* Tehran, June 27, 2006.

8. Bakhash, *The Reign,* p. 4

9. Shirin Ebadi and Azadeh Moaveni, *Iran Awakening* (New York: Random House, 2006), p. 146.

10. Ali Ansari, *Confronting Iran* (New York: Basic Books, 2006), p. 210.

11. Wilfried Buchta, *Who Rules Iran?* (Washington, D.C.: Washington Institute for Near East Policy and Konrad Adenauer Stiftung, 2000), p. 17.

12. Simon Tisdall and Ewen MacAskill, "Iran in Turmoil as President's Purge Deepens," *The Guardian*, Tehran, Nov. 18, 2005.

13. Bakhash, *The Reign,* pp. 242–243.

14. The 2005 Transparency International Corruption Perceptions Index, Transparency International, Berlin.

15. Farideh Farhi, "What Does the Ninth Presidential Election Say About Iranian Politics" (occasional paper series, Woodrow Wilson International Center for Scholars, Middle East Program, Summer 2005).

5. GUARDIANS OF THE REVOLUTION

1. Wilfried Buchta, *Who Rules Iran?* (Washington, D.C.: Washington Institute for Near East Policy and Konrad Adenauer Stiftung, 2000), p. 67.

2. Shaul Bakhash, *The Reign of the Ayatollahs* (New York: Basic Books, 1984), pp. 63, 89.

3. Kenneth Pollack, *The Persian Puzzle* (New York: Random House, 2004), p. 156.

4. Kenneth Katzman, *The Warriors of Islam: Iran's Revolutionary Guard* (Boulder, Co.: Westview Press, 1993), p. 36.

5. Ibid., p. 57.

6. Pollack, *The Persian Puzzle,* pp. 200–201.

7. Ibid., p. 203.

8. Barbara Slavin, "Khobar Is Unsolved, Unresolved," *USA Today,* Nov. 2, 1999, p. 11A.

9. Louis J. Freeh, "Khobar Towers: The Clinton Administration Left Many Stones Unturned," *Wall Street Journal,* June 25, 2006.

10. *The 9/11 Commission Report* (Washington, D.C.: U.S. Government Printing Office, 2004), p. 61.

11. Ibid.

12. Ibid.

13. Ibid., pp. 240–41.

14. Ali Ansari, *Confronting Iran* (New York: Basic Books), p. 187.

15. Patrick Clawson and Michael Rubin, *Eternal Iran: Continuity and Chaos* (New York: Palgrave Macmillan, 2006), p. 147.

16. Michael Gordon, "Iran Aiding Shiite Attacks Inside Iraq, General Says," *New York Times,* June 23, 2006.

17. Katherine Shrader and John Solomon, "Intelligence Gathers Growing Evidence of Terrorists Hiding in Iran," Associated Press, Washington, June 4, 2005.

18. Iranian Student News Agency, "Iran Commander Says Islamic States Have Potential to Become Global Power," Dec. 11, 2005, Federal Broadcast Information Service translation.

19. Katzman, *The Warriors of Islam,* p. 101.

20. "Iran's Conservatives Are Now Underpinned by Military Ideologues," *The Economist,* Tehran, June 17, 2004.

21. Frederic Tellier, "The Iranian Moment" (policy focus # 52, Washington Institute for Near East Policy, February 2006), p. 18.

22. Ibid., p. 10.

23. Siavosh Ghazi, "Arm of Iran Military Set to Enter Energy Sector," Agence France Press, Tehran, June 28, 2006.

24. Ibid.

25. Bakhash, *The Reign,* p. 244.

26. Tellier, "The Iranian Moment," p. vi.

27. Abbas William Samii, "The Iranian Nuclear Issue and Informal Networks," *Naval War College Review,* vol. 59, no. 1 (Winter 2006).

28. Tellier, "The Iranian Moment," p. vi.

29. Ali Gheissari and Vali Nasr, "The Conservative Consolidation in Iran," International Institute for Strategic Studies, *Survival* vol. 47, no. 2 (Summer 2005), pp. 175–90.

30. Buchta, *Who Rules Iran?* p. 125.

31. Ibid., pp. 189–90.

32. Daniel Byman, Shahram Chubin, Anushiravan Ehteshami, Jerrold D. Green, "Iran's Security Policy in the Post-Revolutionary Era" (report by the Rand Corporation, 2001), p. 47.

33. Buchta, *Who Rules Iran?* p. 93.

34. Ibid., p. 125.

35. Elaine Sciolino, *Persian Mirrors* (New York: Free Press, 2000), p. 288.

36. Ibid.

37. Behzad Yaghmaian, *Social Change in Iran* (Albany: State University of New York Press, 2002), p. 122.

6. THE REFORMERS

1. Wilfried Buchta, *Who Rules Iran?* (Washington, D.C.: Washington Institute for Near East Policy and the Konrad Adenauer Stiftung, 2000), p. 163.

2. Abdulkarim Soroush interview with Dariush Sajjadi, broadcast on Homa TV, March 9, 2006, and posted on Soroush's official Web site, drsoroush.com.

3. Robin Wright, *The Last Great Revolution* (New York: Alfred A. Knopf, 2000), p. 35.

4. Shaul Bakhash, "Letter from Evin Prison," *The New York Review of Books,* Sept. 22, 2005, as reprinted by drsoroush.com.

5. Scott MacLeod, "Abdolkarim Soroush: Iran's Democratic Voice," *Time,* April 2005, as reprinted by drsoroush.com.

6. Abdulkarim Soroush, CNN interview, June 1997, drsoroush.com.

7. Mohammad Khatami, *Islam, Liberty, and Development* (Binghamton: Institute of Global Cultural Studies, State University of New York, 1998), p. 14.

8. Buchta, *Who Rules Iran?* p. 142.

9. Ibid., p. 194.

10. Ibid., p. 159.

11. Shirin Ebadi and Azadeh Moaveni, *Iran Awakening* (New York: Random House, 2006), p. 139.

12. Ibid., p. 153.

13. Vali Nasr, "Shirin Ebadi's Troubled History," *The New Republic Online,* June 12, 2006 (tnr.com/doc.mhtml?i=20060612&s=asr061206).

14. Buchta, *Who Rules Iran?* p. 189–90.

15. Ibid., p. 190.

16. Laura Secor, "Fugitives," *The New Yorker,* Nov. 21, 2005.

17. Scott Peterson, "Are Hardliners Taking Aim at Reformists?" *Christian Science Monitor,* Amman, Jordan, March 13, 2000.

18. Azadeh Moaveni, *Lipstick Jihad* (New York: PublicAffairs, 2005), p. 132.

19. Ali Gheissari and Vali Nasr, *Democracy in Iran* (New York: Oxford University Press, 2006), p. 141.

20. Nasr, "Shirin Ebadi," *The New Republic Online.*

21. Crane Brinton, *The Anatomy of Revolution* (New York: Vintage Books, 1965), p. 145.

22. Saeed Hajjarian, interview, *Dowran-e Emrooz* newspaper, March 21, 2001, as translated by the BBC.

7. CHILDREN OF THE REVOLUTION

1. Ali Akbar Mahdi, *Encyclopedia of Islam and the Muslim World,* Richard Martin, ed. (New York: Macmillan Reference USA; Thomas/Gale, 2004), pp. 740–44.

2. Malihe Maghazei, Iran chapter, *Teen Life in the Middle East,* Ali Akbar Mahdi, ed. (Boulder, Co.: Greenwood Press, 2003), p. 22.

3. Behzad Yaghmaian, *Social Change in Iran* (Albany: State University of New York Press, 2002), p. 66.

4. Sanam Vakil, "Iran: The Gridlock Between Demography and Democracy," *SAIS Review,* Johns Hopkins University Press, 2004.

5. *Iran* newspaper, "Labor Minister Gives Youth Unemployment Figures," Jan. 29, 2006.
6. Maghazei, *Teen Life,* p. 19.
7. Ali Akbar Mahdi, "The Student Movement in the Islamic Republic of Iran," *Journal of Iranian Research and Analysis,* vol. 15, no. 2 (Nov. 1999).
8. Shaul Bakhash, *The Reign of the Ayatollahs* (New York: Basic Books, 1984), p. 110.
9. United Nations Office on Drugs and Crime, *World Drug Report 2006,* p. 74.
10. Ibid.
11. Statistics from *Entekhab* newspaper as quoted by Thomas Friedman, "Iran by the Numbers," *New York Times,* June 23, 2002.
12. *Iran* newspaper, "Shadows That Become Taller," Feb. 4, 2005 (Foreign Broadcast Information Service translation).
13. Official Summary of the State of the World's Children 2006, UNICEF, "Iran at a Glance."
14. *Iran Daily,* as quoted by the Mideast Mirror, London, June 22, 2006.
15. Shirin Ebadi and Azadeh Moaveni, *Iran Awakening* (New York: Random House, 2006), p. 149.
16. Ibid., p. 178.
17. Nicolas Pelham, "Iran's Soccer Fervor Turns Political and Violent," *Christian Science Monitor,* Nov. 15, 2001.
18. Ali Akbar Dareini, "Iran Frees Academic Who Was Twice Condemned to Death for Blasphemy," Associated Press, Tehran, July 31, 2004.
19. Michael Rubin and Patrick Clawson, "Patterns of Discontent: Will History Repeat in Iran?" *Middle East Review of International Affairs* (March 2006).
20. Internet indicators, International Telecommunications Union, Geneva, 2004.
21. Lara Sukhtian, "Blogs on the Internet Now Under Attack by Iran's Hard-line Regime," Associated Press, Dubai, March 28, 2006.
22. Ibid.
23. "Inside Iran," Reader's Digest/Zogby International poll, May–June 2006.
24. Ibid.
25. Bill Samii, "Iran: Youth Movement Has Untapped Potential," Radio Free Europe/Radio Liberty, April 13, 2005.
26. Ebadi and Moaveni, *Iran Awakening,* pp. 182–83.

8. THE MULLAHS

1. Vali Nasr, *The Shia Revival* (New York: W. W. Norton, 2006), p. 217.
2. Ibid., p. 218.
3. Roy Mottahedeh, *The Mantle of the Prophet* (Oxford, UK: Oneworld Publications, 2000), p. 74.
4. Ibid.
5. Baqer Moin, *Khomeini* (New York: St. Martin's Press, 1999), p. 4.
6. Ibid., p. 12.

7. Ibid., p. 36.

8. Ibid., p. 19.

9. Ibid., p. 28.

10. Ibid., p. 123.

11. Ibid., p. 186.

12. Mottahedeh, *The Mantle,* p. 15.

13. Moin, *Khomeini,* pp. 252–53.

14. Ibid., p. 281.

15. Wilfried Buchta, *Who Rules Iran?* (Washington, D.C.: Washington Institute for Near East Policy and Konrad Adenauer Stiftung, 2000), p. 86.

16. Ibid., p. 97.

17. Elaine Sciolino, "Iran Dissident Alarms Clerics with Calls for Islamic Democracy," *New York Times,* Sept. 19, 2001.

18. Nicholas Kristof, "Overdosing on Islam," *New York Times,* May 12, 2004.

19. Excerpts from the letter of resignation of Ayatollah Taheri, Radio Free Europe/Radio Liberty, June 8, 2002.

20. Jackson Diehl, "In Iran, Apocalypse vs. Reform," *Washington Post,* May 11, 2006.

21. Trudy Rubin, "Iranian Democracy Alive but Weak," *Philadelphia Inquirer,* Feb. 8, 2003.

22. Gian Micalessin, "Iran: Ayatollah Yusuf San'ei Says Dialogue Only Solution," *Il Giornale,* April 23, 2006.

23. Colin Freeman, "The Rise of Prof 'Crocodile'—A Hardliner to Terrify Hardliners," *Daily Telegraph,* Nov. 20, 2005.

24. Mehdi Khalaji, "The Last Marja," Washington Institute for Near East Policy, Sept. 2006, pp. 10–11.

9. THE OPPOSITION

1. Akbar Ganji, "Boycotting All Elections and Insisting on Referendum," Iran Press Service, May 22, 2005.

2. sazegara.net/english/archives/2006/06/an_open_letter.html.

3. *E'temad e Melli* editorial, as translated by the Mideast Mirror, June 19, 2006.

4. Human Rights Watch report, "Iran: Police Attack Women's Day Celebration," March 9, 2006.

5. Ali Akbar Mahdi, "The Student Movement in the Islamic Republic of Iran," *Journal of Iranian Research and Analysis,* vol. 15, no. 2 (Nov. 1999).

6. Letter from Ahmad Batebi, Amir Abbas Fakhravar, and other imprisoned students, Feb. 4, 2003, fakhravar.com/content_03_1.html.

7. Trudy Rubin, "Aggrieved Iranians Ineffective, Unable to Join Forces," *Philadelphia Inquirer,* May 31, 2006.

8. Reuters, "Jailed Student Dies on Hunger Strike in Iran," Tehran, July 31, 2006.

9. Nazila Fathi, "Iran President Facing Revival of Students' Ire," *New York Times,* Dec. 21, 2006, p. 1.

10. Amnesty International report, "Iran: New Government Fails to Address Dire Human Rights Situation," March 2006.

11. Farhad Pouladi, "Eight Killed in Double Bomb Attack in Iran," Agence France-Presse, Tehran, Jan. 24, 2006.

12. Reuters, "Iran Denies Media Reports of Attack on President," Tehran, Dec. 19, 2005.

13. Buchta, *Who Rules Iran?* p. 109.

14. Maryam Kashani, "Interview with the Commander of Jondollah and His Hostage," roozonline, May 14, 2006.

15. Ibid.

16. Buchta, *Who Rules Iran?* p. 108.

17. Shaul Bakhash, *The Reign of the Ayatollahs* (New York: Basic Books, 1984), p. 224.

18. Amnesty International report, "Iran: New Government Fails to Address Dire Human Rights Situation," March 2006.

19. Ibid.

20. Ibid.

21. komala.org/english/sidor/060625abaM.htm.

22. Ali M. Koknar, "Iranian Azeris: A Giant Minority" (PolicyWatch No. 1111, Washington Institute for Near East Policy, June 6, 2006).

23. Ibid.

24. Adnan Khan, "The Back Door to Tehran," *Maclean's*, July 31, 2006.

25. Brian Ross, Christopher Isham, "The United States' Secret War Against Iran," ABC News, April 3, 2007.

26. Maryam Rajavi speech, July 1, 2006, ncr-iran.org/content/view/1860/1/.

27. Buchta, *Who Rules Iran?* p. 184.

28. Shirin Ebadi and Azadeh Moaveni, *Iran Awakening* (New York: Random House, 2006), p. 91.

29. James Bill, *The Eagle and the Lion* (New Haven: Yale University Press, 1988), p. 191.

30. Buchta, *Who Rules Iran?* p. 113.

31. Baqer Moin, *Khomeini* (New York: St. Martin's Press, 1999), p. 278.

32. Nicolas Pelham, "Iran's Soccer Fervor Turns Political and Violent," *Christian Science Monitor,* Nov. 15, 2001.

33. Agence France Presse, "Detained Iran Intellectual Linked to CIA, Mossad," Tehran, May 9, 2006.

34. Rasool Nafisi, "Ramin Jahanbegloo: A Repressive Release," www.opendemocracy.net/content/articles/PDF/3867.pdf.

35. Vali Nasr, "Shirin Ebadi's Troubled History," *The New Republic Online*, June 12, 2006 (tnr.com/doc.mhtml?i=20060612&s=asr061206.).

10. OUT OF SYNC: IRAN AND THE UNITED STATES

1. Madeleine Albright speech, March 17, 2000, State Department archives.

2. Ibid.

3. Kenneth Katzman, *The Warriors of Islam: Iran's Revolutionary Guard* (Boulder, Co.: Westview Press, 1993), p. 99.

4. Elaine Sciolino, "Phone's Ringing: Wonder Who's on the Line," *New York Times,* Dec. 21, 1997.

5. Indyk speech, "The Clinton Administration's Approach to the Middle East," Washington Institute for Near East Policy Soref symposium, May 18, 1993.

6. Anthony Lake, "Confronting Backlash States," *Foreign Affairs*, vol. 73, no. 2 (March–April 1994).

7. Mohammad Khatami, *Islam, Liberty, and Development* (Binghamton: Institute of Global Cultural Studies, State University of New York, 1998), p. 150.

8. Christiane Amanpour, CNN interview with Khatami, Jan. 7, 1998.

9. Madeleine Albright, *Madame Secretary* (New York: Hyperion, 2003), p. 322.

10. Madeleine Albright speech before the Iranian-American Council, New York, Dec. 17, 2001.

11. THE WAR ON TERRORISM AND THE AXIS OF EVIL

1. Condoleezza Rice, "Campaign 2000: Promoting the National Interest," *Foreign Affairs* (January/February 2000).

2. Confirmation Hearings of General Colin Powell to be Secretary of State, Senate Foreign Relations Committee, Jan. 17, 2001. state.gov/s/index.cfm?docid=443.

3. Ibid.

4. James Dobbins, "Time to Deal with Iran," *Washington Post,* May 6, 2004.

5. Powell remarks to reporters en route to Moscow, Dec. 9, 2001.

6. Chubin lecture to the Woodrow Wilson International Center for Scholars, Sept. 14, 2006.

7. See appendix (pages 229–231) for Iran's 2003 offer to the United States.

8. Karl Vick, "U.S. Talks Possible, Iranian Aide Says," *Washington Post,* Jan. 8, 2004.

12. UNINTENDED CONSEQUENCES AND WHAT LIES AHEAD

1. Philip Sherwell, "Iranian Says Tehran Tricked EU on Nukes," *London Sunday Telegraph*, March 5, 2006.

2. Condoleezza Rice, interview with Reuters News Agency, Washington, March 11, 2005.

3. Stephen Hadley, remarks by National Security Advisor to the U.S. Institute of Peace on the President's national security strategy, March 16, 2006.

4. Guy Dinmore, "Iran Ready for High-Level Talks, U.S. Resists," *Financial Times,* April 6, 2006.

5. Hadley to the U.S. Institute of Peace, March 16, 2006.

6. Rice testimony before the Senate Foreign Relations Committee, Feb. 16, 2006.

7. Burns testimony before the House International Relations Committee, March 8, 2006.

8. Carla Anne Robbins, "U.S. Policymakers Weigh Options for Handling Iran," *Wall Street Journal,* Oct. 6, 2005.

9. See annex to U.N. Security Council resolution 1747, March 24, 2007.

10. Elaine Sciolino, "Iran Seeks Talks but Rejects Nuclear Freeze," *New York Times,* June 12, 2006.

11. Richard Perle, "Why Did Bush Blink on Iran? (Ask Condi)," *Washington Post,* June 25, 2006.

12. *E'temad Melli* editorial as translated by Mideast Mirror, London, Aug. 16, 2006.

13. Jim Michaels, "Military: Iran Ships Weapons to Shiite Extremists," *USA Today,* Feb. 12, 2007.

14. Bush press conference, www.whitehouse.gov/news/releases2007/02/20070214-2 .html.

SELECT BIBLIOGRAPHY

Bakhash, Shaul. *The Reign of the Ayatollahs*. New York: Basic Books, 1984.

Bill, James A. *The Eagle and the Lion*. New Haven: Yale University Press, 1988.

Buchta, Wilfried. *Who Rules Iran?* Washington, D.C.: Washington Institute for Near East Policy and Konrad Adenauer Stiftung, 2000.

Cordesman, Anthony H., and Khalid R. Al-Rodhan. *Iran's Weapons of Mass Destruction*. Washington, D.C.: Center for Strategic and International Studies, 2006.

Ebadi, Shirin, and Azadeh Moaveni. *Iran Awakening*. New York: Random House, 2006.

Gheissari, Ali, and Vali Nasr. *Democracy in Iran*. New York: Oxford University Press, 2006.

Katzman, Kenneth. *The Warriors of Islam: Iran's Revolutionary Guard*. Boulder, Co.: Westview Press, 1993.

Moin, Baqer. *Khomeini*. New York: St. Martin's Press, 2000.

Mottahedeh, Roy. *The Mantle of the Prophet*. Oxford, U.K.: Oneworld Publications, 2000.

Nasr, Vali. *The Shia Revival*. New York: W. W. Norton, 2006.

Pollack, Kenneth M. *The Persian Puzzle*. New York: Random House, 2004.

Sciolino, Elaine. *Persian Mirrors*. New York: Free Press, 2000.

Yaphe, Judith S., and Charles D. Lutes. *Reassessing the Implications of a Nuclear-Armed Iran*. Washington, D.C.: Institute for National Strategic Studies, National Defense University, 2005.

INDEX